Annual Review of High Performance Coaching & Consulting 2009

Contents

EDITORIAL

In 1967, legendary American football coach Vince Lombardi addressed 2,000 members of the American Management Association (AMA) on leadership and character. [1, 2] Since then, football coaches have been in demand to speak to audiences in the business and management world. But it's not just a one-way flow of knowledge – when another football coach, Bill Walsh, spoke to computer companies in the Silicon Valley: "They would pepper Bill with football questions, and he would pepper them with business questions. They would use his ideas, and he would use theirs" [3], wrote Mike Shanahan, whose mentor was Bill Walsh.

One of the most successful books written by a coach outside of the USA is Sir Clive Woodward's *Winning!*. Woodward, who led England to victory in the 2003 Rugby World Cup, stated: "There is absolutely no doubt in my mind that England won the World Cup because we applied business principles to the management of professional sport. And I firmly believe the principles found in the England story can be applied to any sport or business situation." [4, p. 412] Woodward also sought to learn from other sports; in fact, in 1998 he made a visit to Mike Shanahan at the Denver Broncos. [5] Woodward's success with England Rugby, but subsequent failure with the British & Irish Lions Tour to New Zealand in 2005 and Southampton Football Club (2005/2006), raised the 'expert versus generalist' debate in leadership that has been well articulated in a book about Admiral Nelson's leadership by Stephanie Jones and Jonathan Gosling. These authors noted that: "The idea of vocation is less popular these days with the increase in corporate job hopping and non-expert leaders" [6, p. 201] and conclude that "there is no simple formula for balancing technical and managerial expertise in all circumstances, but being clear about your vocation is the main thing" [6, p. 202].

The *Annual Review of High Performance Coaching and Consulting* has a particular interest in the transfer of knowledge from one domain to another, especially from sport to business (and vice versa). This inaugural issue of the journal features a leading article about Sir John Whitmore, a former motor racing champion and businessman, who is now arguably the most well known business coach in the world. There is also a review article about Lane 4's High Performance Environment Model, which was developed from research funded by Knowledge Transfer Partnerships (KTP), a UK-Government funded programme to help businesses improve their competitiveness. One of the co-authors, performance psychologist Professor Graham Jones, was a co-founder of Lane 4 in 1995 along with swimmer Adrian Moorhouse, MBE, who won a gold medal for Great Britain in the 1988 Olympic Games. A research paper on leadership has as a co-author, Kai Peters, who is Chief Executive of Ashridge, a business school in the UK which "explores and applies the transferable lessons between business and sport creating powerful analogical learning experiences in the classroom" [7].

REFERENCES

1.   Clary, J., Vince Lombardi: A Coach for All Seasons, *Fordham Magazine*, 1967, June
      http://www.fordham.edu/campus_resources/enewsroom/fordham_magazine/fordham_online/vince
      _lombardi_a_coa_26512.asp

2.   Walton, G.M., *Beyond Winning: The Timeless Wisdom of Great Philosopher Coaches,* Human
      Kinetics, Champaign, IL, 1992.

3.   Gladwell, M., True Grit, *New York Review of Books*, 2000, 47(3), February 24
      http://www.nybooks.com/articles/207

4.   Woodward, C., *Winning!* Rev. and Updated, Hodder, London, 2005.

5.   Kervin, A., *Clive Woodward: The Biography*, Rev. and Updated, Orion, London, 2006.

6.   Jones, S. and Gosling, J., *Nelson's Way: Leadership Lessons from the Great Commander*, Nicholas
      Brealey Publishing, London, 2006.

7.   Ashridge, Ashridge Sport Business Initiative,
      http://www.ashridge.org.uk/Website/Content.nsf/wTLDSBI/Sport+Business+Initiative?opendocum
      ent

Simon Jenkins (Leeds Metropolitan University, UK)

The Impact of the Inner Game and Sir John Whitmore on Coaching

Simon Jenkins
Carnegie Faculty of Sport and Education
Leeds Metropolitan University, Leeds, LS6 3QS, UK
E-mail: S.P.Jenkins@Leedsmet.ac.uk

ABSTRACT

The purpose of this article is to raise issues concerned with "coaching psychology" and the tension between psychologists and non-psychologists in the field of coaching. In particular, it will be shown how coaching has been influenced by Timothy Gallwey's Inner Game approach – the prominent disciples of which are non-psychologists - and, in turn, by the Human Potential Movement. The Inner Game, as applied and developed by Sir John Whitmore and others, appeared to flourish in the business world of the 1980s and 1990s when "empowerment" became a buzzword. Whitmore has continued to develop his career well into the new millennium, particularly through his passionate desire to make a difference in the world, which goes hand-in-hand with his advocacy of transpersonal psychology and coaching.

Key words: Coaching Psychology, Empowerment, Evidence-Based Coaching, GROW Model, History of Coaching, Humanistic Psychology, Human Potential Movement, Inner Game, Maslow's Hierarchy of Needs, Scientist-Practitioner, Transpersonal Psychology

INTRODUCTION

The new millennium has seen the emergence of psychologists in the fast-growing area of coaching in business. The work of psychologists Anthony Grant in Australia and Stephen Palmer in the UK has been particularly influential. The *Handbook of Coaching Psychology* (2007) is billed as an "essential resource for practising coaching psychologists, coaches, human resource and management professionals, and those interested in the psychology underpinning their coaching practice" [1]. It includes chapters on the application of eleven different psychological approaches to coaching practice (e.g., behavioural coaching, NLP coaching, and Gestalt coaching).

Reviewer: Sir John Whitmore (Performance Consultants International, UK)

It is edited by Stephen Palmer and Alison Whybrow, who were co-proposers of the British Psychological Society Special Group in Coaching, which was launched in 2004.

In considering whether there is a difference between "coaching" and "coaching psychology", Palmer and Whybrow first present descriptions of coaching from three "well-known authors and practitioners" [2, p. 2], two of whom (Sir John Whitmore and Myles Downey) are Inner Game disciples (although Palmer and Whybrow do not state this). Common to the descriptions by Whitmore [3] and Downey [4] is that coaching is "a facilitation approach". The third description, by Eric Parsloe [5], appears to be at odds with those of Whitmore and Downey in that it relates to an "instructional approach". However, a recent book on coaching psychology distinguished between a facilitation approach ("helping them to learn rather than teaching them") and an instructional approach ("directly concerned with immediate improvement of performance and development of skills by a form of tutoring or instruction") [6, p. 51].

Palmer and Whybrow state that "definitions of coaching psychology which have developed since the beginning of the new millennium usually include attention to psychological theory and practice" [2, p. 2]. It is shown how the definition of coaching psychology by members of the British Psychological Society evolved. Common throughout was reference to enhancing well-being and/or performance in personal life and work domains. Whereas the initial definition referred to "normal, non-clinical populations" and "established therapeutic approaches", the second definition stated by Palmer and Whybrow excluded reference to any particular population and referred to "established adult learning or psychological approaches" instead of "established therapeutic approaches":

> Coaching psychology is for enhancing performance in work and personal life domains with <u>normal, non-clinical populations</u>, underpinned by models of coaching grounded in established <u>therapeutic approaches</u>.
> [2, p. 2; underlining added]

> Coaching psychology is for enhancing well-being and performance in personal life and work domains underpinned by models of coaching grounded in established <u>adult learning or psychological approaches</u>.
> [2, p. 2; underlining added]

Palmer and Whybrow state that "the foundations of modern day coaching psychology developed from the Humanistic movement of the 1960s" at the same time that cognitive-behavioural therapies were also developing [2, p. 3], but note a difference in terms of the qualifications of practitioners in these two areas:

> The Humanistic approach did not put up barriers on who could practise client-centred or person-centred counselling or other forms of Humanistic therapies whereas the cognitive behavioural training centres in North America and the UK expected trainees to be qualified health professionals. [2, p. 4]

Having laid bare the issue of qualifications, the authors proceed to highlight the distinction between psychologists and non-psychologists with reference to the GROW model. In doing so, the authors make no explicit reference to Whitmore, who popularised this model, even though the authors had earlier cited Whitmore and his statement that, "In too many cases they [coaches] have not fully understood the performance-related psychological principles on which coaching is based." [[3, p. 2; cited in [2, p. 1]]:

> Non-psychologists are more likely to use the GROW model (Goal(s), Reality, Options, Way forward) without having any underpinning psychological theory taught to them on their training programmes whereas coaching psychologists report using a wide range of therapeutic approaches that have been adapted to the coaching arena... [2, p. 4]

Having stated that "modern-day coaching and coaching psychology has its roots back in the 1960s", Palmer and Whybrow argue that "the formal systematic study of the psychology of coaching goes back to the 1920s, if not earlier" [2, p. 4]. Furthermore:

> The study of the psychology of coaching should be seen as distinct from the development of the profession of coaching psychology... [2, p. 4-5]

In discussing the work of Coleman Griffith, who is regarded as the 'father of sport psychology' [7] and carried out research on coaching in sport, Palmer and Whybrow state that Griffith's "great contribution, which often goes unrecognised, was to emphasise the importance of the psychology in coaching" [2, p. 6][1]. Later in the chapter, the authors state that Dr. Anthony Grant is "often considered as the father of modern coaching psychology" [2].

Having left school at the age of 15 with no qualifications, Anthony Grant trained to become a carpenter and ran his own contracting business. He later embarked on a second career in direct sales and marketing before enrolling on a psychology degree at university in 1993 at the age of 39 [9], because he wanted "to learn theoretically-grounded and empirically-validated ways of working with people to help them...create change, and better reach goals" [10, p. 117]. When he completed his Ph.D. in 1999, he approached the Dean in the School of Psychology at the University of Sydney with the idea of a Coaching Psychology Unit, where he is now the director.

PSYCHOLOGISTS VERSUS NON-PSYCHOLOGISTS

Coaching psychologists argue that most coaches do not have a background in psychology and that most commercial coach training programmes are based on "proprietary models of coaching with little or no theoretical grounding" [11, p. 26] or with "little published research underpinning its efficacy" [2, p. 8]. In advocating

---

[1] The reference to Coleman Griffith is testimony to the importance of sport psychology in the development of coaching psychology, but it is one that should be regarded critically. The labelling of Griffith as 'the father of sport psychology' has been described as a disciplinary "origin myth" [8, p. 267] in that there is no direct connection between Griffith and those who developed sport psychology from the 1960s.

coaching psychology, Palmer and Cavanagh state:

> We bring more than just a framework for a conversation with a client, such as the famous GROW model. We bring a host of <u>psychological theories and models that underpin, and bring depth to, the coaching relationship</u>. These include an understanding of mental health; motivation; systems theory; personal and organisational growth; adaptation of therapeutic models to the field of coaching; research into effectiveness, resilience and positive psychology. [12, p. 1; underlining added)

Grant couches this issue in terms of professionalism and the following criteria of professional status: i) significant barriers to entry; ii) a shared common body of knowledge rather than proprietary systems; (iii) formal qualifications at university level; iv) regulatory bodies with the power to admit, discipline and meaningfully sanction members; v) an enforceable code of ethics; and (vi) some form of state-sanctioned licensing or regulation [13, p. 3].

The statement below concerns the second and third criteria:

> The main difference between coaching psychology and coaching, is that the coaching psychology is explicitly grounded in psychological theory, psychological science and psychological research, and its practitioners have had rigorous university level training in psychology, [and] use the 'scientist-practitioner' or 'informed practitioner' approach. [10, p. 118]

Grant notes that there are a number of universities that offer programmes in coaching. With regard to the criterion of formal qualifications at university level, however, John Whitmore has been quoted as follows:

> ...coaches with psychological knowledge are better equipped to deal with [the psychological side of personal development]. I am cautious though of purely academic psychology: there is a difference between the intellectual understanding of psychology and the practice of it. People who are trained in applied psychology practices such as psychotherapy are more able to use psychological principles in coaching. [14, p. 13]

Grant could respond to Whitmore by pointing to the notion of a 'scientist-practitioner', by which is meant a "consumer of research"; i.e., a practitioner who has been trained in how to use research [13, p. 4]:

> Movement towards a scientist-practitioner model required that coach training programs explicitly address the theoretical and empirical foundations of coaching, and provide training in sound research methodologies, basic statistical and data analysis skills, and foster informed critical thinking skills in student coaches. Such an approach

would form the basis of an <u>evidence-based</u> coaching paradigm. [13, p. 4; underlining added]

The concept of "evidence-based coaching" needs to be elucidated, especially as Stephen Palmer has indicated that more research is needed to inform practice in coaching:

> What has been noticeable is the gradual increase in the number of published papers showing the effectiveness of using solution-focused and cognitive-behavioural coaching approaches with non-clinical populations. There are plenty of published research papers highlighting how effective these approaches are with clinical populations but the real challenge has been to prove that they are effective with non-clinical populations. [15, p. x]

In clinical psychology, the concept of scientist-practitioner appears to have been in circulation since the Boulder Conference on Graduate Education in Clinical Psychology in 1949 when a call was made for clinical psychologists to be trained both as scientists and as practitioners. However, there was a lack of consideration given to the integration of science and practice in everyday clinical work. Monte Shapiro [16] originally expressed the scientist-practitioner model in terms of it being a model of the discipline of clinical psychology rather than a model of education and training [17]. Later, Shapiro [18] discarded the notion of clinical psychology as an applied science. In the words of his son, David Shapiro:

> He now considered there were insufficient well-validated methods of assessment or treatment for these to form the mainstay of the discipline. He therefore emphasised more strongly than before the value of applying the findings and methods of psychology to understanding clinical problems. He also highlighted the use of scientific method in every aspect of clinical work. ... As before, the clinician must work scientifically, but this is now defined exclusively in terms of strategy, rather than relying upon (previously validated) procedure. [17, p. 232-233]

With regard to the priority of strategy over procedure, David Shapiro states:

> The evidence base will always be incomplete, and its application to many clinical situations uncertain. The most compelling need for scientist-practitioner skills arises when the evidence is equivocal or lacking...
> [17 p. 232-233]

The criterion of "a shared common body of knowledge rather than proprietary systems" stated by Grant would provoke a response such as the following from a coaching practitioner concerned with marketing of coaching and making psychology accessible to the lay person:

Many successful techniques used in coaching are based on sound psychological research but have only been made accessible through the efforts of disciplines such as neuro-linguistic programming (NLP) which have very successfully encapsulated, labelled and marketed ranges of insights into human relationships and behaviours. For example, it is infinitely more attractive for a layperson to discuss anchoring and its use in advertising than to review data about stimulus-response theory. [19, p. 19-20]

NEURO-LINGUISTIC PROGRAMMING (NLP)

NLP can be regarded as "a method for understanding the structure of subjective experience of human beings, and for utilizing that knowledge in communications" [20, p. 108-109]. It claims to be "a methodology through which effective practices from other fields can be identified and coded" [20, p. 108-109]. The initial NLP work of Richard Bandler and John Grinder [21] was based on observational studies of 'excellent communicators' - Gestalt therapist Fritz Perls, family therapist Virginia Satir, and hypnotherapist Milton Erickson. Bruce Grimley indicates that NLP is informed by a number of theoretical and philosophical roots:

> Neuro-linguistic programming (NLP) coaching is an <u>atheoretical</u>, pragmatic approach which shares a philosophy with constructivist, behaviourist and experiential psychology. It is unashamedly <u>eclectic</u> in its orientation drawing on many psychological approaches. The founders of NLP unlike Kurt Lewin would not say 'there is nothing so useful as a good theory'. They made no commitment to theory, regarding such as being more complex and not as useful. Instead they described NLP as a meta-discipline. As they studied the structure of subjective experience, their prime concern was *description* of how somebody worked without needing to understand why they worked that way. [22, p. 193; underlining added]

Michael Hall has discussed how NLP arose in the early 1970s during the heyday of the Human Potential Movement (HPM) as one of many new therapies and fields [23]. HPM has been described as "a psychological philosophy and framework, including a set of values" [24] that grew out of humanistic psychology and is a term that was first used for humanistic psychotherapies that became popular in the 1960s and early 1970s in the USA. HPM was associated with 'growth centres' such as the Esalen Institute, which was founded in 1962 at Big Sur, California by Michael Murphy and Richard Price. Abraham Maslow became affiliated with the Esalen Institute in 1966. [25] Along with Carl Rogers, Rollo May and Charlotte Buhler, Maslow founded the American Association of Humanistic Psychology. The *Gale Encyclopedia of Psychology* has stated that while "the flashier and most eccentric aspects" [26] of HPM, such as Erhard Seminars Training (est) have been largely relegated to fads of the 1960s and 1970s, it endures in other forms. In fact, est and related practices continue under a variety of new names such as the Landmark Forum. Founded by Werner Erhard in 1971, est has been described as drawing from "a highly eclectic variety of spiritual and psychological development theories and models, apparently the personal selection of Erhard" [20, p. 56].

While stating above that NLP is "atheoretical", Grimley states that theories which NLP draws from include general semantics, systems theory, reattribution theory, social comparison theory, cognitive dissonance, clinical hypnosis, family therapy, ego state theory, cognitive theory, and psychodynamic theory [22, p. 199].

Grimley notes, for example, how goal setting theory is essential to NLP coaching:

> For the NLP coach goals need to be stated in the positive, based upon sensory evidence, measurable, within a timeframe, owned by the coachee, and they need to be something which really accords with the beliefs and values of the coachee. For NLP coaching the most important aspect of goal setting is to ascertain whether or not the coachee really wishes to obtain this goal, compared with them being obliged to do so because of societal, organisational or parental approval. [22, p. 195]

It will be seen in the following section that goal setting theory is essential also to coaching based on the GROW model.

GROW

A number of definitions of coaching are centred around 'conversation' [27, p. 4; 4, p. 99; 28, p. 8; 29, p. 24; 30, p. 177]; albeit a conversation that is qualitatively different to a coachee's everyday conversations [29, p. 24]. Myles Downey indicates a range of different conversational approaches that a coach might take during a coaching session: instructing, giving advice, offering advice, giving feedback, making suggestions, asking questions that raise awareness, summarising, paraphrasing, reflecting, and listening to understand [4, p. 23]. These conversational approaches sit well with the International Coach Federation (ICF) Professional Coaching Core Competencies [31].

The GROW model has been widely used to structure a coaching conversation. This model was developed by Graham Alexander in 1984 [32] and popularised by Sir John Whitmore, who summarised it as follows:

> GOAL setting for the session as well as short and long term
> REALITY checking to explore the current situation
> OPTIONS and alternative strategies on courses of action
> WHAT is to be done, WHEN, by WHOM and the WILL to do it
> [3, p. 54]

Downey has noted that the first stage of the model is identifying the *topic* for the session ('What do you want to talk to me about?') before asking about the *goal* for the session, but that "attempts to include this stage in the mnemonic have, without exception, been clumsy – the best was the To Grow model, borrowing the 'To' from topic" [4, p. 26]. Downey provides insight into how the GROW model developed:

> The practice of effective coaching was already in place before the GROW model was 'discovered'. The early practitioners of coaching

worked more or less intuitively. Over time it became apparent that in the more successful sessions there was a certain sequence of key stages. The pattern was discussed and formulated as the GROW model. The model grew out of best practice and not theory. [4, p. 25-26]

A number of models with "a useful acronym as an aide mémoire" [33, p. 71] have developed from the GROW model; e.g., ACHIEVE[2], POSITIVE[3], OSKAR[4], SPACE[5], and PRACTICE[6]). Citing his earlier work [38, 39], Stephen Palmer recommends that clients who are experienced at using the seven-step, PRACTICE model can use shorter models such as STIR or PIE[7] but "the outcome may be less satisfactory" [33, p. 75].

Ho Law and his colleagues show how different approaches to coaching can be mapped on to each element of the GROW model to serve as a guide for coaches in applying different techniques in different contexts [6, p. 136]. Similarly, Jonathon Passmore, who places the GROW model within "behavioural coaching", argues that:

> ...coaching practice in reality integrates a range of different models and processes. Thus, the behaviourist coach uses humanistic elements to build rapport, create empathy and operate non-judgementally towards their coachee. They may equally draw on cognitive coaching elements; encouraging the coachee to reflect on the beliefs which enhance or inhibit their performance. The coach may also challenge client motivation, or encourage reflection on past experiences and bring into conscious awareness issues from the unconscious. [40, p. 79]

MODELS AND THEORIES

In the above sections, the terms theory and model are used in various ways. Coaching psychologists Carol Kaufman and Tatiana Bachkirova define theories as "coherent, scientifically based descriptions and explanations of phenomena we are interested in exploring":

---

[2] ACHIEVE represents: Assess the current situation; Creative brainstorming of alternative to current situation; Hone goals; Initiate options; Evaluative options; Valid action programme design, Encourage momentum. [34]

[3] POSITIVE represents Purpose, Observations, Strategy, Insight, Team, Initiate, Value and Encourage. [35]

[4] OSKAR represents Outcome, Scaling, Know-how and resources, Affirm and action, Review. [36]

[5] SPACE represents Social context, Physiological, Action, Cognitions and Emotions. [37]

[6] PRACTICE represents Problem identification; Realistic, relevant goals developed (e.g., SMART goals); Alternative solutions generated; Consideration of consequences; Target most feasible solutions; Implementation of Chosen solutions; Evaluation. [33]

[7] STIR: Select a problem; Target a solution; Implement a solution; Review outcome.
PIE: Problem definition, Implement a solution; Evaluate outcome.
[33, p. 75]

> …theories of coaching try to describe and explain the coaching process and outcomes, how change happens, how it can be sustained, what forces keep change from occurring and what galvanises growth. [41, p. 2]

This definition fits with the view in science and academia that a theory is not simply a hypothesis, but rather an explanatory structure that is supported by empirical evidence and can be used to make valid predictions.

In science, models are often used along with analogical reasoning as the basis of theories. For example, Charles Darwin generated his theory of natural selection using an analogy to artificial selection through a model of how stock breeders and gardeners produce new breeds of animals and new plant forms by selecting stock and plants with the characteristics they desired. [42]

Alberto Greco notes that while clinical psychology tends to construct big theoretical systems, experimental psychology tends to use models:

> …these "models" frequently are interested in a single cognitive process or even in some particular aspect of a cognitive process, rather than in old general issues such as the relationships between perception and motivation or memory and intelligence. [43, p. 1]

What Greco refers to as "big theoretical systems" are more commonly known as 'schools of thought in psychology'; e.g., behaviourism, psychoanalysis, cognitivism:

> The psychological schools are the great classical theories of psychology. Each has been highly influential, however most psychologists hold eclectic viewpoints that combine aspects of each school. [44; underlining added]

In coaching, the GROW model can be regarded as a simplified representation of a complex real world process; i.e., 'coaching conversation'. A model in this sense is simple in order to have practical utility. It is what can be referred to as a "heuristic device", which is:

> …a map or model that does not purport to be true, but which enables a learner to explore and discover. It may be a rule of thumb that allows for exploration through trial and error, or a model such as Maslow's hierarchy of needs.[20, p. 74]

Maslow's hierarchy of needs is arguably the most familiar model in the whole field of personal and professional development, but as a number of authors have pointed out "it is not only poorly understood but also promulgated as established theory rather than as the speculative map of human development that Maslow originally seems to have intended." [20, p. 74] As Maslow himself pointed out, his theory lacks empirical support. [45] Maslow's [46, 47] theory of motivation, represented by "the ubiquitous triangle" has been grossly simplified and decontextualised from Maslow's original vision:

> Presented as a tool for understanding and thereby motivating employees, the hierarchy barely resembles Maslow's vision of the hierarchy as a ladder, ultimately leading to societal change and the empancipation of humankind… . His self-acknowledged theoretical placement between Freud and Marx seems far from evident in this pared-down version of what was initially a comprehensive theory of motivation… [48, p. 149]

While Maslow is most closely associated with humanistic psychology, the so-called 'third force psychology', he believed in theoretical eclecticism in that other psychological schools have contributed to human understanding:

> I consider Humanistic, Third Force Psychology to be transitional, a preparation for a still 'higher' Fourth Psychology, transpersonal, transhuman, centered in the cosmos, rather than in human needs and interest, going beyond humanness, identity, self-actualization, and the like. [49, p. iii-iv]

Transpersonal theory was pioneered by Carl Jung, who was originally in the 'second force psychology' with Freud. Along with Robert Assagioli, Maslow was a major contributor to the emergence of transpersonal psychology, after which Ken Wilber, Stanislav Grof and David Levin have been influential, according to Michael Washburn, who has provided a potted history:

> Transpersonal theory came into its own as a movement with the founding of the *Journal of Transpersonal Psychology* in 1969. In the early years, transpersonal theory was predominantly humanistic in its psychology and Eastern in its religion, a synthesis of Maslow and Buddhism (primarily Zen). These identifications, however, have loosened over the years, and transpersonal theory is now more open to a diversity of psychological and spiritual perspectives. [50, p. 3]

THE INNER GAME

Sir John Whitmore, Graham Alexander and Myles Downey are all disciples of Timothy Gallwey, who is author of the Inner Game series [51-54]. The Inner Game can be understood in the context of both humanistic and transpersonal psychology. Indeed it has been shown by Jenkins [55] how Gallwey used ideas from Zen and Yoga.

The influence of Gallwey and his disciples is captured in Peter Bluckert's list of seven "sound coaching principles' of which the first four are: "From tell to ask" [facilitated learning], "Performance and Potential" [unlocking potential], "Awareness and Responsibility", and "Building Self-Belief" [56, p. 4-5]. Furthermore:

> [The importance of awareness and responsibility] is the common ground between most, if not all, coaching authors and is captured in the proposition that awareness is the starting point for growth and change. As people become more aware of their assumptions, belief systems,

attitudes and behavioural patterns they move into a position of choice – to stay with them or to change. The responsibility for this choice is with them. … The coach may facilitate the heightening of a client's awareness through running a 360-degree feedback exercise providing an ocean of rich data but if the individual doesn't own any of it, then the prospect of learning and change is low. …[The coach has] to help people to believe and trust in themselves and others. [56, p. 5]

Downey refers to the facilitation approach as "Non-Directive Coaching", which was developed by himself and other Inner Game disciples, as relying not on "the knowledge, experience, wisdom or insight of the coach" but rather on "the capacity of individuals to learn for themselves, to think for themselves and be creative" [4, p. 9-10]. Downey describes this 'school' of coaching as being "an offshoot of The Inner Game" but having "borrowed much from other sources, not least Carl Rogers" [4, p. 20]. He notes, however, that he has never heard Gallwey use the term 'non-directive' and that, in any case, it is neither possible nor desirable to be completely non-directive [4, p. 37]. Downey also notes that using the GROW model is "a directive act" [4, p. 188]. In the terms used below by Sir John Whitmore, the GROW model is part of the *context* of coaching:

> When you call your coaching non-directive, you are pretending if you believe that you are 100% responsive to the coachee agenda. The mere fact that you are present has an influence. The *content* is what the coachee wants, but the *context* in which it takes place is the presence of the coach. So if I have a global vision, or spiritual vision, I will ask different questions, even about something mundane.
> [14, p. 15; italics added]

Downey distinguishes between 'off-line' and 'on-line' situations in coaching. Off-line situations such as planning and reviewing are where the GROW model is applicable. On-line situations, which are concerned with consideration of performance issues such as making a presentation, bring the Inner Game into place; especially what Downey refers to as the "model" of 'Potential minus interference is equal to performance' [4, p. 11]. This model is the basis of what can be referred to as the Inner Game *theory*, which is based on the premise that a person has two selves, Self One and Self Two:

> Self One is the internalised voice of our parents, teachers and those in authority. Self One seeks to control Self Two and does not trust it. Self One is characterised by tension, fear, doubt and trying too hard.
>
> Self Two is the whole human being with all its potential and capacities including the 'hard-wired' capacity to learn. It is characterised by relaxed concentration, enjoyment and trust. [4, p. 45]

The aim of the coach is to help the coachee get into Self Two, especially in critical situations such as making presentations.

SIR JOHN WHITMORE

The remainder of this article will examine the impact of the Inner Game through the career of John Whitmore[8]. The account that is given appears to have a good fit with Lucy West and Mike Milan's analysis of how coaching developed. These authors make a distinction between "supply" and "demand" factors. The supply factors are: i) the role of psychology; ii) social trends (the personal development movement and the sports analogy); and iii) business trends (outplacement and career management). The demands factors are: i) the diminishing of corporate and individual security; ii) the growing imperative for continuous organisational and individual learning; iii) and the need for new leadership. [31]

The account of Whitmore's career bears heavily on the second of the supply factors and the third of the demand factors. West and Milan [31] refer to the rapid growth of the 'human potential movement' (HPM) that originated in the USA during the 1960s and role of the Inner Game in the concept of coaching being transferred from sport to business. With regard to the third demand factor, West and Milan state that, "The notion of leadership that derives from a 'command and control' model does not work in a world that has become substantively unpredictable." [31, p. 24-25]

WHITMORE AND THE INNER GAME

Born in 1937, Whitmore was educated at Eton College, Sandhurst Royal Military Academy, and Cirencester Agricultural College. His first career was in motor racing and in 1965 he won the European Saloon Car Championship. He retired from motor racing the following year in order to run a large agribusiness, a product design company and a Ford Main Dealership. [58-61]

In 1968, Whitmore sold all his business interests to study physics, psychotherapy and sports psychology. [58, 59] He felt there was more to life: "I had material success from both business and racing, even including my own plane and airstrip, but this did not seem to satisfy me." [62] He went to the Esalen Institute in 1970 at a time when it was visited by Carl Rogers and Abraham Maslow. He studied humanistic psychology and met Timothy Gallwey. [62]

In 1971, Whitmore shot a full-length feature film at the Esalen Institute which was shown at the Cannes and Edinburgh film festivals. It featured a week-long 'encounter group' led by Will Schutz, who had developed a system called Fundamental Interpersonal Relations Orientation (FIRO) [63]. He brought Werner Erhard to the UK in 1974 to present the first est training in Europe. [65, p. 423] Vikki Brock has indicated that the "Gallwey / Whitmore" group was connected to Erhard through Esalen and personal relationships. [65] Erhard has been quoted as follows: "Tim [Gallwey] was one of the coaches that I studied . . . and I really learned a lot working with him . . . [as a tennis coach and] . . . John [Whitmore] came to visit and gave me some support coaching [in race car driving]" [65, p. 423].

---

[8] Sir John Whitmore was presented with an award by the Association of Coaching (AC) in 2005 for having had the most impact on the coaching profession: "This award recognises an individual who has pioneered the development and use of coaching based philosophies that significantly benefit society, along with ethically demonstrating the benefits coaching based relationships can deliver to the wider community." [57] In 2007 he received the President's Award from the International Coach Federation (ICF) and in 2008 he was awarded an honorary Ph.D. in Business Administration by the University of East London (UEL) for his contribution to the development of the coaching profession.

Brock discusses the role of the Human Potential Movement in the 1960s, out of which the Esalen Institute emerged:

> The spread of coaching was fueled through interdisciplinary mingling in venues available at ...[locations such as Esalen]. The key figures in these movements connected through face-to-face conferences, workshops, and forums. [65, p. 487]

The emphasis was therefore on non-formal and informal learning rather than formal learning. In sports coaching, Lee Nelson and his colleagues concluded that coaches learn from a wide range of sources, but formal and non-formal learning episodes are low-impact endeavours when compared to the lifelong process of informal learning. Formal learning is institutionalised and may involve studying for a coaching certificate or university degree; non-formal learning may include coaching workshops and conferences; while informal learning can range from previous experience as an athlete to interaction with peer coaches, as well as independent learning using resources such as journal articles. With regard to informal learning:

> Learning is viewed as distributed among many participants within the community in which people with diverse expertise are transformed through their own actions and those of other participants. ... [It] is largely through such experiences that collective understandings begin to develop and the shared meanings about the occupational culture of coaching start to take shape. Therefore, much of what a new coach learns is through ongoing interactions in the practical coaching context. Such formative experiences carry far into a coach's career and provide a continuing influence over perspectives, beliefs, and behaviours. [66, p. 254]

In 1974, for a series of "May Lectures" in London, Whitmore "brought together the California hippies of Esalen with the British aristocracy of Findhorn [a spiritual community in Scotland]" [67]. Whitmore trained with Gallwey in California and returned to the UK with an agreement to represent the Inner Game in Europe. [65, 68] In 1979, Whitmore and a group of British coaches including Graham Alexander and Caroline Harris took part in the first Inner Game coaching training to be in held in the UK, led by one of Gallwey's trainers. The group set up The Inner Game Ltd. and ran courses in tennis and skiing:

> Enquiries from other sports followed. In the early 80's there began to be noticeably more interest from the business world keen to learn about the principles of Inner Game coaching and sensing the value and potential of their application in the work environment. The original trainees were welcomed into the new field of business coaching. [68]

In 1986, The Inner Game Ltd. and Results Unlimited, which had been founded by Jenny Ditzler in 1981, merged into the Alexander Corporation. Ditzler formerly worked for Erhard. [31] In 1986, Whitmore teamed up with David Hemery and later with David Whitaker to found Performance Consultants:

> We dropped the Inner Game name and called what we did 'Coaching'. Coaching became a business buzz-word quite quickly. Then I felt that some people were leaping on the bandwagon and re-labelling their products as 'coaching' when they did not really understand what the underlying principals of 'coaching' were.
>
> They knew that *questioning* was involved, but not the basis of the whole approach. I wrote 'Coaching for Performance' in order to throw down the gauntlet and say, 'here is the definition of coaching'. It worked because the book became the best seller in the field. Some of the impostors fell by the wayside and we were joined in the market by a number of ex-colleagues from earlier sports 'Inner Game' days. All the successful people in business coaching that I know are now using similar principals to those outlined in my book. [62]

WHITMORE AND EMPOWERMENT

Empowerment has been a buzzword since the 1980s and 1990s [69, p. 404] when it was associated with radical organisational changes. In their research on how organisations are managed when they face decline, turbulence, downsizing and change, Kim Cameron and his colleagues identified twelve negative attributes or attitudes: centralization, threat-rigidity response, loss of innovativeness, decreasing morale, politicized environment, loss of trust, increased conflict, restricted communication, lack of teamwork, loss of loyalty, scapegoating leaders, and short-term perspective [70, p. 403]. Empowerment has been viewed as "a key to unlocking the potential of a successful workforce in an era of chaotic change and escalating competitive conditions" [69, p. 401]. It involves managers removing controls, constraints and boundaries so as to give people the freedom to be more autonomous and self-directed [69, p. 401; 20, p. 53]. From a review of empirical research on empowerment, David Whetten and Kim Cameron identify five core dimensions of empowerment self-efficacy (a sense of personal competence), self-determination (a sense of personal choice), personal control (a sense of having impact), meaning (a sense of value in activity), and trust (a sense of security) [69, p. 406].

Empowerment has not been accepted uncritically by management and personal development scholars, however, as Paul Tosey and Jose Gregory remark:

> There is much talk of 'empowering' people, yet this entails the quite odd idea that some external authority is capable of enabling others to become 'empowered'. Rather like learning, empowerment: may be spoken of as if it were a universal good. This contemporary rhetoric begs analysis also of the restrictions likely to be placed on empowerment in organizations – many employees have found that acting in an empowered way attracts sanctions. [20, p. 53]

Jim Durcan and David Oates report the work of Sir John Whitmore with the Kent County Constabulary in which it was sought to empower lower-rank police officers by encouraging them to generate innovative ways of increasing the crime detection rate, for example. According to Stuart McBride, who was in charge of management and personal development for the Kent County Constabulary, this took place at a time when there was "structural delayering" in police forces and a need to respond to pressures from society for an empowerment approach to be taken; however:

> "It's not true empowerment in the sense that you say 'Here's the mission statement, go away and do whatever it is you want to do'. The coach, in the coaching process, in my view, retains control and responsibility. What he does is recognise that by moving towards the empowering end of the scale people get far more ownership of issues and problems, more enjoyment, more reward. I don't mean that it is a conning approach, that people only think they have control, but they don't really. They do have control, but that doesn't mean the boss loses control. The boss has to be more aware." [71, p. 107]

Whitmore regards The Inner Game as "the purest basis of workplace coaching" and believes that it "is predicated upon us recognising and eliminating the internal obstacles to our becoming what we may be, and fear is the greatest of those obstacles" [72, p. 8]. He defines coaching as "unlocking a person's potential to maximize their own performance" [3, p. 8], and advocates it as "a management style rather than merely a tool for a manager to use occasionally" [3, p. 6].

Awareness and responsibility are the key principles of coaching [3, p. 16]. Awareness is "knowing what is happening around you", while self awareness is "knowing what you are experiencing" [3, p. 35]. Responsibility is concerned with personal choice and control:

> Coaching helps build responsibility into the other person by enriching their capability to make choices and decisions of their own. [14, p. 13]

> Personal responsibility can seem threatening because it means there's someone to blame. But without responsibility you can't make decisions. [73]

Whitmore notes that "many managers withhold responsibility and kill awareness" [3, p. 40]. He believes that "coaching represents and symbolises the collective societal shift from hierarchy towards self-responsibility" and a "paradigm shift from the common culture of fear to one of trust"; and "an emerging shift from the subservient, convenient and automatic following of orders, to the expectation of and demand for more choice by ordinary people at work and elsewhere in their lives" [74, p. 24-25].

He describes empowerment in terms of "encouraging the inner authority of employees" [75], which echoes the words of Tim Gallwey in the foreword to Myles Downey's book:

The goal of coaching is to establish a firmer connection with an *inner* authority that can guide vision and urge excellence and discriminate wisdom without being subject to an 'inner bully', that has established its certification from external dictates and imposes them on you without your authority to do so. [4, p. ix; italics original]

WHITMORE, HIS PARENTS AND EMPOWERMENT

Whitmore has described himself as "the timid son of a benevolent and successful but autocratic father in whose shadow I hid my mediocrity during my school years" [60, 61-62]. He has explained his motivation for motor racing:

I was the 'little guy' and I wanted to break out from behind his imposing shadow. At around 17-18 my rebellious nature came out. I wanted to find myself, and that resulted in a competitive need to prove myself. I was just starting to drive, so the car became the tool of my competitive expression. [62]

In further describing his father, and his mother, Whitmore states:

My father was 65 years old when I was born. He was a Victorian landowning aristocrat and he ruled his estate and his family as a benevolent dictator. Though Norwegian and half his age, my mother's caring and authority were comparable. In my child's eyes they successfully and single-handedly defended England against the Huns during World War II. In their roles as leaders of the district Home Guard and Red Cross respectively, they were indeed renowned and honoured for the contributions they made in material and morale to the war effort.
…
My father was indeed a caricature of a benevolent dictator. He was at times disappointed by the lack of benevolence shown by some of his aristocratic colleagues and by many of the ambitious 'nouveau riche' who rose to commercial or political power when the war was over. Nevertheless he was unable to comprehend the rise of socialism because he cared for his hundred or so employees as if they were his family. They had everything they needed except for the one thing they might have wanted, choice and self-determination. He was incapable of understanding why they would want that. Most of them probably didn't, but other less well-treated workers certainly did. [75]

WHITMORE AND MASLOW'S HIERARCHY OF NEEDS

In 2006 Whitmore formed Performance Consultants International, which is an "international specialist advisory, coaching, leadership and transformation firm" with the purpose being "to share the best leadership, social responsibility and other people skills among different countries and cultures for a sustainable future for all" [76]. Whitmore is also the co-creator with Nick Hart-Williams of the "Be The Change" movement [77], which staged its first event in 2004. He strives in particular "to get businesses to recognise their wider responsibilities and contribute directly to global conditions" [62]. Whitmore promotes the idea of transpersonal coaching, on the basis that we have a "core within ourselves" that is "the fountain from which true values and qualities emerge and, if there is ever a time at which humanity needs to find its values and qualities, it is now" [59]. The following statement would appear to suggest that Whitmore has indeed followed Maslow's original agenda; i.e., of "societal change and emancipation of humankind" [48, p. 149]:

> As we climb the Maslow hierarchy of needs, we meet different needs along the way but its not a linear journey. All people need to have meaning and purpose but often can't define it and so project their need onto the games of life along the way. At first, meaning and purpose for me was to be successful in my sport. Eventually, I left that little game to play a bigger game, first business then the game of life itself. I quickly realised that business was just another game and should not be taken too seriously. Pushing bits of paper around or figures on a screen is fairly pointless and not half as much fun as tennis or racing. We use these games to satisfy an inner need. As we evolve and become more psychologically mature, we get more sophisticated about what gives us meaning. In the early stage we look for recognition from others but that develops into a more profound and discriminating search for self-esteem, self belief and for personal fulfilment. The final stage, at least on the Maslow scale, almost always includes <u>a desire to make a contribution in the wider world</u>, and that is what happened to me. What really gave me satisfaction was to make a contribution.
> [62; underlining added]

CONCLUSION

Stephen Palmer and Michael Cavanagh stated that coaching psychologists "bring more than just a framework with a client, such as the famous GROW model", bringing "a host of psychological theories and models that underpin, and bring depth to, the coaching relationship" [12, p. 1]. Coaching psychologists have had rigorous university-level training in psychology and use the scientist-practitioner approach [10, p. 118]. Notions of 'evidence-based coaching' that are embedded in concepts of scientist-practitioner are not unproblematic, however, not least because (as coaching psychologists acknowledge) more research is needed to inform practice in coaching [15, p. x] and because theory may be conflated with empirical evidence. While coaching psychologists emphasize the need for "a shared body of knowledge rather than proprietary systems" [13, p. 3], coaches argue that their techniques need to be marketed and made accessible to the layperson [19, p. 19-20]. As in psychology, the terms 'model' and 'theory' in coaching are used in a variety of ways. Coaching practice integrates a range of different models, theories, approaches and processes [40, p. 79] - as a consideration of NLP shows [22], coaching is eclectic in its orientation. The GROW model [3] can be regarded as a simplified representation of a complex real world process; i.e., 'coaching conversation'. A model in this sense is simple in order to have practical utility.

The influence of Timothy Gallwey's Inner Game [51] and his disciples such as John Whitmore is captured in Peter Bluckert's list of seven "sound coaching principles" of which the first four are: "From tell to ask" [facilitated learning], "Performance and Potential" [unlocking potential], "Awareness and Responsibility", and "Building Self-Belief" [56, p. 4-5].

Whitmore's success in coaching can be attributed to a number of factors, including his: parents; careers in motor racing and business; involvement in the Human Potential Movement and the Esalen Institute; meeting Timothy Gallwey and learning about the Inner Game; marketing the Inner Game in the UK; finding a synergy between the Inner Game and the empowerment movement in the business world; change in describing what he does from "sport psychology" to "coaching"; distinguishing between "on-line" and "off-line" use of the Inner Game (to use Myles Downey's [4] terminology), commitment to lifelong and shared learning through non-formal and informal means; making a link between spirituality and the workplace; continual search for meaning and purpose in life; and a passionate desire to make a difference in the world, which goes hand-in-hand with his advocacy of transpersonal psychology and coaching:

> In recent years people especially in Western culture are waking up to the transpersonal within themselves through the emerging need to find meaning and purpose in all aspects of their lives and to work in the service of something beyond just making a profit.
>
> This was less urgent when we were more focussed lower down the Maslow hierarchy (on survival, on belonging and material success), and when religion was the preserve of the spiritual. Affluence, global communication and the secularisation of society have now brought the transpersonal onto many people's agenda, both personally and at work. Coaching tends to be viewed in the business world as an action-orientated way of addressing problems.
>
> Transpersonal coaching is an empowering process which helps clients discover the power and effectiveness of who they really are. This core, source of our deepest values and qualities, is a well-spring of real strength, creativity and actualisation. [78]

REFERENCES

1.   Palmer, S. and Whybrow, A., eds., *Handbook of Coaching Psychology: A Guide for Practitioners*, Routledge, London, 2007.

2.   Palmer, S. and Whybrow, A., Coaching Psychology: An Introduction, in: Palmer, S. and Whybrow, A., eds., *Handbook of Coaching Psychology: A Guide for Practitioners*, Routledge, London, 2007, 1-20.

3.   Whitmore, J., *Coaching for Performance: GROWING People, Performance and Purpose*, 3rd edn., Nicholas Brealey Publishing, London, 2002.

4.   Downey, M., *Effective Coaching: Lessons from the Coaches' Corner*, 2nd edn., Orion Business Books, London, 2003.

5.   Parsloe, E., *Coaching, Mentoring and Assessing: A Practical Guide to Developing Competence*, rev. edn., Kogan Page, London, 1995.

6. Law, H., Ireland, S. and Hussain, Z., *The Psychology of Coaching, Mentoring and Learning*, John Wiley & Sons, Chichester, 2007.

7. Kroll, W. and Lewis, G., America's First Sport Psychologist, *Quest*, 13, 1-4.

8. Green, C.D., Psychology Strikes Out: Coleman R. Griffith and the Chicago Cubs, *History of Psychology*, 2003, 6(3), 267-283.

9. Dr Anthony M Grant, http://www.psych.usyd.edu.au/coach/anthony_m_grant.htm

10. Palmer, S., Putting the Psychology into Coaching: Stephen Palmer Interviews the Keynote Speakers from the 3rd BPS SGCP National Coaching Conference, *The Coaching Psychologist*, 2007, 3(3), 115-129.

11. Grant, A.M., Past, Present and Future: The Evolution of Professional Coaching and Coaching Psychology, in: Palmer, S. and Whybrow, A., eds., *Handbook of Coaching Psychology: A Guide for Practitioners*, Routledge, London, 2007, 25-39.

12. Palmer, S. and Cavanagh, M., Editorial – Coaching Psychology: Its Time Has Finally Come, *International Coaching Psychology Review*, 2006, 1(1), 1-3.

13. Grant, A.M. and Cavanagh, M.J., Toward a Profession of Coaching: Sixty-Five Years of Progress and Challenges for the Future, *International Journal of Evidence Based Coaching and Mentoring*, 2004, 2(1), 1-16.

14. Kauffman, C. and Bachkirova, T., The Evolution of Coaching: An Interview with Sir John Whitmore, *Coaching: An International Journal of Theory, Research and Practice*, 2008, 1(1), 11-15.

15. Palmer, S., Foreword, in: Law, H., Ireland, S. and Hussain, Z., eds., *The Psychology of Coaching, Mentoring and Learning*, John Wiley & Sons, Chichester, 2007, ix-xi.

16. Shapiro, M.B., Clinical Psychology as an Applied Science, *British Journal of Psychiatry*, 1967, 113, 1039-1042.

17. Shapiro, D., Renewing the Scientist-Practitioner Model, *The Psychologist*, 2002, 15(5), 232-234.

18. Shapiro, M.B., A Reassessment of Clinical Psychology as an Applied Science, *British Journal of Clinical Psychology*, 1985, 24, 1-11.

19. Leimon, A., Moscovici, F. and McMahon, G., *Essential Business Coaching*, Routledge, New York, 2005.

20. Tosey, P. and Gregory, J., *Dictionary of Personal Development*, Whurr Publishers, London, 2001.

21. Bandler, R. and Grinder, J., *The Structure of Magic 1: A Book about Language and Therapy*, Palo Alto, CA: Science and Behavior Books, 1975.

22. Grimley, B., NLP Coaching, in: Palmer, S. and Whybrow, A., eds., *Handbook of Coaching Psychology: A Guide for Practitioners*, Routledge, London, 2007, 193-210.

23. Hall, L.M., Was NLP Really a Child of the Human Potential Movement? *Resource Magazine*, 2006, 11 http://www.self-actualizing.org/articles/NLP_as_a_child_of_HPM.pdf

24. Puttick, E., The Human Potential Movement, in: Partridge, C., ed., *New Religions: A Guide*, Oxford University Press, New York, 2004; cited in: http://www.lcms.org/graphics/assets/media/CTCR/Web%20Site%20Evaluation%20Human%20Pot ential%20Movement%20091807.pdf

25. Anderson, W.T., *The Upstart Spring: Esalen and the Human Potential Movement: The First Twenty Years*, Addison Wesley, Reading, MA, 1983.

26. *Gale Encyclopedia of Psychology*, http://findarticles.com/p/articles/mi_g2699/is_/ai_2699000166

27. Starr, J., *The Coaching Manual: The Definitive Guide to the Process, Principles, and Skills of Personal Coaching*, 2nd edn., Pearson Education Limited, Harlow, UK, 2002.

28. McDermott, I. and Jago, W., *The Coaching Bible: The Essential Handbook*, Piatkus, London, 2005.

29. Alexander, G. and Renshaw, B., *Super Coaching: The Missing Ingredient for High Performance*, Random House Business Books, New York, 2005.

30. Gallwey, W.T., *The Inner Game of Work: Overcoming Mental Obstacles for Maximum Performance*, Texere, New York, 2002.

31. International Coach Federation, Coaching Core Competencies, http://www.coachfederation.org/ICF/For+Current+Members/Credentialing/Why+a+Credential/Competencies/

32. West, L. and Milan, M., *The Reflecting Glass: Professional Coaching for Leadership Development*, Palgrave, New York, 2001.

33. Palmer, S., PRACTICE: A Model Suitable for Coaching, Counselling, Psychotherapy and Stress Management, *The Coaching Psychologist*, 2007, 3(2), 71-77.

34. Dembkowski, S. and Eldridge, F., Beyond GROW: A New Coaching Model, *International Journal of Mentoring and Coaching*, 2003, 1(1).

35. Libri, V., Beyond GROW: In Search of Acronyms and Coaching Models, *International Journal of Mentoring and Coaching*, 2004, 2(1).

36. Jackson, P.Z. and McKergow, M., *The Solutions Focus: Making Coaching and Change SIMPLE*, 2nd edn., Nicholas Brealey, London, 2007.

37. Edgerton, N. and Palmer, S., SPACE: A Psychological Model for Use Within Cognitive Behavioural Coaching, Therapy and Stress Management, *The Coaching Psychologist*, 2005, 1(2), 25-31.

38. Neenan, M., and Palmer, S., Cognitive Behavioural Coaching, *Stress News*, 2001, 13(3), 15-18.

39. Neenan, M. and Palmer, S., Rational Emotive Behaviour Coaching, *Rational Emotive Behaviour Therapist*, 2001, 9(1), 34-41.

40. Passmore, J., Behavioural Coaching, in: Palmer, S. and Whybrow, A., eds., *Handbook of Coaching Psychology: A Guide for Practitioners*, Routledge, London, 2007, 73-85.

41. Kauffman, C. and Bachkirova, T., Editorial: An International Journal of Theory, Research & Practice: Why Does It Matter? *Coaching: An International Journal of Theory, Research and Practice*, 2008, 1(1), 1-7.

42. Harré, R. and Tissaw, M., *Wittgenstein and Psychology: A Practical Guide*, Ashgate Publishing Ltd., Aldershot, UK, 2005.

43. Greco, A., Heuristic Value of Simulation Models in Psychology, Http://cogprints.org/285/0/HEURIST.HTM

44. Wikipedia, List of Psychological Schools, http://en.wikipedia.org/wiki/List_of_psychological_schools

45. Lowry, R.J., ed., *The Journals of A.H. Maslow*, Vol. I, Brooks/Cole Publishing Co., Monterey, CA, 1979.

46. Maslow, A.H., A Theory of Human Motivation, *Psychological Review*, 1943, 50, 370-396.

47. Maslow, A.H., *Motivation and Personality*, Harper & Row, New York, NY, 1954.

48. Weatherbee, T., Dye, K. and Mills, A.J., There's Nothing as Good as a Practical Theory: The Paradox of Management Education, *Management & Organizational History*, 2008, 3(2), 147-160.

49. Maslow, A.H., *Towards a Psychology of Being*, Wiley, New York, 1968.

50. Washburn, M., *The Ego and the Dynamic Ground: A Transpersonal Theory of Human Development*, 2nd edn., SUNY Press, New York, 1995.

51. Gallwey, W.T., *The Inner Game of Tennis*, Jonathon Cape, London, 1974.

52. Gallwey, W.T., and Kriegel, R., *Inner Skiing*, Random House, New York, 1977.

52. Gallwey, W.T., *The Inner Game of Golf*, Jonathon Cape, London, 1979.

54.   Gallwey, W.T., *The Inner Game of Work*, Random House, New York, 1999.

55.   Jenkins, S., Zen Buddhism, Sport Psychology and Golf, *Annual Review of Golf Coaching*, 2008, 215-236.

56.   Bluckert, P., *Psychological Dimensions of Executive Coaching*, Open University Press, Maidenhead, UK, 2006.

57.   Association for Coaching, Press Release,
       http://www.associationforcoaching.com/news/M50101.htm

58.   Association for Coaching, Press Release,
       http://www.associationforcoaching.com/news/ACMay04.pdf

59.   Action Resources Ltd, http://www.motor-sport.uk.com/news.php?news_id=945

60.   Whitmore, J., *The Winning Mind*, Fernhurst Books, Steyning, West Sussex, UK, 1987.

61.   Ingenium Conference, 2006, http://conference.ingenium.org.nz/ing-web-06/keynotes/keynote-whitmore.htm

62.   McLeod, A., Sir John Whitmore Interviewed: Passion for Coaching
       www.angusmcleod.com/articles/passion%20for%20coaching%20%20sir%20john%20whitmore%20interviewed.doc

63.   Schutz, W.C., *FIRO: A Three Dimensional Theory of Interpersonal Behavior*, Holt, Rinehart & Winston, New York, 1958.

64.   Werner Erhart, Http://www.wernererhard.com

65.   Brock, V.G., *Grounded Theory of the Roots and Emergence of Coaching*, Doctoral Disssertation, International University of Professional Studies, Maui, HI, 2008.

66.   Nelson, L., Cushion, C. and Potrac, P., Formal, Nonformal and Informal Coach Learning: A Holistic Conceptualisation, *International Journal of Sports Science and Coaching*, 2006, 1(3), 247-259.

67.   Brock, V.G., Historical Facts about the Evolution of Coaching, The Foundation of Coaching, http://www.thefoundationofcoaching.org/chronicle-05302007

68.   Knibbs, A., Harris, C. and Farthing, P., The Evolution of Inner Game Coaching in the UK, http://www.innerworkscoaching.org/about.htm

69.   Whetten, D.A. and Cameron, K.S., *Developing Management Skills*, 6th edn., Pearson Prentice Hall, Upper Saddle River, NJ, 2005.

70.   Cameron, K.S., Whetten, D.A. and Kim, M.U., Organizational Dysfunctions of Decline, *Academy of Management Journal*, 1987, 30, 126-138.

71.   Durcan, J. and Oates, D., *The Manager as Coach: Developing Your Team for Maximum Performance*, Pitman Publishing, London, 1994.

72.   Whitmore, J., The Challenge for the Coaching Profession, *Coach & Mentor*, 2006, Spring, 8-9.

73.   Whitmore, J., Lessons I Have Learnt, *The Times*,
       http://business.timesonline.co.uk/tol/business/career_and_jobs/public_sector/article1571767.ece

74.   Whitmore, J., Freedom at Work: The Move Toward Self-Responsibility in the Corporate World, *Choice* 6(1), 23-25.

75.   Whitmore, J., The Roots and the Reach of Coaching,
       http://www.performanceconsultants.com/coaching/theroots.html

76.   Performance Consultants International,
       http://www.performanceconsultants.com/about/major_business_groups.html

77.   Be The Change, http://bethechange.org.uk/

78.   Performance Consultants International, Transpersonal Coaching in Action,
       http://www.performanceconsultants.com/coaching/transpersonal.html

The Impact of the Inner Game and Sir John Whitmore on Coaching:

A Commentary

Sir John Whitmore
Performance Consultants International Ltd,
93 Ifield Road, London, SW10 9AS, UK
E-mail: johnwhitmore@performanceconsultants.com

INTRODUCTION

This is an important and relevant article, not because it prominently features me, I hasten to add, but because it raises issues far beyond coaching and the psychological profession. The first sentence of Simon Jenkins' abstract clearly states the "local" issue and this is where I will begin my comments: "The purpose of this article is to raise issues concerned with "coaching psychology" and the tension between psychologists and non-psychologists in the field of coaching." (p. 1)

I like the article, as far as it goes, and I think it is a fair and comprehensive assessment of the situation and, along with my comments here, will engender new perspectives, debates and actions. I intend to be challenging; for which I make no apology, because optimal learning takes place on the edge, as most good educationalists will know; i.e., the edge between the comfort zone and the stretch zone. I will assume that you will have read Jenkins' article before reading this, so some of the background of my entry into the coaching field will be familiar.

RESISTANCE FROM THE PSYCHOLOGY ESTABLISHMENT

Not long after I had started the Inner Game organisation, tennis and ski schools, in England during the early 1980s, I gave a presentation at what purported to be the first British sports psychology conference, and I was shocked to discover that I was the only person there demonstrating practical application – in this case on a tennis court. All the other presentations were academic research papers, boring minutiae to me, and none of the presenters actually worked with sports people to help them improve their psychological preparedness to perform.

I was told by a participant that sport provided a convenient, measurable, controlled replicable activity and environment for psychological research; an easy way to meet the expectation for academics to publish papers to maintain their status and tenure. As I had left school at 17 with no 'A' level equivalent, this society was no place for me. Of course I had not been to a conventional University, but I was well into another one, the 'university of life', which included professional sport, the Esalen Institute and many different forms of self-development.

My sport, motor racing, employed no coaches, but I had experienced sports instructors at school and elsewhere. (Why were they called coaches?) It was not until I discovered the Inner Game that everything fell into place, and I knew immediately that this was what sports coaching should be. Sport was, however, stuck in the oldest trap in the world of passing from generation to generation obsolete methods that were too entrenched in huge immovable institutions. The good coaches were the mavericks who bucked the system and looked forwards not backwards. Traditional behavioural sports instruction urgently needed to be superseded by coaching based on the emerging, Humanistic and Transpersonal psychologies. I had no idea how tenacious the old guard would be when I came up against them in tennis and skiing, and I was amazed to find that academic psychology lagged so far behind as well when I got involved with workplace coaching.

I am reminded of the time of the emergence of the Humanistic psychotherapies and the resistance that some of the psychological establishment had to them and they even wanted to police them or demand that practitioners acquire academic qualifications. One part of this was that Freudian analysis could take up to five years, and when Behavioural and Cognitive therapies appeared, analysts claimed that they could not be effective that quickly; then the Human Potential movement appeared and the Behaviourists objected for the same reason. Of course each evolution of ideas threatens what has gone on before, and even the livelihood of the practitioners; and I believe that there is an element of this between psychologists and coaches today.

Now let us turn to the big picture of the psychosocial evolution of the collective, and the psycho-spiritual evolution of the individual. I assert that humanity is in a new evolutionary watershed, one that individuals can go through quicker thus revealing the sequence of stages that the collective will reach more slowly. The watershed is the decline in the power and the respect of hierarchy, and its replacement by far greater self-determination and self responsibility. This will only occur after passing through a period of liberation and licensed disorder which may take decades. I believe it is as significant as the Reformation.

Coaching is the only profession whose primary product is self-responsibility, and one which remains non-stigmatised, unlike psychotherapy and spiritual teaching. It can be argued that the coaching profession has emerged and grown so fast in the past 25 years expressly to meet this need for individual and collective self-responsibility. Indeed coaching itself needs to be self-responsible and not be 'controlled' by the psychological hierarchy. The two professions need to stand side by side and learn from each other for the benefit of both. I believe that they both have an equivalent amount to learn from each other about content and methods, but then we come back to their application.

I gave a challenging keynote recently at the Association of Business Psychologists annual conference and asked them what they were up to. I asserted that many businesses and business leaders were dysfunctional today and that they urgently needed psychological help to lift them out of their adolescent, tribal, greed and fear driven behaviours. All the while academic psychologists were busy doing research which would only tell us in two years time what we know already, or some irrelevant other minutiae. A number of them acknowledged the publication problem, and that they had little hands-on knowledge, experience or the confidence to work therapeutically with people or organisations.

Humanity is right now being hit hard by another great watershed, one that education has in part caused and could help to resolve. From the beginning of the industrial revolution 200 years ago, the new-found coal and oil fostered steel and immediate wealth for many, and we deluded ourselves that we could engineer our way to Utopia. We needed engineers and technological experts; and that in turn influenced the focus of education. Bridges, railways and steel ships were followed by cars and aeroplanes and some still believe that electronic marvels will get us there. Meanwhile, education became just about knowledge and was downgraded to league tables, degrees, etc. In the quest for ever more knowledge and technology, we lost the plot. We had focussed on quantity and missed quality. We forgot to teach wisdom, which enables us to use our technology responsibly. The result is that our technological misuse has taken humanity to the brink of self-elimination; first through nuclear weapons and now through non-renewable resources and uncontrollable emissions. We don't even have to foolishly push the nuclear button anymore; just doing nothing will be sufficient to wipe us all out.

Coaching teaches nothing, but evokes that which is within. That is where wisdom resides along with self-responsibility, emotional intelligence, freedom from fear, authenticity, values for the good of all; and so much more. Do we learn those qualities in school? No. Do we learn them in University? No. What about the psychology department? No. Do we learn them in business school? No again. Our education system has much to be accountable for and a great deal to learn.

WHAT VALUE CAN ACADEMIC PSYCHOLOGISTS ADD TO COACHING?

We can learn from each other and with each other. Of course there are coaches who have too little psychological knowledge, but most of the schools of coaching do cover the basics in an experiential format. There could and should be more. However, many coaches also have background experience in psychotherapy, which even if it did not lead to a degree, is often far more useful to a coach than all the psychological theories. For coaching, people skills are paramount, published papers are not. Of course therapists do accumulate a variety of psychological theories through their reading; which is fine, provided the author's views are seen as opinions not the truth, and as useful but not the only way.

The science of psychology is relatively new and is evolving; that which is seen as true today may be superseded tomorrow; that which is true of many people is not true of all, and it may require sensitive eclectic and often intuitive abilities, to choose an effective approach to a client. In those cases, too much adherence to or reliance on academic theories may well be a distraction and do more harm than good. I am tempted to turn the challenge the other way round and ask the academic theoreticians to prove that they can add value to the coaching profession. Of course they do in some ways, and I encourage coaches to pick up all the psychological knowledge they can along their way, but I don't believe that the theoreticians contribute as much practical value as they like to think they do. A little more humility from psychology departments might be in order in the light of these bigger issues about which they seem to know or care little.

EMOTIONAL INTELLIGENCE

I often ask a group of managers or trainee coaches to identify from their childhood an older person, other than a parent, who they still remember today with great affection, and to recall the qualities this person displayed that made him, but usually her, so special. Their answers are so consistent (regardless of culture) that I put them up on the screen before the sub-groups have finished sharing their own examples. This exercise provides a great understanding and illustration of what emotional intelligence is, and this is far easier to relate to and replicate than a written list of qualities that research has shown that emotionally intelligent people possess. I then point out that their grandmother, say, could equally have been described as a good coach, but had she ever done a coaching course or studied psychology? Of course not!

In his article, Jenkins refers several times to Esalen Institute, which is where I learned my psychology; not intellectually but experientially in therapy groups of all kinds but humanistic psychology based in the main. We were specifically invited to leave our brains outside the door and bring our senses and emotions to the table on the basis that analysis blocks or distorts experience, and limits the effectiveness of the therapy. It was of course fine to theorise about it all afterwards, but vital to have the experience first. How many academic psychologists have that luxury? Incidentally the extremes of the processes, the emotions and the catharses evoked by the experimental therapies on trial in those early days where hugely educational, but would scare the hell out of many university psychology students and professors alike. They were good times, and learning times that contributed hugely to my coaching, which followed a year or two later.

TRANSPERSONAL PSYCHOLOGY IN COACHING

I am pleased that Jenkins made clear reference to the application of transpersonal psychology in coaching. I frequently urge all coaches who are likely to work at any level other than the most superficial with clients or groups to gain knowledge and experience of the use of transpersonal models that are so valuable, if not essential, when coaching more conscious and evolved people. These are the people who often seek coaching because they feel unfulfilled in their day job, and they want to have more meaning in what they do now, and also find more purpose to do what they will do in future. These are transpersonal issues and need to be facilitated by coaches or therapists who are knowledgeable and experienced in that area. This is entering the spiritual arena, and it raises the issue of whether that can be facilitated effectively by someone who has not yet addressed their own spirituality? The jury is out on that for me – but I doubt it.

Many universities do not yet even teach transpersonal psychology in their psychology departments and that is an absurd and irresponsible omission. In this area, coaches have something to teach academics for they are ahead of the game. Most eastern cultures do not separate the psychological and the spiritual along the developmental journey. If one works all over the world as I do, you will need to know this. The dividing line between the two in our western world is arbitrary and unreal, the product of scientific reductionism. The largest coaching organisations like the International Coach Federation (ICF) and the Association of Coaching (AC) will, I hope, soon list an understanding of the transpersonal as obligatory for their highest coaching qualifications. If so, they will be showing universities the way. Of course such organisations can often move faster to change their qualifications or adopt new ideas, because they have less bureaucracy and do not have to wait for the results of research into the obvious.

SELF-DEVELOPMENT AND INTUITION

One particularly important point on this subject arises now and it is closely related to the transpersonal. When we work in any situation, but especially in dealing with people, the intuition can play an important role, and it does in coaching. There may be logical, linear or rational reasons for a coach to take a certain direction; either following the rules of coaching or the rules of psychology, but the coach intuitively takes a different route and it results in a breakthrough for the client. The rationalist will dismiss that, and say that it occurred by chance. On the contrary, I believe that as we go through our own self-development journey, we increase our reliance on our intuition, and I encourage coaches to do just that. Correct me if I am wrong, but in academic psychology the intuition does not exist because is not measurable or replicable.

THE GROW MODEL

Jenkins' paper refers to a number of maps and models from Maslow to the GROW model about which I will make some opening remarks before referring to GROW specifically. I emphasise that maps and models provide a lens though which one can explore a subject, but they are neither true, nor absolute, nor imperative. They are also over-simplifications which give them their accessibility to all, thereby making them more usable and useful. Jenkins states that Maslow's well known Hierarchy of Needs is far simpler than his original work and far simpler than the similar model, now called Spiral Dynamics, created by Clare Graves after painstakingly detailed research (see [1]).

In my work I attempt to limit my models to three stages, but no more than four whenever possible; for example: 'Dependence – Independence – Interdependence' (for personal development) [2]; Inclusion – Assertion – Cooperation (for teams) [3]; Need – Greed – Freedom (for everyone) [4]; and 'Forming – Storming – Norming – Performing' (for teams) [5]. Such minimalist models leave more space for discussion, learning is extended, and they also allow for additions. Contrary to what many think, I did not 'invent' the GROW model. GROW was actually first coined by Max Landsberg of McKinsey during a conversation about coaching with my then colleague Graham Alexander. We had been trying to find a 4-stage acronym for a while and that one just appeared in that conversation. It had little significance at the time, but then it caught on. It is, as I have stated before, not copyrighted, definitive, obligatory, exclusive or any of that; though another colleague, Alan Fine, later inappropriately but unsuccessfully laid claim to its exclusive use in the USA. However, I was the first to publish it in my book *Coaching for Performance* (1992), which then went on to become a best seller and coaching text book in many languages and countries [6]. Hence GROW became universal and was attributed to me.

In reality, though, GROW says nothing about coaching. Coaching is about raising awareness and responsibility. GROW is no more than a useful chronological sequence for a coaching conversation that could equally be used in a command and control situation or for addressing an item in a Board meeting. In coaching, the only element of it that is not immediately obvious to the uninitiated is that the Goal comes before Reality. If people consider Reality first, they become drawn towards incremental remedial actions even with some negative connotations. Alternatively if the Goal is explored and established first, the action takes the form of how to get there from here and is orientated more towards the positive or the potential. Furthermore remedial actions may be attractive in the short term, but they may divert attention from the ultimate Goal.

CONCLUSION

As I stated above, I believe that Simon Jenkins' article and these comments between them will engender a serious debate about the role, relationship and responsibilities of coaching and academic psychology; not only 'locally', but in the troubled world today. How can we help to heal the dysfunctional people and institutions that have got us into this mess? We are all a part of the problem, and are therefore able to play a part in the solution.

REFERENCES

1.   Beck, D.E. and Cowan, C.C., *Spiral Dynamics: Mastering Values, Leadership, and Change*, Blackwell Publishing, Oxford, 1996.

2.   Covey, S.R., *The 7 Habits of Highly Effective People*, Simon & Schuster, London, 1989.

3.   Schutz, W.C., *FIRO: A Three Dimensional Theory of Interpersonal Behavior*, Holt, Rinehart & Winston, New York, 1958.

4.   Whitmore, J., *Need, Greed or Freedom: Business Changes and Personal Choices*, Element Books, Ltd., Shaftesbury, Dorset, UK, 1997.

5.   Tuckman, B., Developmental Sequence in Small Groups, *Psychological Bulletin,* 63(6), 384-399.

6.   Whitmore, J., *Coaching for Performance: GROWing People, Performance and Purpose*, 3rd edn., Nicholas Brealey, London, 2002.

The Impact of the Inner Game and Sir John Whitmore on Coaching:

A Commentary

Stephen Palmer[1] and Alison Whybrow[2]
[1]Centre for Coaching, 156 Westcombe Hill,
Blackheath, London, SE3 7DH, UK
E-mail: dr.palmer@btinternet.com
[2]i-coach academy Ltd.
56 Queen Anne Street, London W1G 8LA, UK
E-mail: alison@i-coachacademy.com

INTRODUCTION

Simon Jenkins is to be congratulated on writing an interesting lead article on different aspects of coaching and coaching psychology which acknowledges the important contribution of Sir John Whitmore (and others). We have chosen to comment jointly as we worked closely together (with colleagues) on the development of the UK coaching psychology project as the co-proposers of the British Psychological Society (BPS) Special Group in Coaching Psychology and are the co-editors of the *Handbook of Coaching Psychology* [1] which has been referred to a number of times in Simon Jenkins' article. Jenkins' states in his abstract, 'The purpose of this article is to raise issues concerned with "coaching psychology" and the tension between psychologists and non-psychologists in the field of coaching.' Our commentary will focus on this key theme.

SHAPING OF THE COACHING INDUSTRY OR PROFESSION

Jenkins' article provides an illustrative account of some of the events and people that have shaped aspects of the coaching industry or profession. The 'Inner Game' has captured people's imaginations and engaged their understanding with regard the importance of raising self-awareness and through that, the concept of personal responsibility for outcomes. The GROW acronym [2] provides a straightforward, and as with many such process models, a structure which has clarity and validity for those working in the field enabling a relatively inexperienced coach to start coaching effectively with the complex and inexact science of human performance and potentially deliver beneficial outputs. This is empowerment in action. The Jenkins article storyboard is interesting and engaging.

SHAPING OF THE COACHING PSYCHOLOGY PROFESSION

In a parallel and overlapping story, the development of the coaching psychology profession is covered in the article with particular reference to the work of Coleman Griffith [3], Stephen Palmer and Alison Whybrow [e.g.,1], Bruce Grimley [4], Anthony Grant and Michael Cavanagh [e.g., 5], Ho Law and associates [6], and others. Jenkins highlights how the definitions / descriptions of coaching psychology were revised as the proposal to set up the BPS Special Group in Coaching Psychology passed through different committee stages.

What may be less obvious is how the development of coaching psychology in the UK reflected the input and feedback from the members of the Coaching Psychology Forum (CPF) and the BPS Special Group in Coaching Psychology. (The CPF was the pre-cursor of the BPS Special Group.) Surveys were undertaken (and this still continues) which investigated the views of members and provided information about their coaching psychology practice, such as what coaching approaches they used [7, 8]. The challenge for Palmer and Whybrow was to ensure that the fast developing coaching psychology profession in the UK was accurately reflected in their Handbook [1]. As psychologists from different psychological fields became members, they influenced the development of the profession. Thus the path coaching psychology took in the UK differs somewhat from that taken in Australia.

IS THERE A TENSION BETWEEN COACHES AND COACHING PSYCHOLOGISTS?

One of the key themes that develop in the story is of a possible tension between psychologists and non-psychologists who coach. The precise nature of the tensions are somewhat nebulous. Perhaps the tension is between the two professions, but is this a reality?

Coaching psychology is a domain within the coaching industry[1] that draws on a particular foundation of knowledge and expertise with the intention of enhancing capability and practice standards across the industry. Professional bodies in this domain (such as the BPS Special Group in Coaching Psychology) are inclusive and engaged with professional bodies that represent the coaching profession more broadly.

Coaching psychologists are a distinct group who by virtue of the common threads to their professional development will generally have more psychological knowledge and expertise than the (much larger) group of coaches who are not psychologists. The shared common knowledge of psychologists is developed by undertaking a three year full-time (or longer if part-time) accredited psychology degree with additional postgraduate training and supervised practice. The importance of understanding theory and research in the different fields of psychology is reinforced throughout the years of study. Given this, it would be very difficult for a psychologist to use GROW without considering the underpinning psychological theory and knowledge.

---

[1] During the Association for Coaching (AC), "Embracing Excellence" International Conference in London (March 2008), both Palmer and Whitmore stated in speeches that they believe coaching in the UK has moved from being an industry to a profession. Palmer covered it in more depth at the 1st European Coaching Psychology Conference in London (December 2008).

Against this contextual background, it is important to note that there are likely to be a number of coaches with a similar level of psychological knowledge and expertise by virtue of their training and background. There are likely to be many coaches who are very effective in their practice without any specific psychological training. There will be psychologists who would not make good coaches, and would not claim otherwise. Jenkins' article draws attention to Palmer and Cavanagh's [9] statement that coaching psychologists "bring more than just a framework for a conversation with a client, such as the famous GROW model", bringing "a host of psychological theories and models that underpin, and bring depth to, the coaching relationship" [9, p. 1]. It could also be argued that understanding the underlying theory and research of coaching with additional knowledge of mental health problems, may not always be necessary but become much more important when difficulties arise in coaching. Knowledge of the GROW model alone may not always be sufficient. A typical example would be within executive coaching when the coachee has a personality disorder which may be leading to interpersonal problems at work and/or a block to change.

EMBRACING DIVERSITY

What is interesting as the coaching profession develops, is how coaches can embrace the diversity in their field, learn from each other and access the array of different knowledge bases to support them in developing the coaching practice that fits with who they are and the purpose they hold for coaching. This applies equally to coaching psychologists.

The contribution to coaching and coaching psychology by coaches has been recognised by the BPS Special Group in Coaching Psychology. For example, at their Annual Coaching Psychology Conference in December 2007, Sir John Whitmore received a conference award for his outstanding contribution to the field of coaching. At the recent 1st European Coaching Psychology conference in December, 2008, the BPS Special Group gave their first research award for distinguished research into coaching psychology to Eve Turner (a non-psychologist, as it happens). In her acceptance speech Eve Turner similarly called for coaches to embrace psychological as well as other relevant bodies of knowledge and expertise.

CONCLUSION

We believe the tension alluded to in Jenkins' article between coaches and coaching psychologists and the relevant professions, which may only exist to a small extent, is largely based on misunderstandings. As misunderstandings are also an opportunity for constructive dialogue and exploration, we would encourage coaches and coaching psychologists alike to explore areas of misunderstanding and gain greater insight into the value of the diversity that is offered across the coaching profession.

At the professional body level, the BPS Special Group in Coaching Psychology continues to enjoy a successful reciprocal relationship with the Association for Coaching (AC), one of the leading coaching bodies with a growing National and International membership. We hope this continues.

We thank Simon Jenkins for inviting us to comment on his paper.

REFERENCES

1.   Palmer, S. and Whybrow, A., eds., *Handbook of Coaching Psychology: A Guide for Practitioners*, Routledge, London, 2007.

2.   Whitmore, J., *Coaching for Performance: GROWING People, Performance and Purpose*, 3rd edn., Nicholas Brealey Publishing, London, 2002.

3.   Griffith, C. R., *Psychology of Coaching: A Study of Coaching Methods from the Point of View of Psychology*, Charles Scribner's Sons, New York, 1926.

4.   Grimley, B., NLP Coaching, in: Palmer, S. and Whybrow, A., eds., *Handbook of Coaching Psychology: A Guide for Practitioners*, Routledge, London, 2007, 193-210.

5.   Grant, A.M. and Cavanagh, M.J., Toward a Profession of Coaching: Sixty-Five Years of Progress and Challenges for the Future, *International Journal of Evidence Based Coaching and Mentoring*, 2004, 2(1), 1-16.

6 .   Law, H., Ireland, S. and Hussain, Z., *The Psychology of Coaching, Mentoring and Learning*, John Wiley & Sons, Chichester, UK, 2007.

7.   Whybrow, A. and Palmer, S. Taking Stock: A Survey of Coaching Psychologists' Practices and Perspectives, *International Coaching Psychology Review*, 2006a,1(1), 56-70.

8.   Whybrow, A. and Palmer, S., Shifting Perspectives: One Year into the Development of the British Psychological Society Special Group in Coaching Society in the UK, *International Coaching Psychology Review*, 2006b, 1(2), 85.

9.   Palmer, S. and Cavanagh, M., Editorial – Coaching Psychology: Its Time Has Finally Come, *International Coaching Psychology Review*, 2006, 1(1), 1-3.

DECLARATIONS

Stephen Palmer holds posts in the BPS Special Group in Coaching Psychology, Association for Coaching and the Society for Coaching Psychology. Alison Whybrow holds posts in the BPS Special Group in Coaching Psychology.

The Impact of the Inner Game and Sir John Whitmore on Coaching:

A Commentary

Lynda St. Clair

Department of Management
Bryant University, 1150 Douglas Pike, Suite G
Smithfield, RI 02197-1284, USA
E-mail: Lstclair@bryant.edu

INTRODUCTION

In his analysis of the impact of the Inner Game and Sir John Whitmore on coaching, Simon Jenkins focuses on the historical development of different views of coaching. In particular, he considers the argument put forth by Palmer and Cavanagh that coaching psychologists are better equipped to serve as coaches because they "bring a host of psychological theories and models that underpin and bring depth to, the coaching relationship." [1, p.1]   A key element for Palmer is the fact that coaching psychologists "have had rigorous university level training in psychology…" [2, p. 118]. In contrast, Whitmore has questioned the value of "purely academic psychology" as opposed to the actual practice of psychology [3, p. 13]. At its core, this debate between coaching psychologists and non-psychologist coaches comes down to the question: "Who should be coaching the coaches?"

BARRIERS OF ENTRY INTO THE COACHING PROFESSION

Future research on the outcomes of coaching interventions will continue to help refine our understanding of what makes coaches effective, a primary concern for both coaches and their clients. Unlike their clients, however, coaches have an additional reason for being concerned about who coaches the coaches – establishing criteria for entering the profession not only helps to ensure the quality of the services provided, it also creates barriers to entry that act to improve the economic viability of the coaching profession.

Professional coaches and consultants are in the business of helping others. As the business of coaching continues to grow and attract new practitioners, the field becomes more competitive. Thus, coaches need to find ways to distinguish themselves and establish their own competitive advantage in the marketplace. Whether psychologists or non-psychologists, coaches are not only working to help others, they are also working for themselves. Some may be focused on generating income through the sale of consulting services or books. Others may be focused on publishing journal articles to help build their academic reputations and achieve tenure or promotion. Regardless of the particular context in which they are working, however, even the most altruistic of coaches must face the reality of competition.

Because of concerns about competition, coaching psychologists have an incentive to dismiss the work of coaches who do not have a background in psychology. Similarly, individuals striving to earn a living as coaches have an incentive to create proprietary models. The benefit of a catchy acronym is primarily marketing. It gives one something to trademark and use as a brand. In every profession, creating barriers to entry can help to create a reputation of legitimacy and value – the coaching profession is no different. People whose livelihoods derive from coaching have good reason to be concerned about who coaches the coaches. People who look to coaches for assistance may consider credentials and experience when selecting a coach, but their primary concern is what happens as a result of the coaching process.

COACHING EFFECTIVENESS

From the client's perspective, there appear to be far more similarities than differences when looking at different approaches to coaching. Regardless of the acronyms they use or the theories that they espouse, good coaches listen, ask questions, and try to help those being coached figure things out for themselves. For each individual who seeks out a coach, it is not important whether their coach's techniques are based on neuro-linguistic programming, Gestalt theories, or Sir John Whitmore's experiences as a race car driver. What is important is that the coach can help that individual. Because each individual is unique, the best coaching processes must also be unique – tailored to the needs of a particular individual at a particular time and place.

There is little doubt that both formal education and field experience are valuable sources of information that a coach can draw on when working with a client. Paradoxically, if a coach attempts to use that information in a formulaic way, the value of the coaching experience is reduced. Consider an analogy: When baking bread, is an understanding of the chemical reactions between yeast and sugar and flour necessary? No – having a recipe will suffice. If, however, the baker discovers that they don't have exactly the right ingredients on hand, then understanding what is happening as the different ingredients interact can increase the likelihood that a loaf of edible bread can still be baked.

Just as there are myriad recipes available for baking bread, myriad "recipes" for how to improve performance are available in books, on tape, and online. Yet, just as people seeking to learn to bake bread may choose to go to culinary school or to their grandmothers' kitchens, people seeking help with their personal performance concerns look to coaches to help them. Why? Because they know, whether intuitively or from past experience, that recipes are not sufficient when seeking to make significant personal change.

Effective coaches do not just give instructions or explain theories of mental health, motivation, adaptive systems, and personal growth. Effective coaches do not just offer acronyms to help clients remember a list of steps that need to be followed. Effective coaches find some way to connect with their clients so that their clients can find the courage to change themselves. For some, that courage may come from seeing statistical data on the efficacy of goal setting. For others, that courage may come from listening to a story of how an average tennis player learned to excel by paying attention to the ball, rather than to the conversation in his head.

CONCLUSION

For those who are truly committed to the ARHPCC's mission of bridging the gap between academic, professional and lay discourse on coaching and consulting, it turns out that the real question is not "Who should be coaching the coaches?" but "What can we learn from one another to become better coaches for our clients?"

REFERENCES

1.   Palmer, S. and Cavanagh, M., Editorial – Coaching Psychology: Its Time Has Finally Come, *International Coaching Psychology Review*, 2006, 1(1), 1-3.

2.   Palmer, S., Putting the Psychology into Coaching: Stephen Palmer Interviews the Keynote Speakers from the 3rd BPS SGCP National Coaching Conference, *The Coaching Psychologist*, 2007, 3(3), 115-129.

3.   Kauffman, C. and Bachkirova, T., The Evolution of Coaching: An Interview with Sir John Whitmore, *Coaching: An International Journal of Theory, Research and Practice*, 2008, 1(1), 11-15.

beyond the limiting tensions, to explore and understand more fully what coaching is, and so avoid the destructive and wasteful combat in which so many psychotherapists became caught up as their profession evolved. One of our fears, which this debate touches, is it seems to me the fear of our own ineffectualness. When we coach, we enter the domain where change is possible, but where there is also therefore the possibility of no change and the possibility of disappointment. We re-live, mostly at an unconscious level, all the ways in which we would have liked to make our own lives different, and all the hopes and fears for what we can change and what we cannot. We find it hard to inhabit that frightening space without defences, and one of the defences we clutch most closely to us is the defence of superior knowledge. 'Because I know more than many, I am more effectual than they'. So those of us who are psychologists feel fear when the validity of that superior knowledge is threatened, and those of us who are not psychologists feel rage and envy that we do not have that defence available to us.

COACHING EFFECTIVENESS

This sore point is made yet more tender by virtue of the fact that we cannot know with any degree of certainty how 'successful' our coaching has been. A good outcome for our coachee may have just been coincidental with our coaching of them, rather than the result of our work. What appears to be a good outcome today may not turn out to be good in the long run. A good outcome may not be as good as what would have happened if we had not intervened, or if we had done something different. We are a long way from the kind of scientific evidence which might reassure us on these points, and I am not sure that we will ever reach certainty. We open our hearts and muster our courage to engage in an activity which may at best be irrelevant, at worst damaging. We have to live with that uncertainty.

PSYCHOLOGICAL PRINCIPLES VERSUS LIFE EXPERIENCES

So those of us who are psychologists take refuge in the teachings of psychology: 'We followed all the principles of behavioural change, we attended to the complete set of relationship dynamics so we know we have done a good job.' We are frightened when someone suggests those teachings are not relevant, for then we shall have to face the void again.

And of course we project our own fear of not knowing onto those who are not psychologists: 'You do not have these principles to follow, you are much less sure that your work is good.' So, inevitably, understandably, and classically, we elicit anger in our non-psychologist colleagues. They know that psychology does not guarantee effective coaching, they believe that much of their best work comes from their life experience and not from text books, but they are left alone to wrestle with the difficulty of measuring effectiveness while we psychologists wrap ourselves in the flag of academic respectability.

CONCLUSION

So it seems to me we should face our fears together. It is at present a mystery, how one person can have a conversation with another which enables change. It is a rich mystery too. Sometimes change comes from a conversation with someone who ridicules us. Sometimes from someone who loves us unconditionally. Sometimes from a fool. Sometimes a wise person. For now, we should stay calm and explore together all the phenomena which occur under the banner of 'coaching'. It is not yet time (and maybe never will be) to rule out and rule in, out of fear of the unknown.

REFERENCES

1.   Berglas, S., The Very Real Dangers of Executive Coaching, *Harvard Business Review*, 2002, June, 87-92.

The Impact of the Inner Game and Sir John Whitmore on Coaching:

A Commentary

Jonathan Passmore
Coaching Psychology Unit
University of East London,
Romford Road, London, E15 4LZ, UK
Email: jonathancpassmore@yahoo.co.uk

INTRODUCTION

Simon Jenkins' article raises some interesting and contentious topics that are the subject of debate within coaching and between psychologists and non-psychologists. This commentary explores the notion of difference between psychological and non-psychological practitioners and the application of their knowledge to the arena of coaching. The commentary also reviews the contribution of writers and practitioners such as John Whitmore and Myles Downey to coaching practice.

PSYCHOLOGY: DOES IT MATTER AND WHAT FOR?

Jenkins' paper explores the debate around the nature of coaching psychology. It notes how the definition has been changing and developing over the past decade to reflect the scientists' (academics') and practitioners' thinking, but with a common base of practice being explicitly underpinned by psychological knowledge.

The debate misses the question, 'what is psychological knowledge?'. Many non-psychologists hold the view that 'psychology' is a dark, deep, unknowable knowledge held by a few. Many psychologists take a different view. For many of us psychology is the study of human behaviour, cognition and emotion; i.e., at its simplest, it is what people think, feel and do. As humans, we all have direct experience of observing and thinking about what others are doing, thinking and feeling. We only need to sit at a table in Pizza Express to observe the couple talking, laughing or arguing, with their body language and facial expressions, to have a view about what others think and feel. George Kelly, a humanistic psychologist, suggested the same, when he noted 'we are all psychologists'.

As practicing psychologists, we may formalise some of these processes, observing larger groups or asking their opinions, so we can generalise our opinions from the couple to the wider population. Further, we create experiments to observe outcomes; such as what happens to the couple who have just had an argument when we call one of the couple away for a telephone call and send over a bunch of red roses to the other one with a note which says 'sorry'.

In coaching, I would suggest all coaches are concerned with what their coachee thinks, feels and does. They have views (hypotheses) about why this may be the case and plans (interventions) as to what they might do with their coachee to help them move forward. However, a coaching psychologist or a coach trained in psychology is underpinned by psychological principles and is likely to be able to go further in being able to describe why they have selected this plan rather than another, and what evidence (previous published studies) support the use of intervention A as opposed to intervention B.

From the coachee's perspective, will they do anything different? My own research [1] with a sample of some 250 experienced coaches in the UK drawn from members of the Association for Coaching (AC) (primarily a non-psychologically trained group) and the British Psychologically Society Special Group in Coaching Psychology (BPS SGCP) (primarily a psychologically trained group) found that both psychologically trained coaches (either chartered or licensed with the BPS or an equivalent body) and non-psychologically trained coaches use the same behaviours drawn from a sample of coaching behaviours from humanistic, behavioural, cognitive-behavioural, motivational interviewing, and psychodynamic models. While not conclusive, the research appears to support the argument by trained coaches who are not trained in psychology that they do the same work as those coaches who have psychological background.

So what else may be the difference? The second difference noted in Jenkins' article is that psychological coaches have a psychological underpinning to their work. It is true that chartered psychologists, due to the common aspects in their training, will all share a joint understanding of human motivation, behaviours and change. However, such a body of knowledge is not exclusive to psychologists. Many people, with backgrounds in human resources, consulting and other disciplines have knowledge which overlaps with that held by psychologists, due to the common (doing, feeling and thinking) nature of psychological issues. What can be argued is that the best trained non-psychological coaches are likely to hold much of the knowledge of a psychologist, while less well trained coaches may rely of varying versions of intuition which may be close to, or far from, the reality of the coachee. It is also fair to say that little if any research has been undertaken to explore the knowledge differences between practicing coaching psychologists and non-psychologically trained coaches, and this is an area worthy of further research.

The third area which was not explored in the article, but is worthy of comment, is the difference in the training between psychologists and non-psychologists when working with clients who have as yet undiagnosed clinical needs. Writing about the USA business sector, Berglas [2] suggested that the numbers in this category were sufficiently high to be a cause for concern; i.e., that non-psychologically trained coaches were working with such individuals as if they were 'normal' and on the assumption they would respond to non-clinical interventions. From a UK perspective, Buckley and Buckley [3] made a similar point that mental health issues are widespread and coaches will come into contact with these on a regular and frequent basis. Recognition of such conditions can be difficult, however - even for psychologists. This is particularly true in the UK, where the majority of coaching psychologists have a background and training in occupational settings, where clinical issues are not included as part of their training. As a result, training for coaching should include clinical aspects if we are to equip coaching psychologists and other practitioners with the skills needed to identify and refer such clients.

The final area which has been discussed, but again which is not covered in detail is coaching research. While many practitioners are highly qualified, few have the level and rigour of training found among psychologists. This training provides a background in the scientific methods applied to the human condition and, as a result, much of the recent robust research has been undertaken by psychologists with an interest in coaching practice. This includes qualitative studies using recognised and respected methodologies such as Grounded Theory [1] or Interpretative Phenomenological Analysis (IPA) [4, 5] or quantitative approaches with control groups and random allocation of participants to conditions [6, 7]. It is only through these methods that coaching is going to offer the evidence that it can make a difference to the lives of individual and secondly how it makes this difference [8]. It is this research and peer reviewed publication which will help coaching establish itself as an evidence-based domain of practice.

THE CONTRIBUTION OF NON-PSYCHOLOGICAL WRITERS

In the second part of his article, Jenkins moves to highlight the role of non-psychologically trained practitioners such as Sir John Whitmore and Myles Downey. Both are rightly attributed with taking coaching from what the very best humans naturally do when developing others.

Indeed, coaching has caught the zeitgeist. The new millennium has seen a stronger movement towards the individual and away from treating all employees the same. There has been a parallel movement towards personal learning and towards individuals taking greater responsibility in the workplace. Coaching offers a way by which organisations can deliver a more personalised development agenda.

In this process, Jenkins correctly identified John Whitmore as one of the defining figures of coaching. Whitmore is a writer, thinker and practitioner who maybe has done more than anyone over the past decades to popularise coaching, through his book, *Coaching for Performance*, which has sold more than 500,000 copies and has been translated in to thirty-two languages across the world including Korean and Turkish; and his conference presentations and consulting work with Performance Consultants / Performance Consultants International.

Jenkins summarises the historical development of the coaching approach through Whitmore's work, but at the centre the two key concepts of awareness and responsibility are rightly highlighted. Although less explicit, these principles run through the work of leaders in the field of coaching psychology such as Tony Grant and Stephen Palmer, whose contribution to building the new domain of coaching is considerable.

CONCLUSION

While Jenkins suggests that the divide between psychologists and non-psychologists is a dichotomy, I have suggested in this commentary that this is a false dichotomy, which does no favours to either coaching psychologist or to coaching practitioners.

Instead it has been argued that initial evidence suggests that, in practical terms for the coachee, there may be little difference in the practice between experienced coaches and experienced coaching psychologists. The prime difference may be in their ability to describe what they do or their interest in undertaking and writing research led publications.

REFERENCES

1. Passmore, J., *Workplace Coaching*, Unpublished Doctoral Thesis, University of East London, UK, 2008.

2. Berglas, S., The Very Real Dangers of Executive Coaching, *Harvard Business Review*, 2002, June, 87-92.

3. Buckley, A. and Buckley, C., *A Guide to Coaching and Mental Health: The Recognition and Management of Psychological Issues*, Routledge, Hove, UK, 2006.

4. Gyllensten, K. and Palmer, S., The Relationship Between Coaching and Workplace Stress, *International Journal of Health Promotion and Education*, 2005, 43(3), 97-103.

5. Gyllensten, K. and Palmer, S., The Coaching Relationship: An Interpretative Phenomenological Analysis, *International Coaching Psychology Review*, 2007, 2(2), 168-177.

6. Spence, G. and Grant, A.M., Professional and Peer Life Coaching and the Enhancement of Goal Striving and Well-Being: An Exploratory Study, *Journal of Positive Psychology*, 2007, 2(3), 185-194.

7. Green, S., Grant, A. and Rynsaardt, J., Evidence-Based Life Coaching for Senior High School Students: Building Hardiness and Hope, *International Coaching Psychology Review*, 2007, 2(1), 24-32.

8. Passmore, J. and Gibbes, C., The State of Executive Coaching Research: What Does the Current Literature Tell Us and What's Next for Coaching Research?, *International Coaching Psychology Review*, 2007, 2(2), 116-128.

The Impact of the Inner Game and Sir John Whitmore on Coaching:

A Commentary

Angus McLeod
Angus McLeod Associates
27 Upton Gardens,
Upton-upon-Severn, WR8 0NU, UK
E-mail: am@angusmcleod.com

INTRODUCTION

There is a tangible rivalry between psychologist-coaches and so-called 'non-psychologist coaches'. Let's give the latter their own descriptor, 'practitioner-coaches'. This tension between the psychologist-coaches and practitioner-coaches may be due to differences in their approaches. The psychologists have a tendency to 'a priori', science-based approaches to coaching while the practitioner-coaches come broadly from 'a posteriori' approaches – that is, they use many methods that are generated from practical experience. Simplistically, one might imagine that the psychologists would be thinking and analyzing with reference to proven, academic models, while the practitioner-coaches might be listening and reacting more. But life is more complicated than this.

ANALYSIS VERSUS INSTINCT

Within the practitioner-coach group there is another raft of tension between people whose practice comes largely from instinct and those who (rather like the many disciples of psychology) operate from rational thoughts using a range of models. Models used by practitioner-coaches come from widely different disciplines; for example, emotional intelligence, transactional analysis and neuro-linguistic programming. A question might arise therefore whether the best coaching for most individuals is provided by the thinking analyst (whether psychologist or model-rich, practitioner-coach) or by the quietly-minded, instinctive coach.

QUALITY OF ATTENTION, TRUST AND THE INNER GAME

The main advantage of the instinctive coach is that their head is not busy. Hence the quality of attention to the coachee can be expected to be significantly better than that given by coaches who are analysing what the coachee is saying with reference to their science. Better quality of attention will invariably lead to a deeper level of trust in the coachee; by itself, this trust can have a very significant impact for deeper learning. To my mind the deepening of the trust by the person-centred coach, of any discipline, creates a platform for generative, coaching-performance. In other words, models can get in the way! And that philosophy is close to that of Tim Gallwey, father of the 'Inner Game'.

Tim Gallwey stimulated the modern world of coaching with a disciplined approach to 'keeping out of the way' of the coachee's experiential learning; their 'learning journey'. This honouring of the coachee keeps the responsibility for their learning firmly with the coachee. This is at the heart of best practice in all the practitioner-coach sector (who perform the vast majority of coaching in the market). Regrettably, the disciplines arising from this value of 'keeping out of the way' may not be as well understood or practised by all psychologist-coaches. An exception are those psychologists coming from a Gestalt background, who often find that the Gallwey model, the 'Inner Game', sits well with their professional work in which 'principles not tools'[1] inform the facilitation/coaching process at its extreme. That is, without any goal to inform the progress of the therapeutic experience (which is not coaching per se, as there is no goal or target which is essential to coaching).

In those coaches who have many models and methods at their disposal, many are too involved in internal processing to have adequate attention with their coachees. It appears that there may only be a minority of such coaches whose familiarity with their tool-kit is so integrated and complete, that they can 'let go' and attend deeply to the psychological states of their coachee; if you will, 'subconscious competence'.

Michael Hall, with an ongoing and creative career in the development of NLP-based models, provides numerous and often quite complicated models to trainees on his extensive coach-training programmes. If you want to see the best of his coaches however, you would be well-advised to watch Michele Duval, a former co-developer with Michael, whose ability to park her resources and stay with the coachee (in an intense and co-creational way) produces first-rate coaching as well as motivated action/success in her coachees. I suspect that the same ability to 'park resources' may apply to the best psychologist-coaches too; many others, for all their 'resources/tools' can sometimes be too highly cerebral to take exquisite care of the dynamic space and the human that should be evolving in front of them. From my perspective, the answer to the question, 'where should the coach's attention be?' is 'very predominantly with the coachee and not in mental processing'.

TRANSFERENCE

Psychologist-coaches can sometimes bring vital discipline to coaching that many practitioner-coaches who have graduated from commercial training courses (of any length) may fail to provide. That is, in the area of psychological transference. All coaches would do well to understand and notice transference, whether projection towards them from their coachee or counter-projection tendencies in themselves towards their coachee.

---

[1] Gallwey, T., International Coach Federation (ICF) Plenary lecture, 1999.

COACHING EFFECTIVENESS

A few psychologist-researchers are also helping to measure the effectiveness of coaching using taught disciplines of best practice in statistics. Unfortunately, there is not one best-practice that relates to the journey of any single coaching session. However, bulk statistics ought to throw more light on the general efficacy of particular coaching approaches over time.

A remaining question must be 'how good is a particular coach?' From any discipline where I had the privilege to observe, the effectiveness of any set of coaches (operating from one single methodology) is highly variable. To help unravel this conundrum, we may be well advised then to understand more about both the skills and mind-sets of master-coaches. This knowledge may be achieved by mapping excellence as carried out by the founders of NLP, including the pioneering work of Robert Dilts.

CATHARTIC LEARNING

Another interesting measure of coaching performance might be to map the conversations and body-clues that lead to 'cathartic learning' in the coachee. These episodes, in my experience as a coach and observer, are always preceded by a silent, trance-like state in which the coachee is barely breathing and the eyes are defocused[3]. Poor coaches from any discipline, psychologist-coach or not, never experience catharsis in their coachees, but the best ones, from any discipline or practice, do facilitate these powerful learning experiences.

REFLECTIVE LANGUAGE

A valuable contribution that sits well with a genuine respect for the coachee's-journey comes from the practice of Reflective Language [e.g., 1] where the words of the coachee are reflected by the coach with the dual benefit of showing that their coach is listening but oftentimes, also, by helping to maintain the coachee's psychological 'learning state' achieving deeper self-reflection and learning.

SYMBOLIC MODELING

Yet another enormous contribution to some practitioner-coaches comes from the genius of the late Dr. David Grove. David was an often enigmatic and difficult man to follow, but had an ability to work magic with his clients which remains legendary. Fortunately for us, Penny Tompkins and James Lawley [2] mapped his 'Clean Language' approach, enabling many coaches to use their rendition of it. This powerful and inspiring work, which they call 'Symbolic Modeling', is used by some practitioner-coaches in a disciplined way, as a stand-alone methodology for coaching and with profound results. Along with others, I have let their work advise the language we use in the coaching dynamic, and to great effect also.

---

[3] These signs may include others including a slight nod of the head forwards as the muscle tone in the neck reduces. Sometimes there may be a slight sinking in the chair for the same reason. The pallor of the skin may lighten and any psychological 'leakage', tics and the like, are entirely absent.

GROW

John Whitmore who has promoted GROW as a thumbnail 'process' for coaching has done both his tool-selection and marketing jobs well. For example, we find that where we introduce GROW, about 30% of trainees are still using the model three months following the end of their course; much higher than for any other model we have used, including my own! Of course there is no simple process in a coaching session and, in practice, a session may go back and forth through GROW. However, many coaches, particularly novice coaches, find the GROW method helpful in keeping track of where they are and where they may need to go next in order to help the coachee reach a motivated objective.

CONCLUSION

But where is coaching going? Already we see that the vast majority of sessions are conducted by practitioner-coaches and not by psychologist-coaches. Coaching is generally an expensive intervention in one-to-one work, but we now have coaching 'products' where numerous coaches go into organisations on a full-day basis only and this reduces the coaching-hour rate considerably. Additionally we and others are bringing in facilitation/coaching 'best-practice' into the skill-range of managers as part of management and leadership development within organisations. Our work is supported by planned learning-opportunities (before, during and after the courses) to provide quite rapid culture-change. The approach also reduces perceived over- and under-managing of their staff.

It may be that the psychologist-coach could become more popular than the practitioner-coach within a few years. This could be driven by the market if it is supplied by poor coaches and or yields poor performance results. As the market is now dominated by practitioner-coaches, buyers may look to the universities for more consistent qualities. Unfortunately, the university-based sector is not certain to produce consistently great coaches either. It means that all coaching organisations do need to continue to improve standards and to measure key personal attributes of the coach, not just their technical skills. At the heart of our own best coaches are both psychological and emotional development. A university life does not appear to add any advantage to those two factors in an inquisitive and compassionate coach than life itself.

REFERENCES

1.   McLeod, A.I., The Principal Instruments of Coaching, *Anchor Point*, 2004, 17(12), 11-22.

2.   Lawley, J. and Tompkins, P., *Metaphors in Mind*, Developing Company Press, London, 2000.

The Impact of the Inner Game and Sir John Whitmore on Coaching:

A Commentary

Joseph O'Connor
Lambent do Brasil
Rua Helena 280 cjs 4081409
CEP 0452-050
São Paulo – SP, Brazil
E mail: joseph@lambent.com

INTRODUCTION

Simon Jenkins' article brings to the fore the tension that exists at the moment between coaching and the profession of psychology, with special emphasis on the use of the Inner game, NLP and the GROW model in coaching. This tension concerns me, as an executive coach and a coach trainer. How we frame the tension is important, but it need not be a battle of psychologists versus non-psychologists. In this commentary, I would like to look at this tension from different perspectives and comment on how it might be a source of creativity and cooperation rather than conflict.

HUMAN POTENTIAL MOVEMENT

Here is my formulation of the fundamental tension. Coaching began as a child of the human potential movement in the 1960s. Many other human developmental approaches also were born there; e.g., NLP, but none have achieved the spread, credibility and scope of coaching. Coaching is the human potential movement gone corporate. Unlike many other offspring, coaching has forged a fine mainstream career for itself and has embraced (mostly) and been embraced by both academia and business. Now as it comes of age, and becomes more successful, it encroaches on some domains that are occupied by psychologists. The profession of psychology is uneasy with this young pretender.

I think there is a cultural component as well. Coaching came from the West coast of the USA, with its pragmatic, utilitarian, 'learning by doing' basis. Europe has a more reflective philosophical tradition, thinking more before doing, Europe wants theoretical underpinnings to take coaching seriously.

The extremists on the coaching side might argue that coaching is a practice where the coach helps the client through listening, empathy and questions. Psychologists operate with their own models and theories that are too removed from practice to be useful. Psychologists should stick to their own domain. The extremists in psychology might argue that coaching is getting out of its depth, and that empathy, listening and questions are no substitute for tested psychological theory and knowledge built over the last two hundred years.

Psychology is usually defined as the science or study of the nature and functions of the mind and behaviour. There are many definitions of coaching, one of the most encompassing is the one by Anthony Grant:

> Coaching can be defined as a collaborative, solution-focused, results-oriented and systematic process, in which the coach facilitates the enhancement of performance, life experience, self-directed learning and personal growth of individuals and organizations. [1, p. 73]

Coaching is clearly an application of some aspects of psychology in a particular domain. The GROW model and the Inner game are certainly 'psychological approaches', but perhaps not in the way psychologists understand them.

SCHOOLS OF COACHING

Jenkins gives much of the history of coaching that is useful and enlightening. Let me add some more pieces. Coaching has many roots, the Inner Game being only one. Many approaches to coaching are less achievement oriented than the Inner Game methodology. Gallwey's work was influenced by Eastern philosophy. Indeed, the Inner game was dedicated to his Guru as well as his parents. There is a South American connection through the Ontological coaching built from ideas elaborated by Fernando Flores [2] with contributions from Humberto Maturana [3] and widely disseminated by Julio Ollala and Rafael Echeverria [4]. Coaching in most Spanish speaking countries is equated with Ontological coaching. There are now many other schools of coaching, such as behavioural coaching, integral coaching and NLP coaching. They are different and I have recently made an attempt [5] to find what they have in common to create some shared methods and principles.

MODELS AND THEORIES

Next, there is a helpful distinction between a model and a theory. In science, the word 'theory' refers to a well substantiated explanation of some aspect(s) of the world supported by a body of facts gathered over time and repeatedly confirmed through observation and experiment. Theories also allow scientists to make predictions about as yet unobserved phenomena. Some theories are more robust than others.

A model is a representation of a system that allows for investigation of the properties of the system and, in some cases, prediction of future outcomes. In some ways, models are theories in waiting. A model is not right or wrong, it is purely pragmatic – does it work or not?

Coaching needs some theories to build its models. Psychologists may argue that it should build its models on well-tested theories. But which ones? Can coaching psychologists agree on what theories are relevant and useful to build coaching models? There needs to be relevance criteria. I see this as a major area of work.

I like the metaphor of coaches as chefs and psychologists as nutritionists. A chef does not a need a university degree in nutrition, just as a nutritionist may not be a good cook; but a chef should know something of nutrition that is useful, practical and helps their own profession.

Coaching starts from model(s) of the client/coach/stakeholder system in all its richness. Psychology starts from theories, often generated from controlled experiments. However, both can agree on the use of the basic scientific method. How are theories and models generated? Firstly, there is an injunction, paradigm or model that says, 'If you want to know this, do *that'*. Start with an idea/model/theory and then take action to see how it works in the real world. The injunction needs to be precise in order to give quality data. This data (and human experience is data) can be evaluated and measured within the context it was generated (e.g., you can rate subjective satisfaction on a scale of one to ten.) The quality of the experiment determines the quality of the data. Finally, you need to put this data or experience up for communal confirmation or rejection. You need feedback from different perspectives, but especially from people who have done the experiment or had the experience. Only by doing the experiment do you have the right to contribute fully.

Theories and models can never be proved true, only validated. However, they can be disproven. A validated and therefore robust theory has gone through numerous iterations of those three principles without mishap. Coaching models can be refutable by the three steps outlined above, and I think that this is a point that both psychologists and coaches can agree. Humanistic psychology has many models and theories that have come from pragmatic observation and reflection of human beings in different situations. Just because data is subjective does not mean it cannot be tested, measured and validated.

There are many psychological models and theories (e.g., models of adult development [7, 8]) that are very relevant to coaching, and need some evidence-based research from coaching practitioners to test communally. There need to be case histories, peer-reviewed articles and measurements from many perspectives. On this basis, I fully support research *in* coaching – research from the inside that involves coaches looking at their practice in a critical way in the light of psychological models and theories, making experiments and reporting results for communal testing. I also support research *on* coaching – research from the outside. What does coaching do and how does that relate to other fields?

Evidence-based coaching has been defined as: "Intelligent and conscientious use of best current knowledge integrated with practitioner expertise in making decisions about how to deliver coaching to individual coaching clients and in designing and teaching coach training programs" [9, p. 6]. It should be grounded with specific links to other disciplines on an empirical (experimental and practical) and theoretical knowledge base. I do not see evidence-based coaching as a new school of coaching, nor dominated by psychologists, but an approach to coaching that can and should be used by all serious practitioners.

CONCLUSION

Coaching is not just about knowledge or the application of theories, but about the presence and the being of the practitioner. A coach needs to embody their knowledge and not just know it. Psychology cannot teach them this, perhaps only life can. The experimenter is part of the experiment.

Psychologists can quote Kurt Lewin: 'There is nothing as practical as a good theory.' And coaches might reply: 'In theory, there should not be much difference between theory and practice, but in practice there often is.'

REFERENCES

1.   Grant, A.M., Solution-Focused Coaching, in: Passmore, J., ed., *Excellence in Coaching: The Industry Guide*, Kogan Page, London, 2006, 73-90.

2.   Flores, F. and Solomon, R., *Building Trust*, Oxford University Press, Oxford, 2001.

3.   Maturana, H. and Varela, F., *The Tree of Knowledge: The Biological Roots of Human Understanding*, Shambhala Publications, Boston, MA, 1987.

4.   Echeverria, R., *Ontologia Del Lenguaje*, Domen Ediciones, Santiago, Chile, 1994.

5.   O'Connor, J. and Lages, A., *How Coaching Works*, A & C Black, London, 2007.

6.   Popper, K., *The Logic of Scientific Discovery*, Hutchinson, London, 1959.

7.   Kegan, R., *In Over Our Heads: The Mental Demands of Modern Life*, Harvard University Press, Cambridge, MA, 1994.

8.   Laske, O., *Measuring Hidden Dimensions: The Art and Science of Fully Engaging Adults*, Laske & Associates, Medford, MA, 2006.

9.   Grant, A. and Stober, D., Introduction, in: Stober, D. and Grant, A., eds., *Evidence Based Coaching Handbook: Putting Best Practices to Work for Your Clients*, John Wiley & Sons, New York, 2006.

The Impact of the Inner Game and Sir John Whitmore on Coaching:

A Commentary

Caroline Harris
Optimise
High Trees, Bridge Road,
Levington, Suffolk, IP10 0LZ, UK
E-mail: caroline@optimisepotential.com

INTRODUCTION

In this article, Simon Jenkins directs us to fundamental considerations about the level of knowledge appropriate to being an effective coach and the influence of a significant contributor, Sir John Whitmore, to the art of coaching. The article is a thorough discourse on recent comment and research and will be an extraordinarily helpful reference point for non-academics. As a "non-psychologist coach", I was inspired by Jenkins' exploration of coaching psychology though have always instinctually recognized that good coaching skill can develop from a range of exposures.

In this commentary, my aim is to make some small additions to the story of the Inner Game and the growth of the coaching that has developed from this particular path. Jenkins' knowledge of the background and work of John Whitmore appropriately describes and values the lifelong contribution that John has made and continues to make to coaching and the human potential movement.

THE LABEL OF 'NON-PSYCHOLOGIST'

This is the first time that I have referred to myself as a "non-psychologist" and it is not a label that I found easy to associate with despite its accuracy. For the purposes of Jenkins' article, however, it makes the distinction clear and raises an issue of the inadequacies of calling oneself a coach. Hence the market has spawned: performance coaches, development coaches, management coaches, executive coaches and even life coaches!

THE INNER GAME OF TENNIS

As Jenkins mentions, Caroline Harris' learning about the underlying philosophy and core skills of the Inner Game came directly from Tim Gallwey when the early programmes were run in England in 1979 (initially by an associate). John Whitmore, Graham Alexander, Alan Fine and a number of other early Inner Gamers who gathered in Beaconsfield learned, debated, practised and were consumed by passionate exploration of this "new dimension" in coaching. I was privileged to be among these pioneers and to be taken along on an extraordinary journey of learning from an eclectic mix of national coaches and elite sportsmen who came on our early Inner Game workshops or popped in for coffee in the Inner Game office at West Hampstead, London. Using these skills to teach tennis to numerous individuals and groups over the next 15 years provided significant development. The hour-upon-hour repetition of attempting to use the skills appropriate for each student left me with no doubt about their efficacy. I was aware that this approach accessed the student's innate ability and propensity for learning. It enabled students to learn about *how* they learned and not simply to improve their tennis strokes. The reward of students leaving the lesson with greater confidence in their ability was enduringly powerful. Beyond that, it gave a glimpse of what is possible - the moment of connectedness between coach and student when learning is transformed.

THE GROW MODEL

With the launch of Gallwey's *The Inner Game of Golf* [1] came more invitations to work in different sports. By the early 1980s, The Inner Game Ltd. began to be asked by business companies to design bespoke programmes that would help their managers learn coaching skills. These Inner Game skills were the building blocks of the leadership, manager-as-coach and culture-change programmes that followed. Blended with the educational and life exposures of the pioneers, the Inner Game philosophy underpinned the growth of this path of coaching. While the requisite skills to coach well were adequately demonstrated and taught, the demand for more clarity about what actually happens in the coaching process led to the birth of GROW. The acronym devised with and for a client of Alexander, it simply highlighted the route of the established coaching process "organically" created by the forerunners. It was the map of *some* of the work that occurs between coach and client. Jenkins reflects accurately on GROW that it is a "heuristic device" and is as such a valuable tool for those learning coaching skills. As it moved into the public domain and was taken up by those unfamiliar with its background, there was potential for it to be used as a problem-solving model only. This negates its value and purpose. Whitmore's book *Coaching for Performance* has contributed to a much greater understanding of the model and its position within the coaching conversation. I concur with Jenkins' reference to Myles Downey's book that in particular draws attention to the fundamental aspect of awareness and responsibility and that the GROW model is underpinned by focusing attention – the core skill of the Inner Game.

PSYCHOLOGICAL ASSESSMENT AND BUSINESS COACHING

Another development in coaching history that was perhaps less noticed came in the mid 1980s. After being recipients of the extraordinary coaching and consulting work of the late Ben Cannon, Stephen Bampfylde and Anthony Saxton of the leadership search firm Saxton Bamfylde set up a coaching company, Cannon Rosen. They partnered psychologists with coaches; the process of psychological assessment with individual business coaching programmes. Ben Cannon had joined the Inner Game prior to university and became one of coaching's greatest exponents. Saxton Bampfylde had used psychological assessment in their search work for a number of years and saw both the value and marketing potential of such a marriage. It has been a long, productive and sympathetic liaison with this method of assessment and coaching both inviting self-reflection. Positioned after the initial goal setting, the assessment was focussed upon those internal structures that influence change and how the individual relates to the "outside world". The information gained acted as a springboard for the coaching sessions that followed. The marriage allowed the two aspects of client development to be "held" and for the client each aspect was distinguishable. With regular dialogue between coach and psychologist, there was little doubt of the union's effectiveness for the client. Respect for and contextual understanding of one another's different skill base grew exponentially through the live process of working together.

"COACHING DANCE"

A further contribution came in 2005 when David Hemery, Olympic gold medallist in the 400m hurdles in Mexico and performance consultant, published *How to Help Children Find the Champions within Themselves* [2]. In this book, he describes eloquently the polarities of coaching. With regard to both coach-centred and performer-centred styles of coaching, his "Coaching Dance" draws out the essential components of improving performance as goal setting, learning, listening, questioning, motivation and feedback. While the Coaching Dance, like GROW, may be a "heuristic device", it provides a clear picture for most coaches and enables understanding of the importance of balance. More especially perhaps, the majority of coaches who attend coaching workshops are engaged by this simple, visual model rather than threatened by the perception that what they have done until now is "wrong". The entrenched or reluctant coach is inspired to broaden their knowledge to develop the ability to move flexibly across the spectrum according to the needs of the student. With this model, Hemery has captured the space in which flexible coaching occurs.

CONCLUSION

There are many avenues leading to the creation of an effective coach. Simon Jenkins has described current questions and the potential tensions as the paths of coaching psychologists and those he names "non-psychologists" meet. Both of course push the boundaries of understanding and thus make valuable contributions. No doubt my commentary itself reveals some personal preference towards the value of learning through practice of the art. The increasing number of coaches practising performer-centred skills worldwide is a tribute to the work of John Whitmore. The enduring gift of the Inner Game is to have brought awareness of skills in coaching that are catalysts for self-belief, optimise learning and performance, and demonstrate trust in the potential of all students.

REFERENCES

1.   Gallwey, W.T., *The Inner Game of Golf*, Jonathon Cape, London, 1979.

2.   Hemery, D., *How to Help Children Find the Champions Within Themselves*, BBC Worldwide Ltd, London, 2005.

The Impact of the Inner Game and Sir John Whitmore on Coaching:

A Commentary

Vikki Brock
VB Coaching & Consulting
1198 Navigator Drive PMB 132
Ventura, CA 93001, USA
E-mail: vikki@callmecoach.com

INTRODUCTION

This article presents a clear picture of the tension between the psychologists and non-psychologists in the field of coaching in the UK. From my research, this tension is global in nature and is present when any new field which deals with people emerges. In my commentary, I will focus on the links that existed between the individuals pioneering the Inner Game, involved in Werner Erhard's est trainings, and linked to Sir John Whitmore. The information for the statements below has been gathered from interviews with Werner Erhard, Sir John Whitmore, Graham Alexander, Jinny Ditzler, Myles Downey, and Chris Morgan.

THE INNER GAME

Graham Alexander was a junior tennis champion at Wimbledon who was involved in Werner Erhard's est from 1969. In 1970, he began to look at what the great sports coaches did to bring out performance and how this related to developing people in business. He further developed these ideas by running workshops and working with people one-to-one through a non-profit charitable trust he established in 1972. A personal friend of John Whitmore from 1969, Graham also helped John on the May Lectures in 1974, which is when he came across and got involved with the Inner Game. Graham and John met with Tim Gallwey and suggested a BBC TV show in the UK about Tim's work. Graham was there in the beginning with John, pioneering a different coaching approach in sports, which they brought into business. Seeing an exact parallel between coaching in sport and coaching in business, by 1981 Graham was focusing primarily on one-to-one and team coaching in the business community.

PERSONAL EFFECTIVENESS PROGRAM

Jinny Ditzler took Werner Erhard's est in November 1972 and by 1974 was leading graduate seminars and opening up regions in the USA to est. She moved to England in 1979 to work in the est office and left est in January 1981. Working with individuals to identify and accomplish goals for the upcoming year, she perfected her

PEP (Personal Effectiveness Program) process and developed The Goals and Planning Workshop. By the end of 1981, she was approached by other people who wanted to use the process, so she formed Results Unlimited to train and employ coaches. The first person she trained was Graham Alexander, who she had known from est.

RESULTS UNLIMITED

While partnering John Whitmore in The Inner Game, with its focus on coaching in sports and business, from 1981 Graham was a partner with Jinny Ditzler in Results Unlimited, a coaching business primarily for individuals to get in touch with their life goals and, through dialogue, to experience and realize their potential. Both these partnerships influenced Graham's coaching approach. The awareness based way of coaching from The Inner Game included the proposition that if you help to raise someone's awareness about different aspects of themselves and their lives, they can advance. This included the mental – or inner side - of success which still influence Graham today. Results Unlimited helped people grow their will, their determination, and their confidence by turning hopes and dreams into tangible actions. Both The Inner Game and Results Unlimited coach approaches were complementary to each other.

ALEXANDER CORPORATION

Graham merged these approaches, and the GROW model he developed while working with one of his business clients around 1984, into the Alexander Corporation in 1986 with the purpose to build a substantial organization offering coaching to business. The individuals working for the Alexander Corporation did not think of themselves as either consultants or psychologists. According to Graham, they were in a different domain; as people who catalyzed performance, learning, development and satisfaction in people. The influences of Tim Gallwey and Werner Erhard were strong in the beginning of coaching, with NLP becoming influential in the late 1990's.

MYLES DOWNEY

Myles Downey, who founded the first coach training school in London, entered the picture in the mid-1980's. A practicing architect in Dublin, Ireland, he had been a good tennis player in his youth and read Gallwey's 1974 book, *The Inner Game of Tennis* [1]. Through a series of coincidences he met up with Graham Alexander, and within a year had given up his job and was training as an Inner Game coach in London. Myles' path was from tennis player to tennis coach to sports coach to business coach. In 1987, Myles and Chris Morgan (a former ski instructor who was introduced to The Inner Game by John Whitmore in 1979) joined the Alexander Corporation, which was providing business coaching and manager-as-coach training in corporations. Chris, whose father had been Chief Operating Officer for Werner Erhard for three years, had also worked for KRW International, which was a company of 16 Ph.D. clinical therapists who had been practicing business coaching in the USA since the 1980s. This appreciation for the psychological was also shared by Myles, who believes it is critical for any coach to have "psychological literacy" so they understand the territory and can read the signs when they are in or out of their depth, or the client is in or out of their depth.

CONCLUSION

From the 1970's, the influence and connections of Sir John Whitmore and the Inner Game have clearly shaped the field of coaching in the UK. What is also apparent is that coaching emerged in the post-modern era through individuals who collaboratively, synergistically and eclectically combined theories, models and practice from sports, business, and psychology (through the Human Potential Movement). While the dynamic tension spoken of in this article has always been there, it has become a focus with the bi-directional influences of coaching with its root disciplines, and the resulting creation of coaching psychology.

REFERENCE

1.   Gallwey, W.T., *The Inner Game of Tennis*, Jonathon Cape, London, 1974.

The Impact of the Inner Game and Sir John Whitmore on Coaching:

A Commentary

Glenn Whitney
ECD Insight
8-9 New Street,
London, EC2M 4TP, UK
E-mail: gwhitney@ecdinsight.com

INTRODUCTION

While Sir John Whitmore and the GROW Model have been very influential on coaching over the past 20 years, they are unlikely to remain so. That is because the model is unhelpfully simplistic and is insufficiently focused on objective and externally validated performance measures.

GROW

Most problematic is the establishing of Goals in the first instance and the assessment of Reality. The coaching client relies implicitly on the coach being sufficiently grounded, objective and impartial to facilitate insight and make judgments on the clients' own assertions.

Counselling psychologists and psychotherapists (I will dare to use the terms interchangeably) – when well trained and well supervised – bring the insight and self-awareness that enable them to challenge the client on his or her goals. Are they appropriate? Are they realistic? Are these shorter-term goals actually likely to lead to the client achieving a desirable long-term vision? Do the goals suggest a mentally healthy individual? Some excessively goal-driven behaviour may be counter-productive or downright dangerous to the person's physical health. Inappropriate goals may also have undesirable consequences to the client's family system, colleagues, etc. Psychologists can also challenge the client's interpretation of reality, having studied what constitutes normal and abnormal behaviour and ideation.

PSYCHOTHERAPEUTIC PROCESSES

Whitmore, and particularly those who have been influenced by him, tend to have a view of the coach as a largely neutral, always benign presence in the mental world of the coachee. Those adequately trained in psychotherapeutic processes consider this to be simplistic at best and reckless at worst. A broad range of emotions are often experienced by the coachee in and around their work with a coach, including envy, irritation, anger, hatred and physical and/or romantic attraction. In addition, the coach can and often does experience similarly complex and contradictory emotions, which are understood in the psychodynamic framework in concepts such as 'projection', 'transference,' 'splitting', and 'parallel process.' A thorough and *experiential* understanding of these processes enables a coach to minimise the disruptive and/or counter-productive effect these emotions can have on the coaching alliance.

BEYOND INDIVIDUALISM

Looking ahead to the next 20 years of coaching, it seems likely that organisational development and coaching specialists such as Marshall Goldsmith and Patrick Lencioni will be of far greater influence than Whitmore and Gallwey. Their understanding of the personal and professional development processes are informed by a more comprehensive and nuanced understanding of the individual in his or her social and political environment.

It is worth noting that Whitmore and Gallwey built their models and approaches based on the largely individual-oriented performance sports of tennis, golf and motor racing. Extensive use of phrases like "inner" underline a somewhat introverted cast to Whitmore's thinking; but to be fair to Whitmore, he is not alone. Most theorists in the 20th Century saw the person through the lenses of the ideology of Western individualism, which reached its apotheosis in the 1980s and 1990s through the leadership of the likes of Ronald Reagan and Margaret Thatcher.

Of course a predominately one-person model is prevalent across most psychological and psychotherapy theories, including those derived from Sigmund Freud. These are not socially (or 'systemic') oriented models in which the individual is viewed within the context of his various relationships (family, friends and colleagues). Neither are they hierarchical, taking account of an individual's rank within the organisation and within the context of prevailing cultures, both national cultures and organisational and departmental cultures.

Rather than the loneliness of the long-distance runner or the individual heroics of solo mountain climbers, the reality of most people who work in and around companies and other organisations is very different. Their experience is not at all like an individual athlete competing against the clock or against other individuals. Their day-to-day interactions are more analogous to being part of a football, cricket or rugby team, with different roles to play but a constant flow of overlapping responsibilities, rivalries, and inter-dependencies.

There is not space, other than in summary terms, to discuss Goldsmith's and Lencioni's ideas. Goldsmith focuses on the imperative for leaders to continually recognise how their many habits and behaviours impede their success. He encourages leaders to learn from others, especially from those they seek to lead (their subordinates). Modesty and courageous honesty with oneself are themes that emerge throughout Goldsmith's writing. They reflect the direct influence of his training in education and his practice as a Buddhist, specifically as a student of the Vietnamese teacher Thich Nhat Hanh, who emphasises ideals of community and disciplined mindfulness in everyday interactions.

Lencioni's work reflects the extensive time he spent earlier in his career as a strategic management consultant for a large consultancy. He has an acute awareness of the politics and interpersonal complexities that leaders must understand and adjust for when they seek to lead and influence. He places great emphasis, of course, on the leader's clarity of thought and strategy, but perhaps more importantly on the forms that the leader must use to effectively communicate organisational imperatives, to inspire improvements in the behaviour of others, and to create organisations that are self-correcting.

Goldsmith and Lencioni share a complex view of organisational life. In the organisations they describe, things go wrong; and anxiety, resistance and apathy are constantly present as negative forces. And yet they are optimistic that, with a broad and deep understanding of themselves and the people they work alongside, leaders can make hugely beneficial contributions to their organisations and society as a whole.

Other writers who are likely to prove highly influential well into the 21st Century include Martin Seligman and others who are developing the theories and methodologies of Positive Psychology; and Daniel Goleman and colleagues, with their focus on heretofore under-valued forms of intelligence, including emotional intelligence, social intelligence and cultural intelligence. None of these writers seem to have been influenced by Gallwey or Whitmore.

FROM SPORT PSYCHIATRY TO BUSINESS

It is interesting to note a recent development in elite sports coaching – the arrival of the psychiatrist as "mechanic of the mind." While this trend only dates back to about 2003, it seems likely to grow given the phenomenal success of the British Cycling Team in the 2008 Beijing Olympics. A substantial portion of that success has been attributed to the work of Steve Peters, a psychiatrist who formally specialised in the profiling of dangerous criminals and working with prisoners. His approach has been to help athletes gain control over their emotional responses and strengthen their ability to remain rational and objective even amidst tremendous performance pressure and in intensely distracting environments. Peters' successes, in cycling as well as rugby, point to the likelihood that others trained in psychiatry and psychotherapy will increasingly become involved in the development and coaching of high-performance athletes.

In the high-performance world of the Olympics, the goals, realities, options and ways forward are usually crystal-clear and relatively uncontroversial. This is something that is rather less often the case for leaders of business and other non-sporting areas. The challenges in elite sport – and this is where Peters and others in this vein focus – are related to motivation, compliance with training regimes, respect for authority, consistency, focus and mental toughness.

CONCLUSION

The likelihood of Peters' increasing influence in British sport and business (he is now a highly sought-after corporate speaker and consultant) is part of a larger trend that Whitmore might find amusing and even reassuring. Sports psychologists now proudly display their credentials when working in business and other non-sporting organisations. At the same time, it is my personal experience that high-performance sport is very open to borrowing tools and techniques from business, including evaluation protocols and internal communication practices. There is a creative convergence process taking place that is likely to benefit all who are open to challenging the status quo and learning from others.

The Impact of the Inner Game and Sir John Whitmore on Coaching:

A Commentary

Simon Robinson
School of Applied Global Ethics
Leeds Metropolitan University, The Grange,
Beckett Park Campus, Headingley, LS6 3QS, UK
E-mail: S.J.Robinson@leedsmet.ac.uk

INTRODUCTION

I am pleased to be given this chance to respond to Simon Jenkins' fascinating article. It focuses on the deeper perspectives of coaching and in particular the transpersonal approach of John Whitmore's work. This in turn shows how coaching can relate to a wider, more generic, view of spirituality [1]. In this commentary, I want to reflect on those connections. I then want to raise some questions of Whitmore's approach in the light of these connections. First, how does Whitmore's approach relate to ethical meaning? Second, is this approach to coaching based in community or is it individualistic? Third, if there is so much overlap with spirituality, what makes the role of coach different from a spiritual director or advisor? Finally, and related, how does coaching in this light relate to failure and to second best?

PURPOSE AND MORAL BASIS

I want to begin with the first part of Jenkins' article and the interesting issue of the relationship of psychology to coaching. Part of this is couched in conversation about the professional status and the definition of professions. It is interesting to note that Anthony Grant's criteria for the professions would exclude many professions, not least engineers in the UK who in general do not have state-sanctioned licensing (i.e., 'engineer' is not a legally protected title), and in many of the different professional bodies do not have the power to exclude members of the profession. Airaksinen [2] and others would argue that an equally, if not the most, important aspect of the identity of the profession is about purpose and the moral basis of the profession. Hence, medical practice is based on healing and law is based on justice. Purpose takes one beyond the simple adherence to professional codes into questions of the underlying world view of the profession and how that relates to identity and value. Browning [3] writes about this level of discourse as to do with pre-moral goods. They are, nonetheless, goods. They embody value, and invite others to appreciate that value through the narrative of vision and value statements. That level of value then relates directly to the ethical code of the profession, providing a rationale for the code and a basis for how the code is to be interpreted. Hence, a world view that stresses the importance for autonomy and rational human agency, for instance, will look to interpret codes in such a way that autonomy is developed, and develop codes that set standards around areas such as informed consent and confidentiality.

When it comes to the profession of coaching, Whitmore is clearly uneasy; especially about an uncritical view of the science of psychology as distinct from the use of therapeutic psychology. He accepts the importance of coaching psychology, not least in clarifying theory and developing the skills of coaches. However, theory does not of itself determine value, be it moral or pre-moral. At best, it will confirm or deepen our understanding of the values. Jenkins' reflection on Maslow's hierarchy of needs underlines this thinking. The hierarchy is not a theory, but simply articulates needs around physical and emotional survival. However, if, for instance, you have an ascetic world view that does not value physical survival, you might actually want to invert the hierarchy, or even ignore all the needs.

It is interesting then that Whitmore should give attention to the therapeutic side of psychology, rather than the strictly scientific, and in particular to positive psychology. Not surprisingly, because positive psychology focuses on therapy, it is teleological (focused in purpose), with core values of health and well-being. It is equally not surprising that positive psychology shares its therapeutic stage with philosophy and spirituality (some would suggest theology). The philosophy is found in the focus on developing Aristotelian virtues such as courage and practical wisdom, the theology (mediated through spirituality) is focused in virtues such as faith, hope, care, serenity and even forgiveness (around which specific therapies have been developed). The development of such virtues is associated with the core purpose of health and healing.

AWARENESS AND RESPONSIBILITY

None of this is an attempt to establish academic turf for philosophy or theology, any more than psychology. It simply suggests that the world of the spiritual, defined in generic or transpersonal terms, relates strongly to health and to other core human values, and that this, in turn, relates to the everyday ethics of the profession. All of this feeds into the first question of Jenkins and Whitmore. How do they see this transpersonal world (which cannot be exclusively owned by any academic discipline) relating to moral meaning? I want to argue that coaching should look to connect the two, professional ethical practice with the underlying values, purpose and related world view, and with the underlying level of consciousness and awareness. Whitmore's stress on responsibility and awareness would seem to suggest the same thing. Generic spirituality is often characterised as involving value-neutral consciousness of the self and the other. However, consciousness itself involves choice about the limits of consciousness, about whom or what I decide to be aware of, and who or what I decide to be responsible for. That in itself is a moral choice, in that it will exclude proximate people who may be in need [4]. In turn, this raises questions about how spirituality relates to responsibility (to the self and others).

SPIRITUALITY AND PRACTICAL WISDOM

The second question is related. How far is Whitmore's approach to spirituality instrumentalist and individualistic? At one level, one might interpret his view on awareness and responsibility in that light. The coach has to enable the client to develop awareness and to locate belief in order to make the most effective choices and thus to function most effectively. However, how does such effectiveness relate to the development of health and well-being? And how does health and well-being relate to service to others as much as to the self? The element of service is there in Whitmore, through the idea of 'contribution' and I am wondering how this thinking will be developed and what difference it might make. I would want to argue that this means enabling the client to develop in particular what Aristotle refers to as practical wisdom, the capacity to reflect on purpose and how this is embodied in practice. For the professional coach as much as the client, this is an ongoing reflection – part of a continuing reflection on and development of significant life meaning. In this sense, the life coach is providing the kind of space that can help the client to take such reflection seriously.

COACH AS SPIRITUAL DIRECTOR

The idea of finding space for focused reflection has relevance to the third question. In one sense, the spiritual director is doing much the same as the coach, as set out in Whitmore's terms. The spiritual director is very much a Christian concept, and there are different views about what it involves. However, it is broadly about enabling the person to reflect on Christian-based values and work through purpose and meaning in relation to life planning. Coaching has a much broader value base and enables the client to reflect on and develop his or her basic values and world view in relation to a life plan. The difference then is in context and in the particular sets of values. Both are enabling significant reflection are purpose and value, which in turns leads to questions about awareness, responsibility and practice.

QUESTIONING PURPOSE THROUGH EXAMINATION OF CORE VALUES

Finally, if coaching is based in core values, such as human fulfilment, along with values and health and well-being; and if, as Rawls [5] and others suggest, self worth is core to this, how does all this relate to excellence and success, and to lack of achievement and failure? Isn't the coach's task ultimately to enable the client to be successful? Or is it to enable that more elusive experience of happiness or well-being that so dominated the ancient Greeks? Whichever it is, the conversation comes back to role and purpose. These have to be part of the conversation with the client, and thus part of any ongoing contract. The fact that this is a contractual relationship might well raise the question of what the client wants. Doesn't the choice of the client trump the attempt to develop this deeper form of coaching? If the client wants to be a successful entrepreneur regardless of any teleology, then does all the talk about purpose go out of the window? I would argue that it doesn't. The person-centred approach to coaching enables the client to reflect more deeply and to question what or he or she wants, and thus to question purpose. If the purpose is defensible for the client, then at the least it will have been confirmed through examination of core values. It might also lead to a development or change of purpose, not least when competing values are examined, such as family and work success.

CONCLUSION

Jenkins' article prompts these and many other questions on the relationships of the transpersonal / spiritual to values and ethics. I would suggest a special issue of the journal, to include contributions from Whitmore, and others for and against these ideas.

REFERENCES

1.   Parry, J., Robinson, S., Nesti. M. and Watson, N., *Sport and Spirituality*, Routledge, London, 2007.

2.   Airaksinen, T., Service and Science in Professional Life, in: Chadwick, R.F., *Ethics in the Professions*, Avebury, Aldershot, UK, 1994, 1-13.

3.   Browning, D., *Christian Ethics and Moral Psychologies*, Eerdmans, Grand Rapids, MI, 2006.

4.   Robinson, S., *Spirituality, Ethics and Care*, Jessica Kingsley, London, 2007.

5.   Rawls, J., *A Theory of Justice*, Rev. Ed., Harvard University Press, Cambridge, MA, 1999.

The Impact of the Inner Game and Sir John Whitmore on Coaching:

A Response to Commentaries

Simon Jenkins
Carnegie Faculty of Sport and Education
Leeds Metropolitan University, Leeds, LS6 3QS, UK
E-mail: S.P.Jenkins@Leedsmet.ac.uk

INTRODUCTION

I would like to thank all eleven colleagues for writing excellent commentaries that shed light on a variety of issues raised from my target article. Simon Robinson raises questions on the relationships of the transpersonal / spiritual to values and ethics; while John Whitmore expresses his hope that an understanding of the transpersonal will become obligatory in the highest coaching qualifications of the largest coaching organisations. Vikki Brock and Caroline Harris, as well as Whitmore, provide historical detail related to the Inner Game and coaching; while Joseph O'Connor notes that coaching has many roots, the Inner Game being only one. Glenn Whitney acknowledges the influence of John Whitmore on coaching, but argues his influence is unlikely to remain so. Rather, Whitney points to "a more comprehensive and nuanced understanding of the individual in his or her social and political environment" (p. 62). Several authors, including Whitmore, discuss the GROW model. Issues related to mental health and psychotherapy, especially transference, are also discussed by several authors.

This Response to Commentaries will focus on "the tension between psychologists and non-psychologists in the field of coaching" (p. 1).

PSYCHOLOGISTS VERSUS NON-PSYCHOLOGISTS: A FALSE DICHOTOMY?

Advocating the role of psychologists in the development of coaching as "an evidence-based domain of practice", Jonathan Passmore argues: "While many practitioners are highly qualified, few have the level and rigour of training found among psychologists" (p. 43). Emphasising his own experiential rather than intellectual learning, John Whitmore argues that "too much adherence to or reliance on academic theories may well be a distraction and do more harm than good" (p. 25). Nevertheless, he believes that the coaching and psychology professions "need to stand side by side and learn from each other for the benefit of both" (p. 24). Similarly, in terms of knowledge bases, Stephen Palmer and Alison Whybrow advocate "the value of diversity that is offered across the coaching profession" (p. 31) and Passmore makes the point that there are many people with backgrounds in human resources and professional areas who have knowledge that overlaps that of psychologists. Vikki Brock argues that tension between psychologists and non-psychologists is "global in nature and is present when any new field which deals with people emerges" (p. 57).

Passmore suggests that the divide between psychologists and non-psychologists is a false dichotomy in that "there may be little difference in the practice between *experienced* coaches and *experienced* coaching psychologists" (p. 43; italics added). In support, Passmore cites his own research [1], and it would be interesting to see how he deals with the issue that "experienced" does not necessarily imply "expert" or "effective". Passmore argues that 'we are all psychologists', but does not make clear the distinction between 'everyday (or commonsense) psychology' and 'scientific psychology'. It is implied, however, in his concluding statement that: "The prime diference [between coaches and coaching psychologists] may be in their ability to describe what they do or their interest in undertaking and writing research-led publications, which help us to take the scientific aspects of this emerging domain forward" (p. 44). As Harré et al. [2] have indicated, "the task of scientific psychology consists of making the implicit psychologies of everyday life explicit, and then, in light of that understanding, applying the techniques of *theory-guided* empirical research to develop, refine and extend that body of knowledge and practices" [2, p. 16; italics original].

FEAR AND PROTECTIONISM

Lynda St. Clair notes that whether psychologists or non-psychologists, coaches are in the "<u>business</u> of helping others" (underlining original), and thus need to "distinguish themselves and establish their own competitive advantage in the marketplace" (p. 33). Acronyms can be trademarked and used as a brand, while "creating barriers to entry can help to create a reputation of legitimacy and value" (p. 34). Joseph O'Connor argues that coaching is "the human potential movement gone corporate" and that the profession of psychology is uneasy with the fact that coaching "encroaches on some domains that are occupied by psychologists" (p. 49). As Caroline Harris makes us aware, the term 'non-psychologist' can be construed as protectionist in that she sees it as a "label" that "raises an issue of the inadequacies of calling oneself a coach" (p. 53).

Alison Hardingham shows how fear and protectionism go hand in hand, referring to her student-coaches' perception of Steven Berglas' article "The Very Real Dangers of Executive Coaching" [3] as taking "a nakedly protectionist and self-interested stance" (p. 37). Writing as a psychologist and a coach, Hardingham points to "the fear of our own ineffectualness"; "we enter the domain where change is possible, but where there is also therefore the possibility of no change and the possibility of disappointment" (p. 38). Knowing that psychology does not guarantee effective coaching, Hardingham states, "we project our own fear of not knowing onto those who are not psychologists" (p. 38).

COACHING EFFECTIVENESS

Palmer and Whyrow note that: "There will be psychologists who would not make good coaches, and would not claim otherwise" (p. 31). Making an analogy to baking bread, St. Clair indicates that "recipes are not sufficient" and that effective coaches need to "find some way to *connect* with their clients so that their clients can find the courage to change themselves" (p. 34; italics added). There are many ways in which this connection or rapport can occur, but, in Hardingham's words, it is "a mystery how one person can have a conversation with another which enables change" (p. 38). It certainly involves, as O'Connor concludes, "the presence and the being of the practitioner" (p. 51).

Angus McLeod argues that "the instinctive coach" (i.e., non-psychologist), who might be "listening and reacting more" can be expected to have a better quality of attention and deeper level of trust in the coachee than the psychologists "who are analysing what the coachee is saying with reference to their science" (p. 45). As O'Connor states, however: "The extremists in psychology might argue that coaching is getting out of its depth, and that empathy, listening and questions are no substitute for tested psychological theory and knowledge built over the last two hundred years. (p. 50)"

CONCLUSION

Jonathan Passmore, and Stephen Palmer and Alison Whybrow are at pains to emphasise what psychologists and non-psychologists have in common, but they also draw attention to important differences and, in doing so, they advocate coaching psychology. Beyond the value of "embracing diversity" in the coaching profession or industry, Palmer and Whybrow do not really develop their argument (albeit due to lack of space) that the tension between psychologists and non-psychologists is based on "misunderstandings" (p. 31). Nevertheless, their point about the two sides working together is well made. The bottom line, as Lynda St. Clair makes clear, is that dichotomies (with their tendency to promote 'black-and-white' thinking) render distinctiveness and competitive advantage in the marketplace to, say, coaching psychologists; but also, as Alison Hardingham explains, they give rise to fear and protectionism.

REFERENCES

1.   Passmore, J., *Workplace Coaching*, Unpublished Doctoral Thesis, University of East London, UK, 2008.

2.   Harré, R., Clarke, D.D. and De Carlo, N., *Motives and Mechanisms: An Introduction to the Psychology of Action*, Methuen, London, 1985.

3.   Berglas, S., The Very Real Dangers of Executive Coaching, *Harvard Business Review*, 2002, June, 87-92.

Developing Women Athletes: Insights from Business and Management

Deborah A. O'Neil[1], Margaret M. Hopkins[2] and Diana Bilimoria[3]

[1]College of Business Administration
Bowling Green State University
Bowling Green, OH 43403-0001, USA
E-mail: oneild@bgsu.edu
[2]College of Business Administration
The University of Toledo, Toledo, OH, USA
[3]Weatherhead School of Management
Case Western Reserve University, Cleveland, OH, USA

ABSTRACT

This review presents the unique needs of women in the dual domains of business and sports, and proposes that there are parallels between the talent development of women in management and women in sports. We first describe the specific development needs and characteristics of women in both the business and sports arenas. Next, we examine three leading practices in business and management (executive coaching, mentoring, and emotional intelligence skills development) and discuss their relevance to women's development in business as well as in sports. Recommendations for how each management practice informs the effective development of women athletes are then made. Finally, we offer suggestions for future research directions regarding the effective development of women athletes.

Key words: Emotional Intelligence, Executive Coaching, Gender, Mentoring, Sport, Women

Reviewers: Christina Geithner (Gonzaga University, USA)
Alison Hardingham (i-coach academy, UK)
Jim McKenna (Leeds Metropolitan University, UK)
David Selchen (Personnel Decisions International, USA)
Sue Slocombe (Performance Consultants LLP, UK)
Mike Voight (Central Connecticut State University, USA)

INTRODUCTION

The development of organizational talent is arguably one of the most important responsibilities of leaders, managers and coaches. The ability to effectively lead, coach, mentor, and develop individuals is of paramount importance in the business world as well as in the sports world. Challenges facing leaders in the business arena in many ways parallel what confronts the sports coach. For example, corporate leaders deal with staff performance and development, personnel assessments for recruitment, retention and promotion of staff, relations with upper management, strategic decisions for the short-term and the long-term, maintaining a competitive advantage, and their own performance and development [1]. Sports coaches tackle similar issues, namely: the performance and development of athletes, assistant coach and other personnel choices, management hierarchy issues, strategic decisions, controlling the competitive environment, and their own performance and development [2]. A primary focus in both sports and business is the development of an individual's performance and leadership capabilities. This is accomplished by fostering greater self awareness, self management, and relationship management in order to assist the individual in becoming more effective; whether at leading a global business or becoming a better sports player.

The purpose of this article is to extrapolate what we know of best practices for the development of women in the business and management worlds and translate those practices into insights for the effective development of women athletes in sports. Our recommendations are targeted at amateur and professional athletes at all levels in both individual and team sports. We believe that coaches, athletic administrators, and women athletes can benefit from leadership development practices applied in the workplace due to the similar nature of women's experiences in both business and sports venues. We believe it is important to apply these workplace strategies to women athletes because providing women with the skills and experience to perform at their best, whether in an organizational or sporting context, results in more diverse, inclusive, and ultimately successful organizations. In the sections that follow, we discuss development issues germane for women in business and sports, offer brief summaries of the research on executive coaching, mentoring and emotional intelligence skills development, and provide practical suggestions for the application of these practices to the development of women in sports.

DEVELOPING WOMEN IN BUSINESS AND SPORTS

There is evidence to suggest that while women and men may share similar goals of realizing their dreams and achieving lives of purpose, the manifestation of these desires may look and feel different [3], requiring a differential developmental focus [4]. In a study of high-achieving managerial women, researchers at the Center for Creative Leadership proposed five key themes that influence how women approach their lives and their careers: acting authentically, making connections, living agentically (controlling one's own destiny), achieving wholeness, and gaining self-clarity (understanding one's values and behaviors in the context of organizational perceptions of women and men) [5]. These authors propose that these life patterns can be used effectively to guide development efforts targeted specifically for women.

It has also been noted that women's work experiences differ from men's due to three primary factors - the salience of relationships in women's developmental processes, the impact of the dearth of women at senior levels of organizations, and the differential impact of family responsibilities on women and men [6]. Evidence suggests that women's career histories reflect more of a relational nature than men's careers [7], that women and men define career success differently [3], and that gender differences exist in terms of psychological development [8] and organizational and societal norms and expectations [9].

A study of the perceptions regarding female advancement held by senior women leaders and male CEOs in American *Fortune* 1000 corporations found striking differences [10]. CEOs believed the major barriers to women's advancement were that women lacked general management experience and were not adequately represented in the managerial pipeline. In contrast, female executives noted barriers such as stereotyping and exclusion from important networks. This same study also found that the top four success strategies cited by women were to consistently exceed performance expectations, develop a style with which men are comfortable, seek difficult or high visibility assignments, and have an influential mentor [10]. Such disparate perspectives continue to create separate and unequal opportunities for women and men in organizations, necessitating a specific developmental focus for improving women's career and leadership opportunities.

Three aspects of sex-related differences demonstrated by empirical research must be taken into account when considering the systematic development of women's leadership [11]. First, women and men differ in leadership styles [12, 13]. Second, women and men differ on the behaviors of leadership [e.g., 14], and third, sex-related differences emerge in the evaluation of leadership [e.g., 15]. Such gender differences in leadership styles, leadership behaviors and evaluations of leadership have been cited as rationale for creating leadership development practices targeted specifically for women.

Research on leadership styles and gender differences is ongoing and support can be found for positions of both difference and similarity in the leadership styles of women and men [16]. Eagly and Johannesen-Schmidt [16] propose that the normative impact of leadership roles and leader selection criteria may promote similarity, while the intersection of organizational and gender roles may result in differences. They conclude that the differences found over the course of numerous studies are small, but that women tend to have more of a democratic, participative and collaborative style than do men, and that women are more likely to use a transformational leadership style particularly when mentoring and encouraging employees [16].

Research on leadership behaviors also reveals differences between men and women. Studies applying 360 degree feedback processes indicate that women managers consistently scored higher on behavioral skills such as teamwork, empowerment, information sharing, and care for employees [17]. Additional analyses of leadership competencies reveal that women are more empathetic, are more aware of their emotions, and are more adept interpersonally while men are more self-confident, optimistic, adaptable, and able to manage stress [14]. A meta-analysis examining leadership effectiveness, measured by self and other ratings of performance found that male and female leaders did not differ overall in effectiveness [15]. However, the authors found that "in general, leaders of each sex were particularly effective when they were in a leadership role regarded as congruent with their gender" [15, p. 137].

In addition to gender-related differences in characteristics, work experiences as well as leadership styles, behaviors and perceptions, organizational patterns and practices continue to favor male-defined constructions of organizational and career success [18, 19] and male life experiences [4, 20], resulting in gendered organizational contexts. Skills that women tend to demonstrate such as teamwork, collaboration, conflict resolution, emotional expression and developing relationships are not necessarily noticed or valued when exhibited by women in male-dominated organizations [21]. Arguably, business and sports both are predominantly male-dominated arenas. Therefore applying a "gender-neutral/gender-free" strategy for developing women does not adequately address women's specific developmental needs or take into account the gendered contexts in which women work.

Literature in the sports arena also indicates that women athletes differ from men athletes in critical ways. Prescriptive writings, such as by long-standing women's soccer coach Anson Dorrance, highlight these differences, particularly that women athletes are not as innately competitive as men athletes and are more naturally self-reflective and self-critical than their male counterparts [22]. Dorrance drew on his experience to note that women athletes relate through a web of personal connections as opposed to a more traditional male hierarchical style, thus requiring more personal connection, sensitivity, and facilitation of the competitive environment from the coach rather than "force of personality" type coaching [22].

Hays et al. [23] identified that world-class female athletes place more importance on good personal performance than world-class male athletes, who derive confidence from winning. In another study, coaches of collegiate-level women's sports teams indicated that compared to male athletes, the sporting experience for female athletes includes experiences on and off the field, and that to a greater extent than males, good communication between coach and athlete and among athletes is essential for team cohesion [24]. Similarly, Holbrook and Barr [25] reported that team unity was regarded as more motivating for female athletes than for male athletes. A study of 408 male and female student-athletes from ten NCAA Division I and II universities examining the differences of student-athletes' preferred leadership behavior for their coaches identified that male student-athletes significantly preferred autocratic and social support behaviors while female student-athletes significantly preferred situational consideration and training and instruction behaviors [26].

Several differences between coaching female and male athletes have been identified. For example, coaches have observed that female athletes listen better, are more interested in learning techniques and understanding their roles in various situations [27]. Independent of the sport and the gender of the coach, women's teams spend more time on technique drills while men's teams use most of their time on competitive activities. DeBoer [27] proposed that coaching women to their strengths; i.e., cooperative play, along with focusing on the stress of competition will better prepare them.

In addition to the above noted distinctions between female and male athletes, the gendered nature of sports may also impact the development of female athletes in particular. According to Cunningham and Sagas [28], although females have far greater access to sports today than they did in the past, "sports organizations are often places that still reproduce traditional gender roles and male privilege and dominance (p. 3)." For instance, the relative lack of representation of women in positions of leadership in sport has created a social context in which the experience of female sports coaches is referenced from a predominantly male perspective [29]. As such, recurring issues elicited by attendees at the USOC/NCAA sponsored Women in Coaching Conferences focused on coach education strategies in three main areas: i) restructuring the work environment to recognize and value relational work skills; ii) relational mentoring models to navigate career and life transitions and advocate for change; and iii) the continuation of women and sport programs [30]. Given that women athletes rely on their coaches as role models, the predominantly masculine ethos of the sporting world may leave female athletes lacking role models with whom they can readily identify and emulate.

In summary, research in both the business and the sports arenas highlights characteristics and contexts of women that differ from those of men. We believe the primary distinctions are that women tend more toward relational practice [21, 24], are more participative and collaborative [16], focus on exceeding their personal best performance [22], and tend to be more self-reflective and take a holistic perspective toward life and career [5]. There is also recognition that both the managerial [4] and professional sporting worlds are male-dominated arenas [31-33] resulting in unequal playing fields for women. We do not mean to suggest that the development of women in sports should be dictated solely by gender. In any development process, the needs of the individual must be considered. However, we do believe that contexts differ significantly enough for women and men that gender considerations are warranted. Given these realities for women, we propose that there are specific developmental practices from the business world that can inform the effective practice of coaching, leading and developing women in sports. In particular we believe the following areas of business practice apply: *executive coaching*, which relates to the overall development of an individual's skills, abilities and leadership capacity; *mentoring*, which relates to sponsorship, role modeling, individual development, and creating a supportive web of relationships; and *emotional intelligence skills development*, which relates to the development of self awareness, self management, and relationship management skills.

EXECUTIVE COACHING

Coaching in organizations has expanded greatly in the past few decades. According to London [34], there are tens of thousands of professional coaches world-wide and sixty percent of organizations offer their managers some coaching services.

Kilburg [35] defines executive coaching as "a helping relationship formed between a client who has managerial authority in an organization and a consultant who uses a wide variety of behavioral techniques and methods to help the client achieve a mutually identified set of goals to improve his or her professional performance and personal satisfaction and, consequently, to improve the effectiveness of the client's organization within a formally defined coaching agreement" (p. 142). Boyatzis [36] describes coaching as a process of caring for and helping others in their personal intentional change process, and Ford [37] notes that the aim of coaching is "to review and challenge old values, attitudes, styles of dealing with people, and strategies for getting things done" (p. 21). Individual clients report that their chief reasons for seeking coaching services include: to moderate their interaction style; to build trust in their relationships; to deal more effectively with change; to improve their listening skills; and to improve their public speaking [38].

Coaching models vary, but the coaching process typically centers around five key activities: relationship-building between the coach and the client, data gathering and assessments, feedback, implementation of an action plan, and evaluation [39, 40]. Chemistry between the coach and the executive is critical. The quality of their relationship built on trust is the first determinant of the effectiveness of coaching [41]. The purpose of the data gathering and assessment stage is to collect information from a variety of sources on the client's strengths and areas for further development. Typically 360° assessments and other quantitative and qualitative measurements such as leadership styles are used. Honest feedback from the coach is critical to the coaching relationship [42]. Through appropriate feedback, the executive can become more self aware and begin to recognize areas for change. The next step in the process is determining goals for improvement and establishing an action plan to achieve the goals. And finally, an evaluation of the coaching from both the executive and the coach's viewpoints completes the coaching cycle.

In effect, executive coaching is a leadership development process. Leadership development is "expanding the collective capacity of organizational members to engage effectively in leadership roles and processes" [43, p. 582]. Maximum impact from leadership development can only be realized if organizational programs focus simultaneously on both individual and organizational levels of learning [44]. This involves working with individuals to improve their skills and knowledge while building the overall capacity and effectiveness of the organization [45]. Leaders at all levels of an organization share the responsibility of developing the leadership capacity of the organization along with members of the senior leadership team [46]. Also, scholars note that individuals and organizations should work together in support of leadership development whereby organizations should structure developmental opportunities for employees who then have the responsibility to act on them [47]. McCauley and Van Velsor [48] propose that in order to be effective, developmental experiences should incorporate an array of assessments, challenges and support mechanisms. Parallels can be drawn between these three aspects of effective leadership development practices and the primary activities of executive coaching (i.e., data gathering, feedback, implementation of an action plan, and evaluation). The literature describes numerous attributes of the best coaches; for example:

> Good coaching is simply good management. It requires many of the same skills that are critical to effective management, such as keen powers of observation, sensible judgment, and an ability to take appropriate action. [49, p.111]

These authors propose that the coach must take on the role of a teacher and not a judge, and must first reflect before taking action. A coach is one who inspires, models, guides, trains, challenges, and sponsors and who helps people succeed through motivation, enhancing abilities, and providing support [50]. The best coaches are good listeners, give realistic feedback and are results-oriented by providing ideas for action [51]. The abilities to establish relationships and to demonstrate empathy in addition to confront and challenge the executive are all essential skills for coaches in business [40]. Of course, knowledge of leadership and awareness of the organizational environment in which the executive is embedded are also critical.

Studies measuring the effectiveness of executive coaching conclude that increased self awareness, learning, behavior change, development, leadership and organizational productivity are outcomes of coaching [52-54]. An examination of over 1,000 senior managers in one organization followed their progress over the course of a year. Results indicate that those managers who worked with a coach received improved ratings from their managers and direct reports [55]. However, there are still relatively few empirical studies of executive coaching and this field remains ripe for further exploration.

While the discipline of executive coaching has grown and the processes and characteristics of effective coaches have been identified, little is known about the coaching of executive women. One primary reason for this is the fact that women remain in small numbers at senior leadership levels in business organizations and have only recently begun to engage executive coaches. In addition, a survey of more than 3,000 human resource professionals in the USA reported that one-fifth of the respondents stated that women do not receive the same amount of coaching as their male counterparts [56].

The above data suggest that coaching may be of particular value to women in the leadership ranks. Women seek to balance their multiple responsibilities including career and family over the course of their lives [57], and women confront multiple life roles at different stages in their life spans resulting in distinct decision points over the course of a career. For example, O'Neil and Bilimoria [6] discovered that women's careers fall into three phases from early to late career – idealistic achievement, pragmatic endurance, and reinventive contribution – with different developmental concerns and priorities in each. Coaching can also help develop the political skills of women who do not have access to important networks and can help women take advantage of organizational opportunities heretofore unavailable to them [58].

A large amount of research in the sports leadership arena has focused on coaching behaviors and styles of coaching that contribute to positive reactions and successful performance [59]. An analysis of the coaching science research published in the past three decades found that articles concerning sports coaching appeared in a broad range of journals and half of the articles focused on the behaviors of coaches [60]. One conclusion these authors drew from their investigation is that successful coaching depends on effective interpersonal communications and relationships established among all the stakeholders.

The National Standards for Athletic Coaches [61] delineated three competency domains critical for sports coaching: the athlete's development; the psychological aspects of coaching; and the skills, tactics and strategies of coaching. There have been a number of studies in which coaching competency has been measured (see recent reviews by Horn [59] and Myers et al. [62]). An early study by Maclean and Chelladurai [63] proposed that behavioral product factors (team and personal products) and behavioral process factors (including task related and maintenance related behaviors) contribute to coaching performance. More recently, Horn's [59] comprehensive model of coaching effectiveness took into account contextual (e.g., socio-cultural context, organizational climate), psychological (e.g., athlete's motivation, coaches' expectancies, beliefs and goals), demographic (e.g., coaches' and athletes' personal characteristics) and behavioral factors (e.g., coaches' behaviors and athletes' performance). Werthner [64] noted three key qualities or skills that successful coaches possess: being open to learning and seeking out mentors or experts across disciplines; listening to and learning from their athletes; and practicing self-reflection and enabling others to do the same. A study of U.S. Olympic coaches indicated that coaches who were not able to effectively manage crises, pressures, stress, and distractions or failed to establish trust with their athletes perceived themselves as less effective [65].

APPLICATION OF EXECUTIVE COACHING INSIGHTS TO DEVELOPING WOMEN ATHLETES

Three elements of executive coaching appear particularly relevant to the development of women in sports: establishing high quality relationships with teammates and coaches; focusing on holistic personal development; and providing a balanced menu of assessments, challenges and supports.

Whether coaching in a business environment or in an athletic venue, the art and science of coaching require good interpersonal skills in order to establish high-quality relationships. The value that women place on having strong connections with others indicates the essential nature of relationship-building to the development of female athletes. Two central relationships for female athletes are with teammates and coaches. Since team cohesion and team performance are significant for women, developing skills of teamwork and collaboration, conflict management and inspirational leadership would in effect serve a dual purpose: support women's desires for effective working relationships; and maximize their abilities to establish high quality relationships as athletes, teammates, future coaches, and members of society.

The notion that the most effective leadership development occurs simultaneously at the individual and the organizational level suggests that both the coach and the female athlete need to work in tandem to improve the athlete's effectiveness, the effectiveness of the working relationship between the coach-athlete dyad, and overall team effectiveness. Establishing a coach-athlete partnership will likely enhance athletic performance because the female athlete has a critical stake in her performance and will be encouraged to actively participate in the planning and training components if she has a coach who is open to her insights and suggestions for improvement. This is also supported by the concept of relational authenticity [66] which joins a leader and a follower together in a values identification process. Both parties must subscribe to the values of the larger community (team, performance goals, etc.) in order to work together transparently and effectively in support of the common goal.

Since business research suggests that women tend more toward participative or transformational leadership styles, women athletes may likely respond best to an inclusive coaching style. This means that coaches who take an autocratic or dictatorial approach may run the risk of shutting down their female athletes instead of encouraging them to work at optimal capacity. However, it may also be important to utilize both transformational and transactional styles depending on the individual needs of the athlete and the particular context of a given situation. Accurate assessment of the given athlete and the particular coaching situation, and use of the appropriate style to ensure one's message gets across is a key component of effective coaching. This is also an important consideration in developing the leadership and coaching capabilities of the female athlete who may role model her coach as she moves into a future coaching role herself.

A second theme derived from the literature on executive coaching that translates to the development of female athletes is the focus of women on personal development. Individual performance and development along with personal satisfaction are important to women. A balance of coaching to female athletes' strengths; for example, collaborative skills, as well as coaching to win, seems advisable. This balanced strategy would enhance female athletes' overall performance and development, and it would also address women's attention to wholeness.

A developmental balance of assessment, feedback and evaluation contributes to self awareness, a central outcome of effective coaching in the business arena and a pillar of emotional intelligence. Another objective of executive coaching is to have the individual become skilled in reflecting before taking action. Given women's proclivity for self reflection, coaching that includes time and processes for self reflection for female athletes would also be of benefit.

Women have been described as more self critical than men; and coaches providing female athletes with ongoing assessment and feedback would give their athletes a constant barometer for their performance and development. It is as important for feedback processes to include what the female athlete is doing well as it is to address areas for improvement. Focusing on strengths, particularly since female athletes tend to be self-critical, is necessary in order to provide a balanced perspective on performance and capability.

Finally, the combination of assessments, challenges, and support systems that comprise effective developmental experiences [48] provide a good template for developing female athletes for three particular reasons: i) the inclination of women to desire a holistic perspective toward balancing multiple aspects of their lives [5]; ii) their tendencies toward self reflection, self criticism, and self competition [22]; and iii) their inclinations toward creating supportive relationships [22, 67]. Assessment is providing constant information about strengths and development needs; challenges should take the form of experiences that call for stretching both skills and perspectives; and supports should enhance self confidence and provide reassurance about skills and abilities [48]. For female athletes, these activities should focus on the full range of skills from athletic performance to team, leadership, interpersonal, and career development. Assessments, challenges and supports would encompass open communication between coach and athlete, continual dialogue about goals, providing training partners who can offer feedback and encouragement, and fostering strong team relationships. These activities will provide female athletes with opportunities to reflect on their performance and to collaboratively identify ways to improve.

MENTORING

Traditional definitions of mentoring describe a relationship between a more experienced person (the mentor) and a less experienced person (the mentee or protégé) with the purpose of providing the mentee with career development and support [68]. Kram [68] proposed that mentors offer two types of functions to their protégés: career and psychosocial; additional studies note that role modeling may be considered a third and separate function of mentoring [69-71]. Mentoring relationships have been found to be positively linked to career development [69], and individuals who have mentors are often more satisfied, more highly paid, and experience more career commitment than those without mentors [72].

In addition to the traditional definition of an experienced mentor advising a junior level protégé, mentoring research has also focused on the positive effects of multiple mentoring relationships including peer and group mentoring [67, 73, 74]. Higgins and Kram [74] note that individuals likely receive mentoring assistance from multiple sources simultaneously and that given the increasing complexity of contemporary lives, there is relevance in examining mentoring as a "multiple relationship phenomenon" (p. 266). These authors propose a developmental network perspective on mentoring that operates both internal and external to an organization, is based on mutuality and reciprocity, and includes more than just the traditional dyadic relationship. Women in particular find mutual support in establishing a variety of relationships [5].

Mentoring has been found to be beneficial for both men and women, but there is evidence to suggest that it may be of particular importance to women who may have less access to networks and power structures in organizations than men [75-78]. Mentors provide women with three essential benefits: assistance in interpreting masculine organizational cultures, providing help with advancement and successful performance, and enhancing women's sense of belonging to the organization [79]. While the second benefit would also apply to men, women have less overall access to advancement opportunities and thus need additional support from mentors in being recognized for advancement.

Availability of and access to mentors for women in organizations has been found to be more difficult than for men [76, 80]. One reason cited for this difficulty is the lack of women in senior organizational positions who may play the role of mentor and role model to junior women [81]. Researchers have found that women's intentions to mentor are similar to men's [82] and conclude that the relative lack of senior women mentors is due to the lack of women in senior positions, not a lack of desire [83]. Another effect of the lack of senior women is that women are likely to find themselves in cross-gender mentoring relationships. Mentoring relationships with men offer women career benefits, but can be complicated by traditional gender roles and external perceptions. Ragins and Cotton [82] suggest that traditional gender stereotypes lead to women being more passive and submissive with a male mentor than with a female mentor. Also, issues of sexual harassment and misperceptions of sexual attraction between mentors and protégés are cited as hindrances to establishing effective mentoring relationships [84, 85].

Mentoring in sports has been found to positively affect both athletes and coaches. In a study examining the development process of coaches, Bloom et al. [86] found that most coaches were mentored during their athletic and early coaching careers. They noted that their subjects reported gaining insights and experiences that shaped their coaching philosophies and enhanced their athletic performance. They also noted that these mentored individuals in turn became mentors when they reached more advanced levels in their fields.

In a study of athletic administrators in NCAA Division I and III, Weaver and Chelladurai [87] found that an equal number of females and males reported being mentored in contrast to findings in business and management. They speculated that a progressive educational environment and improved status of women in sports may explain their findings. In a recent study of mentor-protégé sex and attitudinal similarity among NCAA Division I women's basketball coaches, Avery et al. [88] found that protégés with sex dissimilar mentors received less psychosocial and career mentoring than did those with same-sex mentors. However, they noted that the presence of a white male mentor mitigated the effects of dissimilarity in career (as opposed to psychosocial) mentoring, and related this to the power perspective [89] that privileges white men, and which they conclude applies even in women's college basketball. The authors suggest that cross-sex mentoring may pose a barrier to the career development of women in sports.

The percentage of women coaching women's teams dropped to 44% by 2000 from a high of 90% in the 1970s [29]. Between 2002 and 2004, men filled 53% of new women's athletic head coaching positions [90]. These data suggest that women athletes interested in career paths that include athletic coaching or administration will likely continue to face stiff competition from men resulting in diminishing numbers of female athletic coaches and administrators to serve as role models for the next generation of female athletes and aspiring coaches.

APPLICATION OF MENTORING INSIGHTS TO DEVELOPING WOMEN ATHLETES

Three insights from the mentoring research appear particularly relevant to the development of women in sports: establishing multiple mentoring relationships in order to address women's needs for personal performance, teamwork, and wholeness, providing assistance in navigating the organizational system, and the deleterious effects of the lack of female role models.

Given the efficacy of multiple mentoring relationships and the preference of women to create a network of relationships, it is important that attention is paid to these aspects of women's development in the sports domain. One avenue for the effective development of female athletes is to offer opportunities for peer mentoring whereby athletes would provide each other assistance in enhancing their skills as well as offering support. These peer mentoring relationships could be established through both formal mechanisms and informal systems encouraged by the coach.

Appropriate mentoring for female athletes should incorporate activities that assist their individual talent development, their concentration on team performance, and their team leadership abilities. These activities are particularly important for female athletes because of women's dual focus on personal performance and team unity. Facilitating the achievements of female athletes in their organizational context(s) includes consideration of intrinsic and extrinsic factors of individual success. Intrinsic success factors for women athletes include beating their personal best and giving an optimum personal performance as opposed to a sole focus on winning which would be an extrinsic measure of success.

The psychosocial functions of mentoring are particularly germane for women athletes because these functions concentrate on enhancing a protégé's personal and professional development and sense of self-esteem and self-efficacy. Given that studies have found that females desire a connection between their personal and professional lives and strive for wholeness [5], the positive influence of a developmental relationship with a senior mentor who is invested in developing the whole person will likely be enhancing for a female athlete in concert with her athletic training regimen. As mentioned previously, female athletic coaches noted that relational mentoring models were important to help them better navigate career and life transitions and advocate for change in the sports world [30]. These same factors would apply to the development of female athletes.

Assistance in navigating and making sense of an organizational system is one of the key career development functions of mentoring. Helping female athletes compete effectively in the male-dominated sporting world is of paramount importance. For example, mentors can work with their female athletes to develop skills of organizational awareness and influence. These skills can help athletes understand and navigate the political dynamics involved in individual and team performance in the world of competitive sports.

Role modeling is a third critical dimension of mentoring applicable for women athletes. Just as in the business world where the dearth of women in senior positions results in fewer role models for women striving for advancement, the relatively few female coaches means that female athletes do not have access to a representation of women in leadership positions in the sporting context. Given the male-dominated context of sports, issues with cross-sex mentors [88], and the discouraging statistics on women in coaching reported earlier [29, 90], creating new opportunities for female athletes to attain assistant and head coaching positions must be addressed in order to provide viable same sex mentoring opportunities for female athletes.

EMOTIONAL INTELLIGENCE SKILLS DEVELOPMENT

The use of emotions, emotional expression, and related constructs has captured our attention for decades. The subject of emotional intelligence is a burgeoning area of interest to practitioners and researchers alike. Emotional intelligence has been defined as the ability to perceive emotions in self and others, to understand emotions, and to effectively manage emotions in self and others [91, 92]. Emotional intelligence is demonstrated by emotional competencies in both the personal and the social domain. Personal competencies of self awareness and self management include such skills as emotional self awareness, self confidence, emotional self control, achievement, transparency, and optimism [93]. Social competencies of social awareness and relationship management include such skills as empathy, organizational awareness, inspirational leadership, teamwork and collaboration, and conflict management [94].

Two primary models of emotional intelligence exist today; one incorporating ability-based models and the other including a mix of traits and abilities [95, 96]. While questions about emotional intelligence have been raised, focused principally around these conflicting constructs of emotional intelligence as well as a high correlation with personality constructs [97-99], Ashkanasy and Daus [95] argue that emotional intelligence is indeed an individual difference variable involving a person's ability to identify, perceive, understand and manage emotions in oneself and in others. Other proponents of emotional intelligence maintain that the "weight of the evidence now supports the claim that EI is distinct from IQ, personality, or related constructs." [100]

Emotions are the primary apparatus we use to coordinate interactions and relationships with others [101]. Individuals with a high degree of emotional intelligence are better able to discern the emotional climate in organizations [102]. Emotional intelligence facilitates a leader's ability to have successful interactions and positive relations with others [103, 104] and to develop collective goals with their colleagues and direct reports [105].

Leaders excel not only through their cognitive ability, but also through their ability to connect with others using emotional intelligence [94]. A steady stream of research has investigated the relationship of emotional intelligence to a variety of performance outcomes. Emotional intelligence has been found to predict leader effectiveness [106], supervisor ratings of job performance [103, 107], and sales performance [108]. It has also been positively associated with performance in such diverse populations as account officers, call center staff, and military and school principals [109-113].

The influence of emotional intelligence on team performance is also considerable [114-117]. Emotional intelligence supports team members in their ability to determine team goals and priorities [105], and fosters positive emotions which have been found to increase creativity and innovative problem solving [118]. The effective management of emotions and the emotional intelligence competencies of influence, empathy and achievement in particular, have been reported to be positively related to cohesive work teams [119, 120].

Team leaders set the tone for the emotional reality of teams, i.e., the experience of being a member of the team and having the capacity to develop emotionally intelligent teams [94]. Leaders with a high degree of emotional intelligence are able to establish strong emotional relationships with team members, to accurately assess the emotions of others, and to manage those relationships effectively [121]. The emotionally intelligent leader, for example, can influence the emotions of team members toward successfully embracing change [105].

Research examining whether there are differences in the emotional intelligence between men and women have yielded equivocal findings. Some authors of empirical studies reported finding no significant differences in the overall emotional intelligence of men and women [122, 123]. In one study, Petrides et al. [124] found no significant gender differences in a total emotional intelligence score, but they found that men gave higher self-estimates on IQ and lower self-estimates on emotional intelligence than women. Participants in this study specifically associated emotional intelligence with two factors: emotional understanding and dependability. Another researcher reported that while women may not demonstrate a higher level of emotional intelligence overall in comparison to men, women do exhibit more social skills such as social expressivity and social control, and more emotional skills such as emotional expressivity and emotional sensitivity than do men [125].

Still other researchers have found that there are indeed gender distinctions in overall emotional intelligence scores, with females rating higher than males [126-128]. For example, significant differences between men and women were detected on an ability measure of emotional intelligence [129], with women scoring higher than men. Interestingly, in this same study it was reported that the self-estimated performance on the emotional intelligence measure by the men was significantly higher than that of the women. Bar-On [130] found that gender differences did exist for specific emotional intelligence components; females seemed to have stronger interpersonal skills, were more aware of their emotions, and demonstrated more empathy.

Scholars have proposed that emotional intelligence may be particularly relevant to the world of sports and this relationship merits further exploration [131-133]. Aberman and Anderson [134] maintain that: "Almost everything we do in sports is about emotional intelligence" (p. 53) and propose that coaches pay more attention to teaching emotional intelligence skills than technical skills. To date, few empirical studies have been published on this potentially significant relationship between emotional intelligence and sports. In one study exploring the connection between the athletic performance of Division I baseball players and emotional intelligence, the authors found a modest link between emotional skills and pitching performance but not hitting performance [133]. In a second study, researchers investigating the relationship between emotional intelligence and leader efficacy on the personal caring of leaders at a summer sports camp found that emotional intelligence (as self reported) significantly predicted the personal caring of the coach [135]. In a third study researchers examined the relationship between emotional intelligence and coaching efficacy with a sample of 99 coaches in a variety of sports in the United Kingdom [136]. Self-reported assessments of efficacy and emotional intelligence were used. The coach's motivation efficacy was found to be significantly related to regulation of emotions and social skills, while character building efficacy was associated with the optimism component of emotional intelligence.

Emotions play a central role in sports. The outcome of a sports contest may be influenced by an athlete's emotions during practice as well as in the competition itself [137]. Athletes experience a range of emotions before, during and after their sports performance [138-141]. For example, researchers investigating the Individual Zones of Optimal Functioning model reported that athletes feel both positive and negative emotions [139]. In order to realize optimal motivation and performance, athletes need to effectively manage their positive emotions as well as their negative emotions [142]. There is a delicate balance between the best possible emotions for performance generating the appropriate amount of energy and dysfunctional emotions resulting in an excess or deficient supply of energy [139]. Botterill and Brown [138] contend that "typically athletes just experience their emotional responses and do not stop to reflect on them critically and constructively" (p. 50).

APPLICATION OF EMOTIONAL INTELLIGENCE INSIGHTS TO DEVELOPING WOMEN ATHLETES

Two global themes from the literature on emotional intelligence are particularly germane to coaching women athletes. The first is the importance of personal competencies, especially emotional self awareness, as this aspect of emotional intelligence directly relates to the inclination of women to be self-reflective as noted earlier. The second principal theme is the significance of teamwork and collaboration, one of the social competencies of emotional intelligence and a particular behavioral strength of women.

There is a growing body of evidence from the business literature that supports the positive association between emotional intelligence and performance. This is true for both individual performance, leader performance and team performance. Given this evidence and the parallel responsibilities between sports coaching and business leadership, it stands to reason that emotional intelligence is an essential ingredient for the effective development of athletes. The power of emotions has been found to significantly impact performance and outcomes in sports, and tapping into those emotions and harnessing them in positive ways will likely lead to increased performance for athletes, coaches and teams. Based on our assessment of the particular development requirements for women, targeting the development of emotional intelligence competencies such as emotional self awareness, self confidence, empathy, and teamwork and collaboration would appear to be especially noteworthy for coaching female athletes and enhancing their individual and team performance.

In examining the impact of emotional intelligence on the female athlete, the literature on women in sports notes that females tend to be self-reflective and self-critical, which differentiates them from the overall characterization that athletes likely do not critically or constructively reflect on their emotions. These self assessment attributes suggest that female athletes seek to be attuned to their emotional states and likely have a predisposition toward developing self awareness, the foundation of emotional intelligence. In addition, self confidence is a critical factor in the performance of women in both sport and business; and coaches must pay particular attention to the tendency of women to be self-critical which may influence their confidence level. Coaches should work with female athletes to help them hone each of these emotional competencies in service of individual performance improvement and team cohesion.

The social and emotional expressivity and emotional sensitivity aspects of emotional intelligence distinguishes women from men. Thus, a female athlete may require a coach who taps into her emotions in a positive way in addition to paying attention to the technical aspects of the sport. Another important factor in the characterization of women is their tendency toward developing interconnected personal relationships as opposed to pursuing a hierarchical model of connection. This suggests that women athletes will benefit from opportunities to demonstrate and develop the social competencies associated with emotional intelligence, skills of social awareness and relationship management. They will also likely respond well to an emotionally intelligent coaching style that motivates and inspires through connection and empathy rather than through conflict and force.

In a team context, higher levels of emotional intelligence facilitate the development of collaborative goals, innovative problem solving and strong bonds within the team. Evidence from the management literature suggests that women tend toward collaboration and a team orientation [16]. There is a relationship between the social awareness and relationship management competencies salient for women and the inclination toward interpersonal relationships and teamwork. Since women athletes desire effective communication with teammates and coaches, and appreciate developing strong team relationships, a coach who supports and nurtures these characteristics should realize benefits in his or her athlete's individual performance as well as the overall team performance. Coaches should also find opportunities to enhance and promote collaborative and team-based performance development strategies such as general team building exercises, active listening and other methods of effective communication, peer coaching activities, and team social interactions to tap into women's highly developed social and relational skills.

The connection between emotional intelligence and leadership performance is relevant in examining the role of the coach in developing female athletes. In order for coaches to be effective, understanding and managing their own and others' emotions are critical. An athletic coach who demonstrates a greater degree of emotional intelligence will more likely be attuned to the specific emotional needs of the athlete being coached. Furthermore, the emotionally intelligent coach will recognize and regulate his or her own emotions prior to being able to understand and effectively manage the emotions of the athlete. These components of emotional intelligence are particularly important in establishing effective relationships and communication between coach and athlete, both of which are essential in creating optimal development conditions for female athletes. A coach who continues to enhance his or her own emotional intelligence will not only recognize these particular skills on the part of women athletes, but also encourage their practice and development by the athletes.

CONCLUSION

This analysis of the parallels between developing women in business and in sports is intended to highlight the distinct advantages of addressing the particular developmental needs of women. We have provided recommendations for the effective development of women athletes based on three areas of business and management best practice: executive coaching, mentoring, and emotional intelligence skills development. Within these three areas of developmental practice, issues of paramount importance for women include the development of personal and social competence focused on developing high quality relationships with coaches and teammates, and a focus on holistic personal development. We believe considering these primary issues in concert with targeted individual development will lead to the effective growth of female athletes.

FUTURE RESEARCH

Future research on the application of executive coaching practices for women athletes might focus on three areas informed by business and management research on the coaching of executive women. First, an examination of the impact of coaching across life roles may offer insights into ways in which women athletes manage multiple priorities. What opportunities for transfer of skills and abilities do women athletes experience from personal to professional and from professional to personal? How do women athletes develop in their sport while continuing to develop as individuals, wives/partners, mothers, etc.? Second, in addition to a coach developing a female athlete's athletic ability, how does the coach help the athlete make sense of and navigate the gendered context of competitive sports? Is it necessary for coaches of women athletes to help them develop proactive career management and political skills? Are coaches that develop female athletes' such skills more effective than those who don't? Third, deeper examination of the factors that facilitate the leadership development of women athletes in individual and team sports would be instructive. Relevant research questions might be: How do women develop simultaneously as individual athletes and members of winning teams? Are women athletes more likely to demonstrate transformational or relational leadership behaviors than male athletes? What are the differential impacts of female versus male coaches' leadership styles on the development of women athletes?

Future research on mentoring in the sports domain should examine the impact of hierarchical mentoring relationships (e.g., between coach and athlete) as well as peer mentoring relationships (e.g., between team members). What types of mentoring relationships yield superior performance from women athletcs? Do female athletes, as compared with male athletes, prefer some forms of mentoring over others? Investigations of the impact of multiple mentors should also be undertaken. It is likely that athletes will have relationships with multiple mentors, both internal and external to the sporting world. What is the impact of these multiple developmental relationships? How do these relationships impact the overall development of the athlete, both personally and professionally?

Further examining the relationship between gender, performance and emotional intelligence for both athletes and coaches would be informative, addressing questions such as: Do female sports coaches demonstrate greater overall emotional intelligence than male sports coaches? What are the similarities and differences in specific emotional intelligence competencies? What is the relationship between emotional intelligence and athletic performance? Do coaches that demonstrate greater emotional intelligence produce more winning teams over time? Do athletes develop greater self awareness, self management, social awareness and relationship management skills when coached by coaches who demonstrate a high degree of emotional intelligence?

In addition to the above suggestions for future research directions, we recognize that it is likely that there are best practices from the world of sports coaching of women that may be informative for the development of women business managers and executives. While we have not explored this directly in the present review, we encourage future scholars to examine these connections as well in order to continue to further the advancement of women in both the business and sports worlds.

REFERENCES

1.   Lorenzi, P., Managing for the Common Good: Prosocial Leadership, *Organizational Dynamics, 2004, 33(3), 282-291.*

2.   National Association for Sport and Physical Education, National Standards for Sports Coaches, 2nd Ed., 2006, http://www.aahperd.org/naspe/template.cfm?template=domainsStandards.html Retrieved 12/16/08.

3.   Sturges, J., What it Means to Succeed: Personal Conceptions of Career Success Held by Male and Female Managers at Different Ages, *British Journal of Management*, 1999, 10, 239-252.

4.   Ruderman, M. N. and Ohlott, P. J., Leading Roles: What Coaches of Women Need to Know, *Leadership in Action,* 2005, 25, 3-9.

5.   Ruderman, M. N. and Ohlott, P. J., *Standing at the Crossroads: Next Steps for High-Achieving Women*, Jossey-Bass, San Francisco, 2002.

6.   O'Neil, D. A. and Bilimoria, D., Women's Career Development Phases: Idealism, Endurance, and Reinvention, *Career Development International,* 2005, 10(3), 168-189.

7.   Mainiero, L. A. and Sullivan, S. E. Kaleidoscope Careers: An Alternate Explanation for the Opt-out Revolution, *The Academy of Management Executive*, 2005, 19(1), 106-123.

8.   Gallos, J., Exploring Women's Development: Implications for Career Theory, Practice, and Research, in: Arthur, M. B., Hall, D. T. and Lawrence, B. S., eds., *Handbook of Career Theory,* Cambridge University Press, Cambridge, 1989, 110-131.

9.   Betz, N. E., Women's Career Development, in: eds., Denmark, F. L. and Paludi, M. A., *Psychology of Women*, Academic Press, New York, 1993.

10. Ragins, B. R., Townsend, B. and Mattis, M., Gender Gap in the Executive Suite: CEOs and Female Executives Report on Breaking the Glass Ceiling, *Academy of Management Executive*, 1998, 12, 28-42.

11. Hopkins, M. M., O'Neil, D. A., Passarelli, A. and Bilimoria, D., Women's Leadership Development: Strategic Practices for Women and Organizations, *Consulting Psychology Journal: Practice and Research*, 2008, 60, 4, 348-365.

12. Eagly, A. H. and Johnson, B. T., Gender and Leadership Style: A Meta-Analysis, *Psychological Bulletin*, 1990, 108, 233-256.

13. Carli, L. L. and Eagly, A. H., Gender Effects on Social Influence and Emergent Leadership, in: Powell, G.N., ed., *Handbook of Gender and Work,* Sage Publications, Thousand Oaks, CA, 1999, 203-222.

14. Goleman, D., *Working with Emotional Intelligence*, Bantam, New York, 1998.

15. Eagly, A. H., Karau, S. J. and Makhijani, M. G., Gender and the Effectiveness of Leaders: A Meta-Analysis, *Psychological Bulletin*, 1995, 117, 125-145.

16. Eagly, A. H. and Johannesen-Schmidt, Leadership Style Matters: The Small, But Important, Style Differences between Male and Female Leaders, in: Bilimoria, D. and Piderit, S., eds., *Handbook on Women in Business and Management*, Edwin Elgar Publishing, Northampton, MA, 2007, 279-303.

17. Sharpe, R., As Leaders, Women Rule, *Business Week*, 2000, November 20, 74-84.

18. O'Neil, D. A., Hopkins, M. M. and Bilimoria, D., Women's Careers at the Start of the 21st Century: Patterns and Paradoxes, *Journal of Business Ethics*, 2008, 80, 727-743.

19. Williams, J., *Unbending Gender: Why Family and Work Conflict and What to Do About It*, Oxford University Press, New York, 2000.

20. Meyerson, D. E. and Fletcher, J. K., A Modest Manifesto for Shattering the Glass Ceiling, *Harvard Business Review*, 2000, 78(1), 126-136.

21. Fletcher, J. K., *Disappearing Acts: Gender, Power and Relational Practice at Work*, MIT Press, Cambridge, 1999.

22.   Dorrance, A. and Averbuch, *G., The Vision of a Champion*, Huron River Press, Ann Arbor, 2005.

23.   Hays, K., Maynard, I., Thomas, O. and Bawden, M., Sources and Types of Confidence Identified by World Class Sport Performers, *Journal of Applied Sport Psychology*, 2007, 19(4), 434-456.

24.   McClain, N., *Unique Aspects of Team Cohesion with Female Athletes*, Dissertation Abstracts International: Section B: The Sciences and Engineering, 2006, 66 (10-B), 5733.

25.   Holbrook, J. F. and Barr, J. K., *Contemporary Coaching: Issues and Trends*, Cooper, Traverse City, MI, 1997.

26.   Beam, J. W., Serwatka, T. S. and Wilson, W. J., Preferred Leadership of NCAA Division I and II Intercollegiate Student-Athletes, *Journal of Sport Behavior*, 2004, 27(1), 3-17.

27.   DeBoer, K. J., Practice Like a Girl, Compete Like a Boy: Training the Total Athlete, *American Swimming Coaches Association Newsletter*, 2007, 3, 12-16.

28.   Cunningham, G. B. and Sagas, M., Gender and Sex Diversity in Sport Organizations: Introduction to a Special Issue, *Sex Roles*, 2008, 58, 3-9.

29.   Reynaud, C., *She Can Coach!*, 2005, Human Kinetics, Champaign, IL.

30.   Kilty, K., Women in Coaching, *The Sport Psychologist*, 2006, 20(2) 222-234.

31.   Bryon, L., Sport and the Maintenance of Masculine Hegemony, *Women's Studies International Forum*, 1987, 10, 349-360.

32.   Fielding-Lloyd, B. and Mean, L. J., Standards and Separatism: The Discursive Construction of Gender in English Soccer Coach Education, *Sex Roles*, 2008, 58(1), 24-39.

33.   Fink, J. S., Gender and Sex Diversity in Sport Organizations: Concluding Comments, *Sex Roles*, 2008, 58(1), 146-147.

34.   London, M., *Leadership Development: Paths to Self-Insight and Professional Growth*, Lawrence Erlbaum, Mahwah, 2002.

35.   Kilburg, R. R., Towards a Conceptual Understanding and Definition of Executive Coaching, *Consulting Psychology Journal*, 1996, 48(2), 134-144.

36.   Boyatzis, R. E. (2003). *Notes from a Coaching Workshop*, Unpublished Paper, Case Western Reserve University, 2003.

37.   Ford, R. G., Professional Coaching in Leadership Development, *Executive Development*, 1992, 5(4), 21-23.

38.   Judge, W. Q. and Cowell, J., The Brave New World of Executive Coaching, *Business Horizons*, 1997, 40(4), 71-78.

39.   Feldman, D. C. and Lankau, M. J., Executive Coaching: A Review and Agenda for Future Research, *Journal of Management*, 2005, 31(6), 829-848.

40.   Kampa-Kokesch, S. and Anderson, M. Z., Executive Coaching: A Comprehensive Review of the Literature, *Consulting Psychology Journal*, 2001, 53(4), 205-228.

41.   Hunt, J. M. and Weintraub, J., How Coaching Can Enhance Your Brand as a Manager, *Journal of Organizational Excellence*, 2002, 21(2), 39-44.

42.   Kilburg, R. R., Facilitating Intervention Adherence in Executive Coaching: A Model and Methods, *Consulting Psychology Journal*, 2001, 53(4), 251-267.

43.   Day, D. V., Leadership Development: A Review in Context, *Leadership Quarterly*, 2001, 11(4), 581-613.

44.   Conger, J. A. and Benjamin, B., *Building Leaders: How Successful Companies Develop the Next Generation*, Jossey-Bass, San Francisco, 1999.

45.   Cummings, T. G. and Worley, C. G., *Organization Development and Change*, 8th edn., Thomson-South-Western, Belmont, 2005.

46.   Cohn, J. M., Khurana, R. and Reeves, L., Growing Talent as if Your Business Depended on It, *Harvard Business Review*, 2005, October, 62-70.

47.   Ready, D. A. and Conger, J. A., Why Leadership Development Efforts Fail, *MIT Sloan Management Review*, 2003, 44(3), 83-88.

48.   McCauley, C. D. and Van Velsor, E., eds., *The Center for Creative Leadership Handbook of Leadership Development*, Jossey-Bass, San Francisco, 2004.

49.   Waldroop, J. and Butler, T., The Executive as Coach, *Harvard Business Review*, 1996, 74(6), 111-117.

50.   Longenecker, C. O. and Pinkel, G., Coaching to Win at Work, *Manage*, 1997, 48(2), 19-21.

51.   Hall, D., Otazo, K. and Hollenbeck, G., Behind Closed Doors: What Really Happens in Executive Coaching, *Organizational Dynamics*, 1999, 27(3), 39-53.

52.   Kilburg, R. R., Trudging Toward Dodoville: Conceptual Approaches and Case Studies in Executive Coaching, *Consulting Psychology Journal*, 2004, 56(4), 203-213.

53.   Laske, O. E., *Transformative Effects of Coaching on Executive's Professional Agenda*, 1, University of Michigan Press, Ann Arbor, 1999.

54.   Olivero, G., Bane, K. D. and Kopelman, R. E., Executive Coaching as a Transfer of Training Tool: Effects on Productivity in a Public Agency, *Public Personnel Management*, 1997, 26, 461-469.

55.   Smither, J. W., London, M., Flautt, R., Vargas, Y. and Kucine, I., Can Working With an Executive Coach Improve Multisource Feedback Ratings Over Time: A Quasi-Experimental Field Study, *Personnel Psychology*, 2003, 56(1), 23-44.

56.   Laff, M., Women Receive Less Coaching, *Training and Development*, 2007, January, 18.

57.   Powell, G. N. and Mainiero, L. A., Cross-Currents in the River of Time: Conceptualizing the Complexities of Women's Careers, *Journal of Management*, 1992, 18(2), 215-238.

58.   Perrewé, P. L. and Nelson, D. L., Gender and Career Success: The Facilitative Role of Political Skill, *Organizational Dynamics*, 2004, 33(4), 366-378.

59.   Horn, T. S., Coaching Effectiveness in the Sports Domain, in: Horn, T. S., ed., *Advances in Sport Psychology*, 2nd edn., Human Kinetics, Champaign, 2002, 309-354.

60.   Gilbert, W. D. and Trudel, P., Analysis of Coaching Science Research Published from 1970-2001, *Research Quarterly for Exercise and Sport*, 2004, 75(4), 388-399.

61.   National Association for Sport and Physical Education, *Quality Coaches, Quality Sports: National Standards for Athletic Coaches*, Kendall/Hunt, Dubuque, 1995.

62.   Myers, N. D., Feltz, D. L., Maier, K. S., Wolfe, E. W. and Reckase, M. D., Athletes' Evaluations of Their Head Coach's Coaching Competency, *Research Quarterly for Exercise and Sport*, 2006, 77(1), 111-121.

63.   MacLean, J. C. and Chelladurai, P., Dimensions of Coaching Performance: Development of a Scale, *Journal of Sport Management*, 1995, 9, 194-207.

64.   Werthner, P., Making the Case: Coaching as a Viable Career Path for Women, *Canadian Journal of Women in Coaching*, 2005, 5, 3, 1-9.

65.   Gould, D., Guinan, D., Greenleaf, C. and Chung, Y., A Survey of U.S. Olympic Coaches: Variables Perceived to have Influenced Athlete Performances and Coaching Effectiveness, *The Sport Psychologist*, 2002, 16, 229-250.

66.   Eagly, A. H., Achieving Relational Authenticity in Leadership: Does Gender Matter?, *The Leadership Quarterly*, 2005, 16, 459-474.

67.   De Janasz, S. C., Sullivan, S. E. and Whiting, V. Mentor Networks and Career Success: For Turbulent Times, *Academy of Management Executive*, 2003, 17(4), 78-91.

68.   Kram, K. E., *Mentoring at Work*, Scott, Foresman, Glenview IL, 1985.

69.   Ragins, B. R. and Kram, K. E., The Roots and Meaning of Mentoring, in: Ragins, B. R. and Kram, K. E., eds., *The Handbook of Mentoring at Work*, Sage Publications, Thousand Oaks, CA, 2007, 3-15.

70. Scandura, T. A., Mentorship and Career Mobility: An Empirical Investigation, *Journal of Organizational Behavior*, 1992, 13, 169-174.

71. Scandura, T. A. and Ragins, B. R., The Effects of Gender and Role Orientation on Mentorship in Male-Dominated Organizations, *Journal of Vocational Behavior*, 1993, 43, 251-165.

72. Allen, T. D., Eby, L. T., Poteet, M. L., Lentz, E. and Lima, L. Career Benefits Associated with Mentoring for Proteges: A Meta-Analysis, *Journal of Applied Psychology*, 2004, 89, 127-136.

73. Baugh, S. G. and Scandura, T. A., The Effects of Multiple Mentors on Protégé Attitudes Toward the Work Setting. *Journal of Social Behavior and Personality*, 1999, 14, 503-521.

74. Higgins, M. C. and Kram, K. E., Reconceptualizing Mentoring at Work: A Developmental Network Perspective, *Academy of Management Review*, 2001, 26, 264-288.

75. Burke, R. J. and McKeen, C. A., Mentoring in Organizations: Implications for Women, *Journal of Business Ethics*, 1990, 9, 317-332.

76. Ragins, B. R., Barriers to Mentoring: The Female Manager's Dilemma, *Human Relations*, 1989, 42, 1-22.

77. Tharenou, P., Does Mentor Support Increase Women's Career Advancement More Than Men's? The Differential Effects of Career and Psychosocial Support, *Australian Journal of Management*, 2005, 30, 77-109.

78. Woolnough, H. M. and Davidson, M. J., Mentoring as a Career Development Tool: Gender, Race and Ethnicity Implications, in: Bilimoria, D. and Piderit, S., eds., *Handbook on Women in Business and Management*, Edwin Elgar Publishing, Northampton, MA, 2007, 154-177.

79. McKeen and Bujaki, M., Gender and Mentoring: Issues, Effects, and Opportunities, in: Ragins, B. R. and Kram, K. E., eds., *The Handbook of Mentoring at Work*, Sage Publications, Thousand Oaks, CA, 2007, 197-222.

80. Burke, R. J. and Nelson, D., *Advancing Women's Careers: Research and Practice*, Blackwell, Oxford, 2002.

81. Rothstein, M. G., Burke, R. J. and Bristor, J. M., Structural Characteristics and Support Benefits in the Interpersonal Networks of Women and Men in Management, *International Journal of Organizational Analysis*, 2001, 9(1), 4-25.

82. Ragins, B. R. and Cotton, J. L., Gender and Willingness to Mentor in Organizations, *Journal of Management*, 1993, 19(1), 97-122.

83. Ragins, B. R. and Scandura, T. A., Gender Differences in Expected Outcomes of Mentoring Relationships, *Academy of Management Journal*, 1994, 37(4), 957-971.

84. Blake-Beard, S. D., Taking a Hard Look at Formal Mentoring Programs, *Journal of Management Development*, 2001, 20(4), 331-345.

85. Clawson, J. G. and Kram, K. E., Managing Cross-Gender Mentoring, *Business Horizons*, 1984, 27, 22-32.

86. Bloom, G. A., Durand-Bush, N., Schinke, R. J. and Salmela, J. H., The Importance of Mentoring in the Development of Coaches and Athletes, *International Journal of Sport Psychology*, 1998, 29, 267-281.

87. Weaver, M. A. and Chelladurai, P., Mentoring in Intercollegiate Athletic Administration, *Journal of Sport Management*, 2002, 16, 96-116.

88. Avery, D. R., Tonidandel, S. and Phillips, M. G. Similarity on Sports Sidelines: How Mentor-Protégé Sex Similarity Affects Mentoring, *Sex Roles*, 2008, 58, 72-80.

89. Ragins, B. R., Diversified Mentoring Relationships in Organizations: A Power Perspective, *Academy of Management Review*, 1997, 22, 482-521.

90. Acosta, R. V. & Carpenter, L. J., *Women in Intercollegiate Sport: A Longitudinal, National Study, Twenty-seven Year Update; 1977-2004*. Retrieved 12/12/08 from http://webpages.charter.net/womeninsport/AcostaCarp_2004.pdf

91.   Goleman, D., *Emotional Intelligence*, Bantam Books, New York, 1995.

92.   Salovey, P. and Mayer, J. D., Emotional Intelligence, *Imagination, Cognition and Personality*, 1990, 9, 185-211.

93.   Boyatzis, R., Goleman, D. and Hay, Inc., *Emotional Competency Inventory, Version 2*, Philadelphia, PA, 2002.

94.   Goleman, D., Boyatzis, R. and McKee, A., The Emotional Reality of Teams, *Journal of Organizational Excellence*, 2002, Spring, 55-65.

95.   Ashkanasy, N. M. and Daus, C. S., Rumors of the Death of Emotional Intelligence in Organizational Behavior are Vastly Exaggerated, *Journal of Organizational Behavior*, 2005, 26, 441-452.

96.   McEnrue, M. P. and Groves, K., Choosing Among Tests of Emotional Intelligence: What is the Evidence? *Human Resource Development Quarterly*, 2006, 17(1), 19-42.

97.   Landy, F. J., Some Historical and Scientific Issues Related to Research on Emotional Intelligence, *Journal of Organizational Behavior*, 2005, 26, 411-424.

98.   Locke, E. A., Why Emotional Intelligence is an Invalid Concept, *Journal of Organizational Behavior*, 2005, 26, 425-431.

99.   Waterhouse, L., Multiple Intelligences, the Mozart Effect and Emotional Intelligence: A Critical Review, *Educational Psychologist*, 2006, 41(4), 207-225.

100.   Cherniss, C., Extein, M., Goleman, D. and Weissberg, R. P., Emotional Intelligence: What Does the Research Really Indicate?, *Educational Psychologist*, 2006, 41(4), 239-245.

101.   Kumar, R., The Role of Affect in Negotiations: An Integrative Overview, *Journal of Applied Behavioral Science*, 1997, 33, 84-100.

102.   Ashkanasy, N. M. and Daus, C. S., Emotion in the Workplace: The New Challenge for Managers, *Academy of Management Executive*, 2002, 16(1), 76-86.

103.   Law, K. S., Wong, C. S. and Song, L. J., The Construct and Criterion Validity of Emotional Intelligence and Its Potential Utility for Management Studies, *Journal of Applied Psychology*, 2004, 89, 483-496.

104.   Lopes, P. N., Salovey, P. and Straus, R., Emotional Intelligence, Personality, and the Perceived Quality of Social Relationships, *Personality and Individual Differences*, 2003, 35, 641-658.

105.   George, J. M., Emotions and Leadership: The Role of Emotional Intelligence, *Human Relations*, 2000, 53(8), 1027-1044.

106.   Rosete, D. and Ciarrochi, J., Emotional Intelligence and Its Relationship to Workplace Performance Outcomes of Leadership Effectiveness, *Leadership and Organization Development Journal*, 2005, 26(5), 388-399.

107.   Slaski, M. and Cartwright, S., Health, Performance and Emotional Intelligence: An Exploratory Study of Retail Managers, *Stress and Health*, 2002, 16, 63-68.

108.   Wong, C. S., Law, K. S. and Wong, P. M., Development and Validation of a Forced Choice Emotional Intelligence Measure for Chinese Respondents in Hong Kong, *Asia Pacific Journal of Management*, 2004, 21, 535-559.

109.   Bachman, J. Stein, S., Campbell, K. and Sitarenios, B., Emotional Intelligence in the Collection of Debt, *International Journal of Selection and Assessment*, 2000, 8(3), 176-182.

110.   Bar-On, R., Handley, R. and Fund, S., The Impact of Emotional Intelligence on Performance, in: Druskat, V. U., Sala, F. and Mount, G., eds., *Linking Emotional Intelligence and Performance at Work: Current Research Evidence with Individuals and Groups,* Lawrence Erlbaum, Mahwah, 2005, 3-19.

111.   Dulewicz, C., Young, M. and Dulewicz, V., The Relevance of Emotional Intelligence for Leadership Performance, *Journal of General Management*, 2005, 30(3), 71-86.

112.   Higgs, M., A Study of the Relationship Between EI and Performance in UK Call Centres, *Journal of Managerial Psychology*, 2004, 19(4), 442-454.

113. Williams, H. W., Characteristics That Distinguish Outstanding Urban Principals, *Journal of Management Development*, 2008, 27(1), 36-54.

114. Druskat, V. U. and Wolff, S. B., Building the Emotional Intelligence of Groups, *Harvard Business Review*, 2001, 79(3), 81-90.

115. Jordan, P. J. and Troth, A. C., Managing Emotions During Team Problem Solving: Emotional Intelligence and Conflict Resolution, *Human Performance*, 2004, 17(2), 195-218.

116. Lopes, P. N., Salovey, P., Cote, S. and Beers, M., Emotion Regulation Ability and the Quality of Social Interaction, *Emotion*, 2005, 5(1), 113-118.

117. Offerman, L. R., Bailey, J. R., Vasilopoulos, N. L., Seal, C. and Sass, M., The Relative Contribution of Emotional Competence and Cognitive Ability to Individual and Team Performance, *Human Performance*, 2004, 17(2), 219-243.

118. Isen, A. M., Daubman, K. A. and Nowicki, G. P., Positive Affect Facilitates Creative Problem Solving, *Journal of Personality and Social Psychology*, 1987, 52(6), 1122-1131.

119. Barrick, M. R., Stewart, G. L. and Neubert, M. J., Relating Member Ability and Personality to Work-Team Processes and Team Effectiveness, *Journal of Applied Psychology*, 1998, 83(3), 377-391.

120. Rapisarda, B. A., The Impact of Emotional Intelligence on Work Team Cohesiveness and Performance, *The International Journal of Organizational Analysis*, 2002, 10(4), 363-379.

121. Sosik, J. J. and Megerian, L. E., Understanding Leader Emotional Intelligence and Performance: The Role of Self-Other Agreement on Transformational Leadership Perceptions, *Group and Organization Management*, 1999, 24, 367-390.

122. Hopkins, M. M. and Bilimoria, D., Social and Emotional Competencies Predicting Success for Male and Female Executives, *Journal of Management Development*, 2008, 27, 13-35.

123. Petrides, K. V. and Furnham, A., Gender Differences in Measured and Self-Estimated Trait Emotional Intelligence, *Sex Roles*, 2000, 42 (5-6), 449-461.

124. Petrides, K. V, Furnham, A. and Martin, G. N., Estimates of Emotional and Psychometric Intelligence, *Journal of Social Psychology*, 2004, 144(2), 149-162.

125. Groves, K. S., Gender Differences in Social and Emotional Skills and Charismatic Leadership, *Journal of Leadership and Organizational Studies*, 2005, 11(3), 30-46.

126. Ciarrochi, J. V., Chan, A. Y. C. and Caputi, P., A Critical Evaluation of the Emotional Intelligence Construct, *Personality and Individual Differences*, 2000, 28, 539-561.

127. Mandell, B. and Pherwani, S., Relationship Between Emotional Intelligence and Transformational Leadership Style: A Gender Comparison, *Journal of Business and Psychology*, 2003, 17(3), 387-404.

128. Schutte, N., Malouff, J., Hall, E., Haggerty, D., Cooper, J., Golden, D. and Dornheim, L., Development and Validation of a Measure of Emotional Intelligence, *Personality and Individual Differences*, 1998, 25, 167-177.

129. Brackett, M. A., Rivers, S. E., Shiffman, S., Lerner, N. and Salovey, P., Relating Emotional Abilities to Social Functioning: A Comparison of Self-Report and Performance Measures of Emotional Intelligence, *Journal of Personality and Social Psychology*, 2006, 91(4), 780-795.

130. Bar-On, R., *Emotional Quotient Inventory Technical Manual*, Multi-Health Systems, North Tonawanda, NY, 2002.

131. McCann, S., Emotional Intelligence: The Secret of Athletic Excellence, *Olympic Coach*, 1999, 9, 8-9.

132. Meyer, B. B. and Fletcher, T. B., Emotional Intelligence: A Theoretical Overview and Implications for Research and Professional Practice in Sports Psychology, *Journal of Applied Sport Psychology*, 2007, 19, 1-15.

133. Zizzi, S. J., Deaner, H. R. and Hirschhorn, D. K., The Relationship Between Emotional Intelligence and Performance Among College Baseball Players, *Journal of Applied Sport Psychology*, 2003, 15(3), 262-269.

134. Aberman, R. and Anderson, J., *Why Good Coaches Quit: How to Deal with the Other Stuff*, Coaches Choice Books, Monterey, 2005.

135. Magyar, M., *The Influence of Leader Efficacy and Emotional Intelligence on Personal Caring and Motivational Climate*, Paper presented at the Association for the Advancement of Applied Sport Psychology, Minneapolis, 2004.

136. Thelwell, R. C., Lane, A. M., Weston, N. J. V. and Greenlees, L. A., Examining Relationships Between Emotional Intelligence and Coaching Efficacy, *International Journal of Sport and Exercise Psychology*, 2008, 6(2), 224-235.

137. Butler, R. J., *Sports Psychology in Action*, Butterworth-Heinemann, Oxford, 1996.

138. Botteril, C. and Brown, M., Emotion and Perspective in Sport, *International Journal of Sport Psychology*, 2002, 33(1), 38-60.

139. Hanin, Y. L., Individual Zones of Optimal Functioning (IZOF) Model: Emotions-Performance Relationships in Sport, in: Hanin, Y. L. ed., *Emotions in Sport*, Human Kinetics, Champaign, 2000, 65-89.

140. Jones, M. V., Controlling Emotions in Sport, *The Sport Psychologist*, 2003, 17, 471-486.

141. Lazarus, R. S., How Emotions Influence Performance in Competitive Sports, *The Sport Psychologist*, 2000, 14(3), 229-252.

142. Skinner, N. and Brewer, N., Adaptive Approaches to Competition: Challenge Appraisals and Positive Emotion, *Journal of Sport and Exercise Psychology*, 2004, 26, 283-305.

Work-Life Imbalance, Stress, and Individual and Organisational Intervention Strategies

Christina A. Geithner, Ph.D.[1], Joseph F. Albert, Ph.D.[2] and Diane R. McKenney[1]

[1]Department of Exercise Science, Gonzaga University, 502 E. Boone Ave., Box 4, Spokane, WA, 99258, USA; E-mail: geithner@gonzaga.edu

[2]Department of Organisational Leadership, Gonzaga University, 502 E. Boone Ave., MSC 2616, Spokane, WA, 99258, USA.

ABSTRACT

Work-life imbalance results in physical and psychological stress, and reduced productivity, performance; and negatively impacts our relationships and quality of life. Work-life balance can be addressed at different organizational levels. As employees and leaders, we can improve our work-life balance by changing approaches to our work and home lives by practicing mindfulness, developing awareness, and building skills that enhance our ability to self-regulate. Individuals have a responsibility not only to themselves with respect to their own well-being, but also to others in modelling healthier behaviours. Organisations can promote a healthy workplace and culture that supports good communication, collaboration, and flexibility in scheduling; education and assistance for employees and their families; opportunities for social engagement and fun; and adequate time-off. Coaches, consultants, and counselors can assist individuals, team members, leaders, and organisations in understanding the importance of work-life balance, developing healthy lifestyle practices, and creating a healthy workplace.

Key words: Healthy Workplace, Leadership, Mindfulness, Resilience, Self-Management, Stress, Work-Life Balance

Reviewers: Jim McKenna (Leeds Metropolitan University, UK)
               Danny Mielke (Eastern Oregon University, USA)
               Srikumar Rao (Long Island University, USA)

INTRODUCTION
OVERVIEW

Work-life balance tops today's agenda for government and business in response to shifts in the labour market and the changing nature of work [1]. According to the Families and Work Institute:

> The fast-paced, global 24/7 economy, the pressures of competition, and technology have blurred the traditional boundaries between work life and home life. [2, p.2]

The way in which we work and live has changed dramatically. Work has intensified in the past 25 years as a result of the boom in information technology, increasing vulnerability to competition, and deregulation of the workplace [3]. The sense of trust and corporate community and long-term loyalty that were status quo a generation ago have been eroded by a culture that places a higher premium on performance, expects more of employees and businesses, and offers less and less security [3]. These changes have occurred over a relatively short period of time and have resulted in greater work stress, stress-related illness, and work-life imbalance. The traditional focus of work-life balance was on family-friendly workplaces, and assisting working mothers to balance childcare responsibilities with their occupations. This focus, however, has shifted to recognition by organisations that work-life balance goes well beyond this to include flexible work arrangements compatible with employees' other responsibilities, lifestyles, and families as well as work [1]. The focus of work-life balance has also expanded to include greater value placed on the health and well-being of individual employees and the nature or healthiness of the workplace environment, as the research has unequivocally shown these to be related to greater job satisfaction, higher worker productivity, and organisational success.

To these issues of work-life imbalance and stress, we, the authors, bring our expertise in kinesiology/exercise science and organisational leadership, and experience in facilitating communication, team building, leadership development and stress management programs and workshops in corporate and academic settings. Our views are influenced by our observations of, and direct experience with, the negative implications of work-life imbalance in academic workplaces and learning environments. Our collective experience and experience from walking our individual paths have taught us that work-life balance is an important issue for individual and organisational well-being, and one that is vital to high performance both personally and professionally. Thus, we have taken a proactive approach in our own lives towards better work-life balance and hope to help others do the same. Our purposes in this paper are to: 1) provide some information about work-life balance – what it is, the benefits of balance, and the causes and costs of imbalance to individuals, leaders, and organisations; 2) have readers think critically about their current state of work-life balance; and 3) offer some tools and strategies (some of which are provided in inserts) that individual employees, leaders, and organisations as well as coaches, consultants, counselors, and other readers outside those realms can use to achieve better work-life balance.

WHAT IS WORK-LIFE BALANCE?

Work-life balance is a popular term, but there is no clear consensus on its meaning [1]. A balanced life is one characterized by a distribution of energy and effort among key areas of importance: intellectual, imaginative, emotional, physical, and spiritual [3]. Work-life balance describes the equilibrium between responsibilities at work and those outside paid work and how this balance impacts the individual concerned [1]:

> The term 'work-life balance' was first coined in 1986 in reaction to the unhealthy choices that many Americans were making in favor of the workplace, as they opted to neglect family, friends and leisure activities in the pursuit of corporate goals. [3, p. 1]

Work-life balance [4, 5] is a concept which refers to healthy amounts of time and energy spent on the job and in work-related endeavors relative to the time and energy spent on and with significant others (spouse/partner, family, friends), in recreational activities, and in renewal. It is also about how we work rather than how much time we spend at work [6]. Work-life balance connotes "having a measure of control over when, where and how you work, leading to being able to enjoy an optimal quality of life" and "is achieved when an individual's right to a fulfilled life inside and outside paid work is accepted and respected as the norm, to the mutual benefit of the individual, business and society" [7].

Kathleen Hall [8] describes work-life balance as "an awareness of your life force, and a discovery of intimacy, serenity, purpose, fulfillment and happiness in every aspect of your life" and that we need "to discover daily sources of inspiration, energy and strength that allow us to find renewal, fulfillment, and balance in new and dynamic ways" [8, p. 87]. Hall indicates that because we have so many responsibilities at work, at home, and in the community, it is very difficult to attain and maintain work-life balance and to nourish a sense of self [8].

As challenging as work-life balance might be to define, taking action to achieve and maintain it is vital to the development of health, well being, vibrancy, and resilience at every level - including individual employees and team members, leaders, and their organisations.

BENEFITS OF WORK-LIFE BALANCE

Work-life balance has many benefits at both individual and organisational levels [5, 9, 10; see Table 1]. But despite the benefits of having a healthy work-life balance, a great many workers are experiencing an out-of-balance lifestyle dominated by increasing stress and related illnesses. Stephen Covey has surveyed thousands of audiences about their greatest personal and professional challenges and has found that work-life balance is always at or near the top [11]. Research is showing, however, that work life and the accompanying stressors are manageable, and workers can regain a healthier work-life balance. This article offers an overview of the challenges in maintaining work-life balance and strategies for moving in a healthier direction.

Table 1. Benefits of Work-Life Balance [5, 9, 10]

For Individuals and Leaders:
- ↓ Stress
- ↓ Risk of chronic disease
- ↓ Worry about work
- ↓ Feeling of overwhelm
- ↓ Unused leave
- ↓ Work taken home
- ↑ Feeling of calm
- ↑ Time to think
- ↑ Feeling more focused at work
- ↑ Ability to react to urgent situations
- ↑ Working in advance of deadlines
- ↑ Scope of work
- ↑ Taking control of long-term career
- ↑ Physical and mental health
- ↑ Morale
- ↑ Quality of life
- ↑ Creativity
- ↑ Decision making

For Organisations:
- ↓ Absenteeism
- ↓ Insurance costs
- ↓ Benefit costs
- ↓ Staff turnover
- ↑ Employee and workplace morale
- ↑ Job satisfaction
- ↑ Happier and healthier staff
- ↑ Recruitment and retention
- ↑ Information sharing with teams and colleagues
- ↑ Ability of staff to cope with changes to priorities and direction
- ↑ Sales volume
- ↑ Productivity
- ↑ Increased organisational effectiveness

WORK-LIFE IMBALANCE - CAUSES AND COSTS

One might first consider all of the opposites of the benefits of work-life balance (provided in Table 1) when identifying the characteristics and costs of work-life imbalance. But before moving into more detail and revealing what the literature on work-life balance and imbalance has to tell us, let's put a face on work-life imbalance with the help of two brief stories. Both Andrew and Joanie (whose names have been changed, but whose stories are true) are facing the challenges of maintaining work-life balance. Andrew is experiencing the impact of it through the voice of his son.

Joanie chose to make some changes in her life to regain balance and live her life in a way that manifested her passions and priorities. These stories help introduce the concept of work-life imbalance, its causes and costs.

Andrew's Story

Andrew sat alone at his kitchen table. It was 8:30 p.m. He felt like he had just been punched in the stomach. As a mid-30's general manager for one of the larger - and thriving - construction firms in town, he had been tagged as a future company leader and maybe an owner. Married, with three children under ten, Andrew was known as the "get it done" guy. He always did.

Unfortunately, Andrew's climb up the ladder to success had come at a price. Just a few minutes earlier his oldest child, Ryan, nine years old, said "Daddy, we know you're busy at work, but when do we get to have you here with us?" Andrew loved his job. He enjoyed the 'rush' of getting a project done on time and under budget. His salary afforded his family a comfortable life style. But the thing that mattered most - his family - was getting the least amount of his attention, time and energy. What could he do, Andrew wondered, to regain some balance in his life?

Joanie's Story

Joanie walked out to her car in the parking lot of the YWCA. She had just finished teaching a Monday night fitness class and was feeling great. Her thoughts turned to a time - just a year ago - when her life was very much out of balance.

Joanie is employed at a college in the IT department. She works at the help desk and is on-call evenings and some weekends. She is a 'pleaser' and loves making people happy. She is frequently involved with work projects well above the standard 40 hours per week. Her boss knows he can count on her to be available to help out on evening and weekends. In addition to her job Joanie has a strong interest in personal fitness and health and recently gained her certification so she could become an instructor at the YWCA.

Last year Joanie realized that her energy level was low, she was frequently sick, and was experiencing some neck and back soreness. Her doctor recommended that she suspend doing her volunteer instruction at the YWCA, and rest. One night after work a group of her friends confronted her about the imbalance that was evident in her life. They challenged her to reflect on her goals, and on the things that made her happy. This questioning led her to become more self-aware and respond differently to requests for more overtime work. She gradually reduced her level of guilt. Eventually her energy and passion returned.

CAUSES OF WORK-LIFE IMBALANCE

Causes of work-life imbalance are numerous and offer target areas for intervention. They include our beliefs about work-life balance [12]; half a dozen workplace factors [13]; role stressors [13] and self-efficacy [14]; job decision latitude vs. psychological demands of the job [15]; effort-reward imbalance [16-18]; technological advances, the global economy, and international business with its 24/7 timeframe [19, 20]; changing family roles [20]; and not enough time off [2] or little or no vacation time [21].

Rosen [12] suggests that our buy-in to various myths are part of the problem and gives several examples along with their accompanying realities:

- *Workaholics are good for business*: While many companies foster the idea that working longer and harder translates into better performance and higher productivity, the research shows that overwork results in reduced productivity and performance at the individual and organisational level.
- *Healthy companies are in competition with healthy families*: In fact, when there is imbalance at home, productivity suffers.
- *Work is rewarding and families are responsibilities*: The truth is that the rewards are different, but equally valuable.
- *Paying attention to what we're feeling prevents us from focusing on our work*: The truth is that not paying attention to what's going on internally is disruptive and distracting, and keeps us from doing our work.

In addition to the myths that we and/or our organisations perpetuate about work-life balance, other contributors to work-life imbalance have been identified. Sauter et al. [13] have noted six workplace factors most likely to influence employees' mental and physical health. These include work scheduling (work pace and unusual work shifts), role stressors (ambiguity, incompatible job-related demands, and role overload), and career security factors (insecurity about one's current job and knowing one has a career path within the organisation), as well as interpersonal relationships (i.e., interactions with subordinates, peers, customers/clients, and/or superiors), work and job content (meaningfulness, responsibilities as related to abilities, and knowledge of performance through feedback from peers and supervisors), and autonomy (e.g., sense of personal responsibility for one's work, degree to which one is able to work and make decisions independently) [13].

Autonomy has also been addressed in Karasek and Theorell's Job Strain Model [15] as job decision latitude available to the worker; i.e., skill discretion (continuing to learn new things and develop skills, skills required for the job, task variety, repetition, and creativity) and decision authority (freedom to make decisions, choice of how to perform work, and having a say on the job). The second element of work stress identified in the Job Strain Model [15] is the psychological demands of the job (i.e., excessive work; conflicting demands; and having to work very fast, very hard, and not having sufficient time to get the work done) [22]. The Job Strain Model suggests that the greatest stress-related health risk occurs when workers face high psychological workload demands or pressures combined with low control or decision latitude in meeting those demands [22]. More than 60 combined studies link high job strain to heart disease and its risk factors (e.g., hypertension) [22, 23]. On the other hand, when psychological workload demands and decision latitude are both high, and workers take an active role in addressing the psychological demands, the results are active learning and motivation to develop new behaviors. This model emphasizes that stress is caused by the interaction between demands and control, and objective constraints on action in the work environment, rather than individual perceptions and experience [22]. The two directions in which outcomes can occur, increased risk psychological strain and physical illness and the more positive direction of active learning and motivation for behavioral adaptation, also serve to illustrate the mediating influence of the worker's level of control over and response (passive vs. active) to the work situation on job strain.

Work-life imbalance also results from failed social reciprocity, as explained by the Effort-Reward Imbalance (or ERI) model [16-18]. Social reciprocity refers to a fundamental principle of interpersonal behavior and is characterized by mutual cooperative investments based on the norm of return expectancy, in which efforts are equalized by respective rewards. When this norm is violated, and rewards do not reciprocate efforts made, strong negative emotions and sustained stress responses are the result. The ERI model suggests: i) an imbalance created by high effort and low reward or non-reciprocity increases health risks above those associated with each of the components; ii) over-commitment increases risk of reduced health; and iii) overcommitted workers who put forth a high degree of effort and do not receive a reciprocal reward are at greatest risk for reduced health.

Other sources of work stress include uncertainty, technological advances, distribution of work, and unemployment [19]. A Mayo Clinic Report [20] suggests additional causes of this increasing problem of work-life imbalance (Table 2).

Table 2. Mayo Clinic Report [20] – Causes of Work-Life Imbalance

- *Global economy.* As more skilled workers enter the global labor market and companies outsource or move more jobs to reduce labor costs, people feel pressured to work longer and produce more just to protect their jobs.
- *International business.* Work continues around the world 24 hours a day for some people. If you work in an international organisation, you might be on call around the clock for troubleshooting or consulting.
- *Advanced communication technology.* Many people now have the ability to work anywhere - from their home, from their car and even on vacation. And some managers expect this.
- *Longer hours.* Employers commonly ask employees to work longer hours than they're scheduled. Often, overtime is mandatory. If you hope to move up the career ladder, you may find yourself regularly working more than 40 hours a week to achieve and exceed expectations.
- *Changes in family roles.* Today's married worker is typically part of a dual-career couple, which makes it difficult to find time to meet commitments to family, friends and community.

In a review of Wainright and Calnan's text on *Work Stress. The Making of a Modern Epidemic* [24], Jones [25] states that the authors "make a convincing case that the work stress epidemic is an individualized and historically specific response to adverse working conditions where problems are internalized and individualized" (p. 1283). Policies instituted in the European Union and elsewhere to address the reconciliation of work and family have also shifted in intention reflecting feminist potential to a market-oriented objective, from sharing family responsibilities between the sexes to encouraging flexible forms of employment [26]. These reflections on work-life balance suggest that work-life imbalance and the resultant stresses are a function of the times, and this seems to be even truer for the present. We live in an "always wired, always on-call world" [27], in a workaholic, out-of-balance culture, and work stress appears to be a global issue.

Research on relationships among role stressors, general self-efficacy and burnout has been carried out in the USA, Germany, France, Brazil, Israel, Japan, China, Hong Kong, Fiji, and Finland [14]. A negative association was found to exist between general self-efficacy and burnout, and general self-efficacy was found to mediate the relationships between role conflict and/or role ambiguity and burnout across eight of the nine cultures [14], indicating that work stress is a universal phenomenon. In addition, increased competition within the global marketplace has caused higher levels of stress for U.S. employees [19]. As more companies outsource domestic jobs, U.S. workers have a growing sense of loss of certainty and job security that has become a large source of stress [19].

Another work-related stressor is not having sufficient time off work to reflect, recover, and renew. This seems to be an issue particularly for Americans. The USA has been called the "no-vacation nation" [21], because it is the only advanced economy in the world that does not provide its workers with a guaranteed paid vacation. Without a legal requirement for paid vacation and paid holidays, approximately one quarter of the U.S. workforce goes without time off during their work year [21]. In contrast, France is the most generous with 30 days of paid annual leave; Finland, Denmark, Norway, and Sweden provide 25 days; Germany, Austria, Portugal, and Spain give 24-22 days; Italy, Belgium, Ireland, Australia, New Zealand, Greece, Netherlands, Switzerland, and the U.K. provide 20 days; and Canada and Japan have 10 days of paid annual leave. However, the number of paid days of holiday vary from 1 to 13, creating greater variability among the 21 countries included in the study [21]. The total sum of the average paid vacation and paid holidays combined – 15 days total – offered in the private sector of the USA would not even meet the minimum paid vacation in 19 other rich countries [21].

A 2001 study by the Families and Work Institute indicated that 44% of U.S. employees were overworked *often* or *very often,* based on past month reports on how much work they had to do and not having time to step back and process or reflect on work; however, of the 79% with access to paid vacations, 36% didn't plan to use their full vacations, and more than 85% did not take at least a two week vacation [2]. In contrast, the majority of industrialized countries, 137 nations in total, guarantee an average of four weeks paid vacation a year by law, and Europeans average vacation time is closer to six weeks [28]. About one-third of those who do take vacation take their work with them, a habit facilitated by cell phones, laptops, and the Internet [28]. Not taking sufficient time off (at least two weeks) to recover and renew ourselves not only results in work-life imbalance and chronic stress, it costs us our health as measured by a greater number of heart attacks and higher rates of hypertension, heart disease, and diabetes [29].

In summary, there are many causes of work-life imbalance, including: the myths we hold about work-life balance [12]; workplace factors [13]; role stressors [13] and self-efficacy [14]; job decision latitude vs. psychological demands of the job [15]; effort-reward imbalance [16-18]; technological advances, the global economy, and international business and its 24/7 timeframe [19, 20]; changing family roles [20]; and not enough time off [2] or little or no vacation time [21]. Each cause has its costs and also serves as a target for intervention, as addressed in later sections of this paper.

COSTS OF WORK-LIFE IMBALANCE

The costs of work-life imbalance for the individual employee or leader include greater physical and psychological stress (working longer hours, with little or insufficient time off, increased worry and feeling of being overwhelmed, reduced sense of control, and reduced morale), increased risk for and prevalence of chronic illness and disease, reduced quality of life, reduced job satisfaction, and reduced performance and productivity (difficulties focusing and making decisions). The costs for the organisation are high as well: reduced workplace morale, greater absenteeism, poorer retention rates, higher insurance and benefits costs, and reduced organisational effectiveness and performance.

The coupling of high demands, such as increased work pressures suggested in the Mayo Clinic Report [20], with inadequate resources to meet those demands causes an imbalance and results in stress [30]. A recent CommPsych poll indicated that 50% of employees missed 1-2 days of work per year due to stress, and 46% came to work too stressed to be effective 1-4 days per year [31]. Estimates indicate that 60-90% of all physician visits are for stress-related complaints [31]. Insurance claims for stress, depression, and burnout have become the USA's fastest-growing disability category [27].

STRESS

Stress is a natural and costly outcome of work-life imbalance. The causes of work-life imbalance serve as stressors, or objective, quantifiable environmental characteristics that pose cognitive, emotional, physical, social, or other challenges, or impose demands on our coping abilities. Stress reflects the subjective interpretation or experience of stressors, thus the perception of stress and the specific responses to it vary among individuals [19]. However, all of us experience stress physically as an integrated, non-specific physiological response to a perceived demand or stressor that results in a cascade of physiological events [33]. The stress response or Selye's General Adaptation Syndrome [33] involves three stages: the Alarm Reaction - the perception of a threat (physical, psychological, social, emotional, vocational) and up-regulation of the sympathetic nervous system in preparation for a "fight-or-flight" response [34]; the Resistance Stage: coping and adaptation – a reversal of most of the changes that occurred in the Alarm Reaction resulting in partial or full recovery, and increased secretion of cortisol (the "stress hormone"); and the Exhaustion Stage – when adaptation no longer occurs, high cortisol levels begin to have negative effects, and the immune system is weakened, leading to illness and, in extreme cases, death [33].

In another model, Lazarus and Folkman [35] consider stress from a psychological perspective as a transaction between an individual and his/her environment, as a relationship between the two appraised by the individual as taxing or exceeding his/her resources or endangering his/her well being. Perceptions of stress and specific responses vary among individuals due to differences in resources. Examples include cognitive skills and appraisals of stressful situations, past experiences, outlook and/or positive or negative emotions [35-38], current health and lifestyle habits, coping strategies [35, 40], sense of control or autonomy regarding our jobs and in making decisions [15], and social support. Additional factors that influence our perception of stress and our chronic responses to it are its frequency of occurrence, severity or intensity, and duration.

Stress contributes to dis-ease (discomfort, upset, and instability) as well as disease or morbidity. Stress has strong, well-documented associations with psychological health issues such as anxiety, burnout, and depression [41]; and headaches, difficulty concentrating, and short temper [42]. Stress is also associated with a variety of physical maladies that include sleep disturbances and fatigue [43]; gastrointestinal upset, ulcers, impaired immune function, and cancer [42]; as well as multiple factors related to coronary heart disease and sudden cardiac death: higher resting heart rate, elevated blood pressure [44, 45], increases in cholesterol and homocysteine, promotion of arterial wall inflammation, constriction of coronary arteries, increased clotting activity, and cardiac arrhythmias [46]. All of these take physical and emotional tolls on us; they impair our ability to function optimally *and* reduce our quality of life. Stress also impacts organisations at every level from leaders, to individual employees, team members, and organisations as a whole.

STRESS AND LEADERS
HOW STRESS IMPACTS LEADERSHIP
Survey research conducted in conjunction with the Ideas2Action project of the Center for Creative Leadership (CCL) (n = 230 responses total, the typical respondent was 41-50 years of age and represented upper-middle or executive level management), Campbell et al. [47] sought the answer to the question: "How does stress impact leadership?" The 10 major findings reported were:

1. Eighty-eight percent of leaders report that work is a primary source of stress in their lives and that having a leadership role increases the level of stress.
2. More than 60 percent of surveyed leaders cite their organisation as failing to provide them with the tools they need to manage stress.
3. More than two-thirds of surveyed leaders believe their stress level is higher today than it was five years ago.
4. Nearly 80 percent of surveyed leaders state they would benefit from a coach to help them manage stress.
5. A lack of resources and time are the most stressful leadership demands experienced by leaders. Stress is caused by trying to do more with less, and to do it faster.
6. Leaders experience stress equally between their bosses, peers, direct reports and customers, but the reasons for the stress are different depending on the source.
7. Physical exercise is the most commonly cited method leaders use to manage stress, yet only 10 percent of responses from surveyed leaders indicate their organisations provide access to gyms or workout facilities.
8. More than 90 percent of leaders cite they manage stress by temporarily removing themselves, either physically or mentally, from the source of their stress. [47, Executive Summary, p. 3]

9. Most leaders use a variety of sensory pursuits, or physical stimuli, to manage stress regardless of the source.
10. Stress caused by task demands such as job responsibilities and decision-making is often managed by engaging in behaviors that help the leader gain focus and perspective on the challenge.

This CCL research indicates that the majority of leaders are affected by stress and that leaders could use help (e.g., tools and coaching) to manage it. Costs of stress for leaders include a loss of awareness, both in reference to self and to their employees and organisations; loss of the ability to empathize with others; and loss of credibility when they fail to respond appropriately to problems in a timely fashion and to find acceptable solutions.

RESPONSIBILITY FOR SELF AND TO OTHERS

In their book about leadership during Shackleton's *Endurance* expedition to the Antarctic, Perkins et al. [48] wrote about "the inherent tension of taking care of one's self – of preserving one's own well-being – and accomplishing the mission at any cost" (p. 56). Perkins et al. [48] caution us about choosing deliberately to make sacrifices of our physical or psychological health:

> As the leader, you are the foundation of your expedition. If you fail to maintain your own stamina, then you will be unable to summon the energy needed to reach The Edge [your goal]. Furthermore, taking care of yourself is essential because others in your team will take their cues from your behavior. If you want others to have the reserves of energy they will need to do their jobs, you will need to reinforce that message by personal example. [48, p. 57]

THE COST OF SUCCESS

Through her research on executive development, Kofodimos [49] found that the very process of becoming successful causes one to be out of balance, and this imbalance often results in a neglect of many personal and family needs:

> The executive's responsiveness to organisational pressures affects his [or her] personal life. As work expands to dominate his time and energy, neglected family relationships degenerate and become increasingly unsatisfying. [49, p. 60]

The challenge is how to achieve and maintain balance – to stay centered and grounded, having a clear sense of self in such a way that health and good judgment are maintained [50], and the rewards of all aspects of one's life are experienced. Often times, executives experience a major life crisis such as a divorce or personal health issues:

> These events cause executives to realize what they stand to lose as a result of their overwhelming focus on work, and subsequently they may make major changes in their allocation of time and energy. [49, p. 62]

STRESS, TEAM MEMBERS AND THE ORGANISATION

Stress within individual workers and in team members impacts the larger organisation and its culture. The specific stress condition that is the core component of job burnout is job exhaustion [51, 52], and this has been identified as a key predictor of negative job outcomes, including turnover and poor performance [53]. The effects of stress on the corporate collective include increased absenteeism [54]; poor morale, and reduced recruitment and retention [9, 55]; and decreased productivity and performance as well as reduced job satisfaction [41, 55]. In addition, work-related stress is associated with an increase in client complaints and an increase in employee compensation claims [55]. These costs can have direct and indirect negative effects on overall organisational success, particularly over the long haul.

Another impact of stress in work organisations is the management of emotions that are manifested in response to the increased pressures. Frost [56] describes the impact of "toxic emotions" and Fredrickson [37] elaborates on the impact of "negative emotions' (e.g., anxiety, sadness, anger and fear). Frederickson's premise is that while negative emotions have the effect of narrowing the behavioral options of the individual experiencing the emotion; positive emotions (e.g., joy, contentment, love and pride) have the opposite effect of broadening the thought-action repertoires of individuals and therefore increase their range of adaptive behaviors [37]. This increased range of creative options can benefit an organisation through increased levels of creativity, innovation, and problem solving [37]. The long-range impact of more positive emotions is increased health and decreased stress [37].

The causes of stress for employees include many of the same pressures faced by those in leadership roles (i.e., greater expectation of employees with fewer resources; increased pace of change, global market uncertainties, and feelings of loss of control). In addition, research has revealed that job design and de-motivating environments also increase stress levels. Thomas [57] has suggested that decreased levels of choice or freedom in doing work, lower levels of task meaningfulness, and increased feelings of incompetence all contribute to higher levels of stress and de-motivation.

Is work-life imbalance a wake-up call or a death knell? We cannot afford the latter, on an individual or corporate level. The costs are far too high. For all that is at stake and for all of the time we spend engaging in work during our lives, creating healthier workplaces and trying to achieve better work-life balance are worthwhile endeavors. So, *how* do we do it?

THRIVING IN THE CURRENT ENVIRONMENT

The pressure to produce and to perform commonly outweighs the value placed on personal and corporate well being [58]. These pressures have resulted, at least in part, from attempts on the part of organisations to improve their profits and success. Demands on individuals, organisations, and leaders have increased as technology has advanced, and one of the results is an unrelenting pace at work [58]. Another response is multi-tasking – we are being asked to do more with less and more in less time. So in response, Helgesen [58] explains:

> We work harder; we strive to become more organized, more efficient.
> We devise ambitious and demanding schedules for ourselves, set the

clock half an hour earlier each morning, resolve to stop dawdling over lunch (or to stop eating it!), and use the time to be more productive. …Yet our heroic efforts at self-discipline often have the effect of robbing us of spontaneity and the capacity for joy, leaving us wondering exactly what our lives are really *about*. [58, p. 3]

Vaill [59] has likened this evolution in work culture to a more fast-paced, chaotic, and turbulent world to whitewater, the turbulence that results as a river moves over and around obstacles in the riverbed. When paddling whitewater, learning how to read a river and navigate the rapids (i.e., chaos and turbulence) requires close attention and innovation at crucial moments [60]. In this "permanent white-water environment" [59] in which we find ourselves, the challenge is not just to navigate the rapids and survive, but to navigate the rapids with intelligence, grace, and style – to thrive.

Thriving may require a new and comprehensive approach to the ways in which we approach work and life; for example, valuing people over hours and money, organisational change [4], and stress management [42]. We may also need to redefine the barriers between work and home, reducing the overlap of personal and work-life networks. The potential outcomes include creating more enjoyable and less stressful lives, workplaces characterized by greater wellness and higher performance, and priorities that are consistent with our values; all of which will allow us to sustain a high quality of function in all of the arenas in which we operate [30].

COGNITIVE APPROACHES TO STRESS AND IMBALANCE

In *Hamlet*, Shakespeare writes the famous line: "*There is nothing either good or bad - but thinking makes it so.*" This statement sheds light on one of the primary causes of both stress and work-life imbalance: our perceptions. One of the more popular approaches to dealing with depression and other mood problems, cognitive therapy, deals with the ways in which we make sense of or think about events and people in our lives. This approach assumes that our emotions - especially the more problematic ones like depression, anger, anxiety and stress, are caused by the ways we think about things.

In our opening story, Andrew believes that he should take on every project offered to him in order to be successful. Making a mistake, he believes, will end his career. "Should" type statements usually result in guilt and act as a drain on our energy. Joanie, for example, believed that the guilt she felt for turning down a boss's request was warranted because she disappointed him. She thought she would lose his approval. Joanie began to realize, through increased self-awareness, that this kind of cognitive approach was not productive for her. Her boss experienced her taking more control of her life as a sign of strength and growth. He actually complimented her on occasionally turning down of his requests. For Andrew, this growth process remains before him as a choice he has yet to make.

Stress and life imbalance are often caused by certain patterns of maladaptive thinking, or what Burns [61] calls cognitive distortions. According to Burns, these distortions lie at the heart of emotions like depression, anxiety and guilt. Look through the thinking patterns provided in Table 3 and see if any of these seem familiar.

Table 3.   Cognitive Patterns That Contribute to Work-Life Imbalance [61]

- *Jumping to conclusions:* In our opening story, Andrew was sure that if he devoted more attention to his family, his work and work reputation would suffer. He made this assumption without checking it out with his bosses or peers.
- *Magnification or catastrophizing into stress:* Both Andrew and Joanie struggled with the belief that if they took better care of themselves through exercise, family time, and rest that their work would suffer. In fact, the opposite proved true for Joanie. The fitness classes she taught gave her time to gain perspective and increased her work efficiency.
- *Should-ing ourselves to imbalance:* Joanie convinced herself that she should always say yes to requests at work. Her assumption was that to be accepted and liked she always had to comply. In fact, when she supported herself and said 'no' to requests to work overtime, her boss confided that he admired her strength.

Oftentimes our internal experiences are automatic and go unnoticed - they are a product of what Langer [62] calls "mindlessness." This lack of awareness is likened to something we do automatically, or without even questioning it. Negative thought patterns such as those identified by Burns [61] become second nature [62]. These stress-creating reactions to work are taken-for-granted realities of work life.

While the benefits of developing and maintaining a more desirable work-life balance are clear, the challenges to actually doing this can be daunting. Both Andrew's and Joanie's stories offer some insight into the binds that employees face as they progress along successful work trajectories. A matrix of myths, global issues, uncertainty, hard-work ethic, and the impact of stress all conspire to throw our lives out of a healthy lifestyle orbit. But there is hope. Solutions and options are available for those seeking a healthier balance.

STRATEGIES FOR ACHIEVING BETTER WORK-LIFE BALANCE

The following sections provide strategies for individuals and organisations seeking better balance, and are organized as follows:

I.   Achieving Work-Life Balance at the Individual Level: Employees and Leaders
    A. Coping
    B. Living with Intention
    C. Mindfulness and Awareness
    D. Balance Sheet
    E. Self-Management and Intrinsic Motivation
    F. Engagement with Renewing Activities
    G. Energy and Empathy
    H. The Contributions and Power of Positive Psychology

I. ACHIEVING WORK-LIFE BALANCE AT THE INDIVIDUAL LEVEL: EMPLOYEES AND LEADERS

Several experts in the field of leadership have cited leading a balanced life and practicing self-renewal as characteristics of successful individuals and effective leaders [48, 50, 63, 64]. These require intention; they do not occur by happenstance. Covey [65] emphasizes the value of exercising the spiritual, mental, and social/emotional dimensions of our nature regularly and in balanced ways as a means of self-renewal. Perkins et al. [48] suggest that the key to the "art of thriving," or "sustaining career achievement and personal well-being throughout the life cycle" (p. 221) is integrating five components of life structure and developing a level of mastery in each: work, relationships, physical health, renewal, and a sense of life purpose:

> The final skill in the art of thriving is the ability to find balance among all five elements…its essence lies in the ability to know when life is out of balance and when you need to restore balance. [48, p. 225]

The leadership literature suggests that work-life balance is multi-faceted, that it requires continued attentiveness to all dimensions in order to sustain it and high performance, and that it is an individual challenge and responsibility. Certainly, the individual plays a key role in his/her own state of work-life balance and its maintenance, and this is a starting place. However, the organization also has a responsibility towards creating a healthy workplace that fosters work-life balance. Research on management practices, work-life balance, and productivity in 732 medium-sized manufacturing firms in France, Germany, the UK, and the USA by Bloom and Van Renen [66] shows that work-life balance outcomes (higher productivity and better workplace conditions for employees) are significantly related to better management. Thus, leaders and managers have a direct impact on work-life balance, as do individuals.

The study of work-life balance and the lack thereof, and the stress that results, has engendered a variety of useful approaches to improving work-life balance; mental, emotional, and physical health; and quality of life. The approaches focus on developing and honing a range of coping skills and living with intention, and incorporate practicing mindfulness and sharpening our awareness, harnessing the power of positive psychology and emotions, utilizing social support, employing stress reduction and management strategies, and building our resilience.

A. Coping

Lazarus [40], in a review of coping theory and research, indicates that there are two approaches to coping: style, which treats coping as a personality characteristic; and process, which treats coping as efforts to manage stress that change over time. Both approaches are essential in that they address different aspects of the problem and supplement each other. In the past, our understanding of coping focused on cognitive processes, such as decision-making; while more recently there is a broader understanding of coping that includes motivation, specific emotions, general goals (or ends), and situational intentions [40]. Lazarus is confident that:

> ...personal meanings are the most important aspects of psychological stresses with which the persona must cope, and they direct the choice of coping strategy. To truly understand coping requires that we zero in on the main threat meanings of a particular stress situation and how they change over time and across situational contexts.... [40, p. 244]

Social and personality characteristics, which are largely unchangeable, mitigate an individual's vulnerability to a stressful situation and help him/her to manage and survive it. Examples of these characteristics are the social support of family and friends, financial support, ego-strength, intelligence, and skills. Other factors which influence our ability to cope include: our level of attention or mindfulness, and awareness; our cognitive appraisal of a situation; our use of positive psychology and emotions; and our behaviors (including self-care behaviors such as healthful eating, adequate rest, regular exercise, meditating, positive self-talk, and other stress-reducing behaviors). It is these factors to which we give attention in the subsequent sections on strategies for individuals in helping to create a healthier work-life balance.

B. Living with Intention

Living our lives intentionally means focusing our efforts on what it is that gives us the most energy and on those activities we feel are maximizing our time and efforts. Richard Carlson [67] challenges us to spend the energy that is wasted being "stressed-out, frustrated and angry over minor things" and focus it towards being "productive, creative and solution-oriented" (p. 3). Being intentional in what we choose to give our attention to provides us with an internal compass and offers freedom and meaning, even in the midst of chaos. Taking the time every day to become aware of those activities, relationships, and thoughts that keep us balanced is the first step towards living with intentionality (Table 4).

Living intentionally and *in balance* is comprised of three components or strategies: i) mindfulness [68] and self-awareness [69, 70], ii) choice [69] or self-regulation [69, 70], iii) and empathy [70].

C. Mindfulness and Awareness

Kabat-Zinn describes mindfulness as follows:

> Mindfulness is an ancient Buddhist practice which has profound relevance for our present-day lives. This relevance has nothing to do with Buddhism per se or with becoming a Buddhist, but it has everything to do with waking up and living in harmony with oneself and with the

---

Table 4. Strategies for Living an Intentional Life

- *Know yourself* – awareness, meditation, quiet time, time to get re-centered.
- *Take time off* – wellness breaks during work hours, sufficient vacation time ($\geq$ 2 weeks).
- *Create an aesthetically appealing and organized work environment.*
- *Set healthy boundaries* re: work projects, say no to opportunities that are not consistent with or aligned with your mission/purpose and priorities.
- *Make choices that support your mission* and are consistent with your priorities.
- *Build relationships*/develop social connections (a network) in and outside of work.
- *Exercise regularly* – aerobic exercise, mind-body exercise (e.g., Yoga, Tai Chi, Pilates, etc.)
- *Eat healthfully* and maintain a healthy weight.
- *Make time for creative endeavors.*
- *Forgive yourself and others.*

---

world. It has to do with examining who we are, with questioning our view of the world and our place in it, and with cultivating some appreciation for the fullness of each moment we are alive. Most of all, it has to do with being in touch. ... Mindfulness means paying attention in a particular way: on purpose, in the present moment, and nonjudgmentally. This kind of attention nurtures greater awareness, clarity, and acceptance of present-moment reality. [68, p. 3; p. 4]

Living in a more mindful way serves as an antidote for cognitive patterns that contribute to work-life imbalance. Kabat-Zinn [71] makes the point that many potential stressors will always exist in our environment over which we cannot have immediate control; however, by changing how we see ourselves in relationship to them, we can change our experience of the relationship and modify the extent to which it challenges our resources and well-being.

Observing ourselves and our actions without judgment is the means by which we develop awareness [68]. When we are more self-aware, we can choose our responses to people and events rather than simply react to them in our automatic sort of way, and consequently be freed from the ruts we so often fall into. This response enhances our sense of control, calmness, and the quality of our work relationships. Self-awareness serves as an internal barometer as to what we are feeling, what we are thinking, and what we want to see happen. This serves us in our workplaces and in our lives outside of work. It also helps us to see the interconnectedness between the two and to be more aware of where we stand with regard to work-life balance. Kabat-Zinn [72] argues that it is time for us to "free ourselves from the deep anguish of our persistent habit of ignoring what is most important" (p. 125), which we often do in giving more of our time and energies to work and forgetting the people and things that mean the most to us in life. Practicing mindfulness and coming to a greater sense of awareness is one strategy towards a healthier work-life balance.

D. Balance Sheet

We can also develop awareness by paying close attention to the things that drain our energy and those that fuel it [73]. We can use a decisional balance sheet that considers pros and cons or pay-offs and costs of the things, activities, and people that we maintain in our lives (Table 5).

Table 5. Balance Sheet (Adapted from Cheryl Richardson's Take Time for Your Life) [73]

On a blank piece of paper, create and label two columns that will represent your life account, as shown below. Create a list using the examples provided as a guide.

Energy-Drainers
(e.g., things, activities, and
people that take energy from you, that tire
excitement, frustrate you,
that demand your time and greater
and attention and that you don't enjoy)

Energy-Fuelers
(e.g., things, activities, and
provide rest, renewal, fun, and/or
healthier relationships, value,
life satisfaction)

After completing the columns in the decisional balance sheet (Table 5), we can consider how well balanced our life account is. When costs exceed payoffs, or the cost-effectiveness appraisal leaves us in the red, we want to make some different choices with regard to our work situations and our lives outside of work. For example, we might replace an energy-drainer with an energy-fueler, or reprioritize so energy-fuelers play a more prominent role. We can shift the balance to a more positive one that favors energy-fuelers over energy-drainers by identifying changes we can make to reduce or eliminate some of imbalance, and take action. Making one change at a time, and starting with something manageable increases our likelihood of success.

We can also consider the things, activities, and people in our lives in light of the bigger contexts of our values and our purposes in life. By living with a clearer sense of vision and purpose, our lives become sharply focused - we can learn to relinquish activities and pursuits that distract our energy and efforts, and to direct focus and energy toward those that are in alignment with our vision and purpose and support what we value in life and in work. We can take more responsibility with regard to our own work-life imbalance by making choices and choosing to manage ourselves to a greater degree than we allow ourselves to be managed by the circumstances in our lives.

E. Self-Management and Intrinsic Motivation

Another strategy for coping has to do with taking greater responsibility for our own motivation at work and seeking work that is more rewarding. Whether it is the lack of responsiveness by management to employee concerns, or lack of clear direction for the organisation provided by management, employees often feel as though they have little control over their own role and set of responsibilities. These feelings of being manipulated and powerless often result in higher levels of stress, burnout, excessive "job strain" [15], and de-motivation [74].

As a response to this negative work experience, Thomas [57] has developed a comprehensive approach to self-management and intrinsic motivation that includes literature from work redesign [75], self-determination [76], competence [77], self-efficacy [78], and others. Thomas' model [57] focuses on the internal rewards that result from doing work that is meaningful, energizing, engaging and satisfying. These internal or intrinsic rewards help workers feel inspired by their work and they also reduce feelings of stress and frustration. Thomas identifies four key dimensions to intrinsically motivated work behavior: choice, competence, meaningfulness, and progress (Table 6).

Table 6. Four Dimensions of Intrinsically Motivated Behavior [57]

1. *Choice:* This is the opportunity you feel to select task activities that make sense to you and to perform them in ways that seem appropriate. The feeling of choice is the feeling of being free to choose-of being able to use your own judgment.
2. *Competence:* This is the feeling that you can be effective in performing the assigned task. You possess confidence in your ability to do the task or to learn how to successfully do the task.
3. *Meaningfulness:* A task is meaningful if one sees doing the task as something worthy of his/her time and effort. Work is meaningful to someone if it in some way gives expression to one's beliefs and values.
4. *Progress:* This is the feeling that comes from realizing that your efforts are accomplishing something. This is a sense of achieving objectives.

Integral to the effective use of Thomas' model is the notion of self-management in which an employee owns his/her own motivation [57]:

> Self-management begins when you commit to a meaningful purpose. You then choose activities to accomplish that purpose. [57, p. 28]

This type of "purpose-driven" work is very much aligned with the kind of intentional living described before in terms of a clear mission and healthy work environment.

F. Engagement with Renewing Activities

Stress and exhaustion are not only about the presence of negative emotions, but the absence of positive ones [53]. Erosion of engagement, a positive emotion, is linked to exhaustion in workplace studies [53]. Engagement can be measured in part by participation in leisure or co-curricular activities. Strategies to enhance engagement and reduce stress include regularly and strategically scheduled breaks [79], participating in activities that are fun and/or meaningful, eating healthfully, exercising regularly, getting adequate sleep, practicing breathing and meditation, participating in mind-body exercise (such as Yoga, T'ai Chi, Pilates, etc.), getting a massage, using aromatherapy, and practicing progressive muscular relaxation; among others [80]. Participating in leisure activities and incorporating stress management and self-regulation strategies on a regular basis help to renew our energy reserves and maintain our overall health and well being. These strategies allow us to contribute as team members and leaders at work *and* as individuals, to our families and other relationships, and to enjoy all aspects of our lives.

G. Energy and Empathy

Another component of living intentionally and *in balance* deals with energy [69] and empathy [70]. The energy that we gain by realizing our passion and pursuing it helps inform our choices and, thus, guide our daily schedules. This energy is what makes life satisfying and joyful. When we have energy, we have the reserves to give to others as team members and as leaders. When we can focus outward and are able to identify what another person is truly experiencing through accurate reading of non-verbal cues rather than anticipating or projecting, we have empathy.

Empathy involves the ability to understand how another person feels. Having empathy includes an ability to tolerate differences and develop healthy skills for conflict management [70]. These capacities are critical for work relationships. So much of what feeds us in our lives emotionally comes from maintaining vibrant, ongoing, and healthy relationships. A lack of empathy prevents us from experiencing the rewarding aspects of relationships. To be present and empathic with others, and to reap the benefits relationships offer, requires us to possess the energy to be present with others. Taking care of ourselves enables us to be more empathic and energetic.

Taking care of ourselves by making good choices and knowing when and how to effectively self-regulate: i) allows us to be available, aware, and empathic with regard to others and the organisation as a whole; ii) serves as a positive role model for others (allows them to take care of themselves); and iii) is critical to the ability to function at an optimal level as a leader, or to "lead with your best self" [81]. Tom Terez [82] has developed *10 Commandments of a Happy Work Life* that address self-care as well as some healthy approaches to achieving greater satisfaction at work (Table 7). The reader might use these as a basis for self-inquiry, turning the "Thou shalt" statements into questions; for example, for the first commandment, one might ask oneself, Do I honor myself? In what ways?

Note that all of Terez's [82] "commandments" (Table 7) are stated in the positive.

Table 7. The 10 Commandments of a Happy Work Life [82] (Tom Terez Workplace Solutions, Inc. 2007)

1. Thou shalt honor thyself
2. Thou shalt be true to thyself
3. Thou shalt speak up
4. Thou shalt strive to simplify
5. Thou shalt assume the best
6. Thou shalt fix processes, not people
7. Thou shalt serve a greater purpose
8. Thou shalt be interested
9. Thou shalt honor time away from work
10. Thou shalt be thine own best manager

Another and perhaps more empowering approach would be to personalize these into affirmations and to own them as "I" statements, e.g., 'I will honor myself, …I will be my own best manager.'

H. The Contributions and Power of Positive Psychology

In this section we have offered a variety of strategies aimed at helping people in organisations, both employees and those in leadership roles, attain a more desirable work-life balance. Many of the suggested strategies include effective coping, living with intention, mindfulness, motivation and empathy. All of these might be grouped under a theoretical umbrella called, *positive psychology* [83, 84]. Rather than a strict focus on pathology or illness, positive psychology focuses on people's strengths and capacities for effective coping. Seligman [85], one of the pioneers in this field, suggests that this approach focuses on well-being, satisfaction, happiness, optimism, hope and faith, rather than pessimism, disease, and suffering:

> At the group level it is about the civic virtues and the institutions that move individuals toward better citizenship: responsibility, nurturance, altruism, civility, moderation, tolerance and work ethic. [85, p. 3]

Some causes of work-life imbalance may not be under our control to change, such as the global economy, economic uncertainty, and international business; and work schedules, work pace, career security, and job mobility. However, other contributing factors are under our control, and focusing on changing these is the basis of positive psychology. Our cognitive patterns fall into the latter category (things we can be change), and are illustrative of Lazarus and Folkman's transactional model of stress [35]. Similarly, our appraisals of stressors can be shifted from the negative end of the spectrum towards the positive. We can change how we appraise and interact with our environment. Cognitive patterns can be reshaped by first recognizing negative self-talk and assumptions that are unfounded, then replacing them with more positive ways of thinking which lead to more positive emotions. In a well-designed experimental study by Davidson et al. [86] incorporating eight weeks of Mindfulness-Based Stress Reduction (MBSR) and meditation training, participants exhibited a shift in the ratio of Left:Right activation of the two halves of the cerebral cortex, a shift associated with a higher level of positive emotions (joy, happiness, contentment) and greater approach or pleasure-seeking behavior in comparison to difficult or negative emotions (fear, sadness, etc.) and avoidance behavior [86]. This study served to show that we *can* retrain our thinking - we can be more mindful not only about how we think, but also in the choices we make and actions we take.

Adopting new psychological strategies to assist us in dealing with stress that results from an unhealthy work-life balance falls under the umbrella of positive psychology. Positive emotions such as joy, interest, contentment, and love [36] have been identified as one of a number of coping strategies that help buffer against stress and depressed mood. Other positive emotions include laughter and humor, and positive emotional disclosure or gratitude [39]. Folkman and Moskowitz [87, 88] have championed the adaptational significance of positive affect as an important factor in coping processes and stress management. Positive emotions involve positive reappraisal, problem-focused thinking, coping, and giving positive meaning to ordinary events [39], or positive reframing. They serve to broaden an individual's temporary thought-action repertoire, which in turn builds the individual's physical, intellectual, and social resources [36, 37, 89]. These resources translate into higher odds of survival and reproductive success [89]. These effects have been described by Fredrickson's broaden-and-build model [36, 37].

Another benefit of positive emotions is their hypothesized "undoing" effect – that is, they loosen the hold that negative emotions take on both mind and body, counteract the fight or flight response or preparation for action in response to a stressor, and undo the physiological effects of negative emotions [89]. Positive emotions and their undoing effects have been linked with enhanced immune system functioning, lower rates of readmission to the hospital for patients with cardiovascular disease, fewer illness-related physician visits, higher positive morale, decreased depression, longevity, and psychological resilience [39]. Research in positive psychology is beginning to help us understand and explain how such transformations occur. Included in positive psychology is an essential human ability that involves bouncing back from setbacks, rejection and disappointments: resilience. We conclude our strategies section with a focus on this powerful and sometimes overlooked ability that encompasses many of the previously mentioned strategies.

Resilience involves "the ability to recover from or adjust easily to misfortune or change" and "the ability to bounce back after being subjected to adversity or stress" [90, p. 628]. The concept of resilience comes from the assumption that in one's journey towards better work-life balance there will be setbacks, challenges, and disappointments. Characteristics of resilient people include: looking for opportunities in problems, having a positive attitude, avoiding a victim mentality, overcoming difficulties, and learning from mistakes [91]. Wainright and Calnan [24] concluded that work stress is a mode of feeling with physiological and cognitive dimensions, and that worker resilience should receive more attention. Resilience speaks to empowerment and autonomy, and of choice in response, counteracting the concept of the employee as a 'work stress victim' [24]. Suggestions on how to increase our resilience have been offered by the Mayo Clinic [92, Table 8] and the American Psychology Association in its brochure, *The Road to Resilience* [93].

According to the American Psychological Association [93], developing resilience is a personal journey characterized by various strategies influenced by our culture. Cultural differences are reflected in how we communicate feelings, deal with adversity, connect with significant others, and utilize community resources [93]. With increasing cultural diversity at work and in our lives outside of work, we have greater access to a variety of approaches for building resilience as individuals and within our organisations.

Positive emotions, a key factor in resilience, can be transformational [84] and trigger upward spirals toward emotional well being and optimal individual functioning [38] and fuel upward spirals in organisational functioning as well [84]. These emotions follow from appraisals of positive personal meaning at work related to competence, achievement, engagement, and social connections. Organisations can foster these types of experiences via their practices (e.g., group size, methods of communication, incentive and reward structures, and opportunities for renewal and reflection) [84]. Careful consideration of the workplace environment, practices, and strategies may help an organisation stay alive and fresh, achieve harmony, raise energy levels, and prosper [84].

Certainly, the individual plays a key role in his/her own state of work-life balance and its maintenance, and this is an empowering place from which to begin. However, the organisation has a responsibility towards creating a healthy workplace that fosters work-life balance.

Table 8. Tips for Improving Resilience [92]

- *Get connected.* Build strong, positive relationships with family and friends, who can listen to your concerns and offer support.
- *Use humor and laughter.* Remaining positive or finding humor in distressing or stressful situations doesn't mean you're in denial. Humor is a helpful coping mechanism.
- *Learn from your experiences.* Recall how you've coped with hardships in the past, either in healthy or unhealthy ways.
- *Remain hopeful and optimistic.* While you can't change events, look toward the future, even if it's just a glimmer of how things might improve.
- *Take care of yourself.* Tend to your own needs and feelings, both physically and emotionally. This includes participating in activities and hobbies you enjoy, exercising regularly, getting plenty of sleep, and eating well.
- *Accept and anticipate change.* Be flexible. Try not to be so rigid that even minor changes upset you or that you become anxious in the face of uncertainty. Expecting changes to occur makes it easier to adapt to them, tolerate them and even welcome them.
- *Work toward goals.* Do something every day that gives you a sense of accomplishment. Even small, everyday goals are important. Having goals helps direct you toward the future.
- *Take action.* Don't just wish your problems would go away or try to ignore them. Instead, figure out what needs to be done, make a plan to do it, and then take action.
- *Learn new things about yourself.* Review past experiences and think about how you've changed as a result. You may have gained a new appreciation for life.
- *Think better of yourself.* Be proud of yourself. Trust yourself to solve problems and make sound decisions. Nurture your self-confidence and self-esteem so that you feel strong, capable and self-reliant.
- *Maintain perspective.* Don't compare your situation to that of somebody you think may be worse off. You'll probably feel guilty for being down about your own problems.

requirements like vacation policies and dress codes.

- At Google, employees can get subsized massages, get a free lunch at a choice of 17 gourmet cafeterias, and bring their dogs to work.
- Employees at Workman Publishing can take afternoon naps (with eye masks and yoga mats provided).
- Patagonia staffers are encouraged to take breaks outdoors, and there's even a "boardroom" for storing surfboards.

In a recent article on the 14 hottest companies in the Seattle, Washington area, Gullo and Voelker [100] identify characteristics of workspaces as well as workplace culture that have positive impacts on employees.

- Google's office has floor-to-ceiling whiteboards throughout the building to encourage casual collaboration among employees.
- SKB Architects seats architects alongside interior designers in a studio filled with natural light, reflecting its holistic design philosophy and emphasis on collaboration. Glass doors that separate the conference room from the kitchen can be thrown open to create an instant dance hall for staffers who get along so well they don't want to go home.
- GordenDerr, a law firm, advocates for work-life balance by encouraging employees to spend time with their families by setting a maximum billable-hour requirement at 250 hours fewer than the average firm.
- Allyis, a technology firm which designs and manages web sites and content management systems, provides a child-care assistance program which offers employees up to $525 per month toward the cost of day care and/or their child's health-care premiums in addition to a full list of benefits.
- Work-life balance is so important to Cascadia Consulting that the term is included in the company's mission statement. It supports this principle in practice by giving every employee the option to telecommute and 25% of employees work from home as part of their regular weekly schedule. In addition, staff hours are closely monitored and available for everyone to see, and all employees attend a mandatory Monday morning staff meeting. This probably helps ensure against a loss of communication and connection that could result from a lower percentage of the workforce being on site at any one time.
- KPS Health Plans pays 100 percent of health care premiums for their employees and their families. In addition, they offer tuition assistance, online wellness programs and pretax flexible-spending accounts on top of generous health benefits. KPS also offer fun events like an annual bowling competition using frozen Cornish game hens.
- Office Nomads, which created Seattle's first co-working environment, provides an open, friendly office space, Wi-Fi, a coffee pot, and a shower to the self-employed who can drop in for $25 a day or $475 a month (unlimited use). In addition, coworkers benefit from the camaraderie that is missing in a work-at-home and work-alone environment via game nights on Mondays, group lunches on Wednesdays, and business seminars offered on site.

- Adaptis, a health care firm, integrates change management into all of its projects and makes it "part and parcel" of all their activities. Adaptis finds that this approach results in happy, informed employees who stay with the company longer.

- F5, a technology firm that serves to keep professional web sites and e-mail systems running, gives its employees up to 25 days of paid vacation per year, not including holidays, and unique perks on top of standard benefits, such as on-site massage, a $300 a year parking stipend for alternative transportation, $3,000 annually for tuition assistance, and discounts at local gyms. F5's staff grew by approximately 32 percent worldwide in 2006 and its revenues rose 33 percent in 2007. Taking care of your employees is good business.

There are many more examples of workplace environments that support work-life balance. For more information and to visit the websites of some of these companies go to: http://money.cnn.com/magazines/fortune/bestcompanies/2007/index.html.

CONCLUSION

Whether the context is work or life, the costs for maintaining an unhealthy balance arc greater stress, wear and tear on both our physical and emotional health, disintegration of our relationships, reduced productivity and performance, and declining quality of life [30]. On the other hand, the pay-offs for creating better balance in our lives are numerous. Balance lends harmony to life [101], it promotes physical and emotional health, it leads to greater creativity and richer social networks, is associated with higher self-esteem and a more positive outlook on life, and results in greater life and job satisfaction. As Joanie discovered and as Andrew will hopefully realize, the costs of work-life imbalance are real, and the work of establishing work-life balance is not easy, but worth our time, effort, and energy.

How we take care of ourselves, our choices and priorities, our balance at home affects our performance at work and our engagement with the work environment and others in it. The reverse is also true: our workplace balance or lack thereof affects our lives and personal balance outside of work. Work-life balance is circular in this respect and we can address it from either end: work or life outside of work. Either approach or direction can work, and the responsibility for enhancing and maintaining work-life balance lies on both ends. The important thing is to takc action where we can to influence the things that can be changed.

Work-life balance can be addressed at different levels within the organisation, and in a myriad of ways. In order to create better work-life balance, we (as employees and leaders) can approach our work and home lives differently starting with developing awareness or mindfulness, self-regulating (prioritizing, making different choices), which leads to increased energy and the ability to be empathic towards others. Individual employees and leaders have a responsibility to themselves with respect to their own health, well-being, and work-life balance. They also have a responsibility to others in modeling healthier behaviors and ways of responding even when the workplace is not particularly tuned into or supportive of work-life balance. In addition, companies can make changes to promote a healthy workplace that are characterized by: an attractive and comfortable physical environment; a culture that supports good communication, collaboration, and flexibility in scheduling; education and assistance to enhance self-care and the health of employees and their families; opportunities for social engagement and fun; and adequate time-off and opportunities to refresh and renew. Businesses have a legal obligation to recognize the warning signs of stress and work-life imbalance and to act to correct the situations that facilitate unhealthy work relationships and environments. They must comply with industry policies and adhere to best practices in order to safeguard their hires and themselves from litigation. Coaches, consultants, and counselors are particularly well positioned to stimulate awareness and serve as change agents. They can assist individuals (employees, students, etc.), team members, leaders, and organisations in understanding the importance of work-life balance, developing healthy lifestyle practices and creating a healthy workplace, and pursuing these endeavors in effective ways.

The authors wish to acknowledge two limitations in this article. First, our training and backgrounds are not in psychology or sociology, although we have attempted to draw on theoretical frameworks and explanations from those disciplines. Second, the topics of work-life balance and imbalance and stress are much broader than can be covered in a single article. While we recognize these limitations, we hope to have provided some strategies and tools that will be useful across individual, leader, and organisational levels and to coaches, consultants, and counselors across a broad range of situations. We also hope to have stimulated some thought, and hopefully, action towards improving work-life balance. For your convenience, a list of additional resources, i.e., books, information sites, and self-assessment tools related to stress and work-life balance (many of which are available on-line), is provided following the references. We wish you a good journey towards better work-life balance.

REFERENCES

1.   Visser, F. and Williams, L., *Work-Life Balance: Rhetoric Versus Reality?* An Independent Report Commissioned by UNISON, The Work Foundation, Leicestershire, UK, 2008, http://www.theworkfoundation.com/research/publications/, accessed 10/20/08.

2.   Galinsky, E., Bond, J.T., Kim, S.S., Backon, L., Brownfield, E. and Sakai, K., Overwork in America: When the Way We Work Becomes Too Much (Executive Summary), Families and Work Institute, 2005, http://familiesandwork.org/site/research/summary/main.html, accessed 10/20/08.

3.   Halpin, N. Work-life Balance – An Overview, Work Life Balance Centre – Articles. http://www.worklifebalancecentre.rog/nickhalpinl.php, accessed 10/20/08.

4.   Duxbury, L., Higgins, C. and Coghill, D., *Voices of Canadians: Seeking Work-Life Balance.* Canadian Department of Social Development, Quebec, Canada, 2003, http://www.sdc.gc.ca/asp/gateway.asp?hr=/en/lp/spila/wlb/vcswlb/51appendix_b.shtml&hs=wnc#top, accessed February 13, 2005.

5.   Employers for Work-Life Balance, Work-Life Balance – Factsheet, The Work Foundation, http://www.employersforwork-lifebalance.org.uk/work/factsheet.htm, accessed February 13, 2005.

6.   McGuire, R., Work/Life Balance, *British Medical Journal Career Focus*, 2002, 324, 47.

7.   The Work Foundation. Employers and Work-Life Balance - accessed 10/20/08 Jargon-buster. http://www.indsoc.co.uk/difference/e4wlb/jargonbuster.aspx, accessed 10/20/08 Making the Case: The Business Benefits, http://www.indsoc.co.uk/difference/e42lb/businessbenefits.aspx, accessed 10/20/08.
     Useful Links, http://www.indsoc.co.u/difference/e4wlb/usefullinks.aspx, accessed 10/20/08.

8.   Hall, K., *A Life in Balance*, AMACOM/American Management Association, New York, 2006.

9.   Public Health – The Grey Bruce Health Unit, A Healthy Workplace Works for Everyone - A Healthy Workplace Program. http://www.publichealthgreybruce.on.ca/WorkplaceWellness/3-benefits.htm, accessed 5/06/07.
     Healthy Workplace Program Ideas, http://www.publichealthgreqybruce.on.ca/WorkplaceWellness/4-FiveEasySteps.htm,   accessed 5/06/07.
     What Makes a Workplace Healthy? http://www.publichealthgreybruce.on.ca/WorkplaceWellness/2-WhatMakesAWorkplaceHealthy.htm, accessed 5/06/07.

10. Work Life Balance Centre, 5 Nethercote, Newton Burgoland, Leicestershire, LE67 2ST, UK, info@worklifebalancecentre.org - http://www.worklifebalancecentre.org/index.php, accessed 10/20/08.
     Active Living & Working, http://www.worklifebalancecentre.org/activliving.php, accessed 10/20/08.
     Making Work Life Balance Happen: A Brief Guide From the Work Life Balance Centre, http://www.worklifebalancecentre.org/freeguidedownload.php, accessed 10/20/08.
     Work Life Balance Related Organisations. http://www.worlifebalancecentre.org/usefulsites.php, accessed 10/20/08.

11. Covey, S.R., *Living the 7 Habits: The Courage to Change*, Simon & Schuster Publishing, New York, 2000.

12. Rosen, R. H., *The Healthy Company: Eight Strategies to Develop People, Productivity, and Profits*, Jeremy P. Tarcher, Inc., Los Angeles, 1991.

13. Sauter, S.L., Murphy, L.R. and Hurrell, J.J., Prevention of Work-Related Psychological Disorders: A National Strategy Proposed by the National Institute for Occupational Safety and Health (NIOSH). *American Psychologist*, 1990, 45, 1146-1158.

14. Perrewé, P.L., Hochwarter, W.A., Rossi, A.M., Wallace, A., Maignan, I., Castro, S.L., Ralston, D.A., Westman, M., Vollmer, G., Tang, M., Wan, P. and Van Deusen, C.A., Are Work Stress Relationships Universal? A Nine-Region Examination of Role Stressors, General Self-Efficacy, and Burnout, *Journal of International Management*, 2002, 8(4), 163-187.

15. Karasek, R.A. and Theorell, T., *Healthy Work*, Basic Books, New York, 1990.

16. Siegrist, J., Adverse Health Effects of High Effort - Low Reward Conditions at Work, *Journal of Occupational Health Psychology*, 1996, 1, 27-43.

17. Siegrist, J., Effort-Reward Imbalance at Work and Health, in: Perrewé, P. and Ganster, D., eds., *Research in Occupational Stress and Well-Being, Vol. 2: Historical and Current Perspectives on Stress and Health*, Elsevier, New York, 2002, 261-291.

18. Siegrist, J., Starke, D., Chandola, T., Godin, I., Marmot, M., Niedhammer, I. and Peter, R., The Measurement of Effort-Reward Imbalance at Work: European Comparisons, *Social Science and Medicine*, 2004, 58, 8, 1483-1499.

19. Hepburn, C.G., Loughlin, C.A. and Barling, J., Coping with Chronic Work Stress, in: Gottlieb, B. H., ed., *Coping with Chronic Stress*, Plenum Press, New York, 1997, 343-366.

20. Mayo Clinic Report, 2008, http://www.mayoclinic.com/health/work-life-balance/WL00056, accessed 10/28/08.

21. Ray, R. and Schmitt, J., No-Vacation Nation, Center for Economic Policy Research, Washington, D.C., May 2007, http://www.cepr.net, accessed May 12, 2008.

22. Schnall, P., A Brief Introduction to Job Strain, Job Stress Network – Job Strain link, 1998. http://www.workhealth.org/strain/briefintro.html, accessed 10/17/08.

23. Schnall, P.L., Landsbergis, P.A. and Baker, D., Job Strain and Cardiovascular Disease, *Annual Review of Public Health*, 1994, 15, 381-411.

24. Wainright, D. and Calnan, M., *Work Stress: The Making of a Modern Epidemic*, Open University Press, Buckingham, UK, 2002.

25.   Jones, I.R., Book Review: Work Stress: The Making of a Modern Epidemic, *International Journal of Epidemiology*, 2002, 31, 1282-1283.

26.   Stratigaki, M., The Cooptation of Gender Concepts in EU Policies: The Case of "Reconciliation of Work and Family," *Social Politics*, 2004, 11(1), 30-56.

27.   Gorman, C., 6 Lessons for Handling Stress, *Time - Mind & Body Special Issue*, January 29, 2007, 80-85.

28.   De Graaf, J., No-Vacation Nation, *Experience Life*, March 2008, 48-53.

28.   Robinson, J., *Work to Live*, 3rd edn., Perigree Trade, New York, 2003.

30.   Geithner, C.A. and Albert, J.F., Balance: A Means to Personal and Cultural Sustainability, *International Journal of Environmental, Cultural, Economic and Social Sustainability*, 2006, 1.

31.   CommPsych Poll, 2006, cited in K. Haugen: Creating Resilient Employees in a Thriving Environment, http://www.awcnet.org/trainmaterials/EmpHealthAcademy/2007/HaugenCreatingResilientEmploy ees.pps, accessed May 12, 2008.

32.   Perkins, A., Saving Money by Reducing Stress, *Harvard Business Review*, 1994, 72(6), 12.

33.   Selye, H., *The Stress of Life*, McGraw-Hill Book Co., New York, 1956.

34.   Cannon, W., *The Wisdom of the Body*, W.W. Norton, New York, 1932.

35.   Lazarus, R.S. and Folkman, S., *Stress, Appraisal, and Coping*, Springer, New York, 1984.

36.   Fredrickson, B.L., What Good Are Positive Emotions? *Review of General Psychology: Special Issue: New Directions in Research on Emotion*, 1998, 2, 300-319.

37.   Fredrickson, B.L., The Role of Positive Emotions in Positive Psychology: The Broaden-and-Build Theory of Positive Emotions, *American Psychologist: Special Issue*, 2001, 56, 218-226.

38.   Fredrickson, B.L. and Joiner, T., Positive Emotions Trigger Upward Spirals Toward Emotional Well-Being, *Psychological Science*, 2002, 13, 172-175.

39.   Tugade, M.M., Fredrickson, B.L. and Barrett, L.F., Psychological Resilience and Positive Emotional Granularity: Examining the Benefits of Positive Emotions on Coping and Health, *Journal of Personality*, 2004, 72(6):1161-1190.

40.   Lazarus, R.S., Coping Theory and Research: Past, Present, and Future, *Psychosomatic Medicine*, 1993, 55, 234-247.

41.   Faragher, E.B., Cass, M. and Cooper C.L., The Relationship Between Job Satisfaction and Health: A Meta-Analysis, *Occupational and Environmental Medicine*, 2005, 62(2), 105-12.

42.   NIOSH (National Institute for Occupational Safety and Health), A Division of the U.S. Department of Health and Human Services, *Stress at Work*, NIOSH Publication No. 99-101, http://www.cdc.gov/niosh/jobstres.html, accessed February 13, 2005.

43.   Bohle, P., Quinlan, M., Kennedy, D. and Williamson, A., Working Hours, Work-Life Conflict and Health in Precarious and "Permanent" Employment, *Revista de Saude Publica*, 2004, 38(6 Suppl), 19-25.

44.   De Vente, W., Olff, M., Van Amsterdam, J.G., Kamphuis, J.H. and Emmelkamp, P.M., Physiological Differences Between Burnout Patients and Healthy Controls: Blood Pressure, Heart Rate, and Cortisol Responses, *Occupational and Environmental Medicine*, 2003, 60(Suppl 1), i54-i61.

45.   Glynn, L.M., Christenfeld, N. and Gerin, W., The Role of Rumination in Recovery from Reactivity: Cardiovascular Consequences of Emotional Stress, *Psychosomatic Medicine*, 2002, 64(5), 714-726.

46.   Piscatella, J.C. and Franklin, B.A., *Take a Load Off Your Heart*, Workman Publishing, New York, 2003.

47.   Campbell, M., Baltes, J.I., Martin, A. and Meddings, K., *The Stress of Leadership: A CCL Research White Paper*, Center for Creative Leadership, Greensboro, NC, 2007, http://www.ccl.org.

48. Perkins, D.N.T., Holtman, M.P., Kessler, P.R. and McCarthy, C., *Leading at the Edge: Leadership Lessons from the Extraordinary Saga of Shackleton's Antarctic Expedition*, AMACOM/American Management Association, New York, 2000.

49. Kofodimos, J., Why Executives Lose Their Balance, *Organisational Dynamics*, 1990,19(1), 58-73.

50. Heider, J., *Tao of Leadership*, Bantam Books, New York, 1986.

51. Maslach, C., Job Burnout: New Directions in Research and Intervention, *Current Directions in Psychological Sciences*, 2003, 12(5), 189-192.

52. Maslach, C., Schufeli, W. and Letier, M., Job Burnout, *Annual Review of Psychology*, 2001, 52, 397-422.

53. Maslach, C. and Letier, M.P., *The Truth About Burnout*, San Franciso, Jossey-Bass, 1997.

54. Sluiter, J.K., de Croon, E.M., Meijman, T.F. and Frings-Dresen, M.H., Need for Recovery from Work Related Fatigue and Its Role in the Development and Prediction of Subjective Health Complaints, *Occupational and Environmental Medicine,* 2003, 60(Suppl 1):162-170.

55. European Agency for Safety and Health at Work, *Research on Work-Related Stress*, Office for Official Publications of the European Communities, Luxembourg, 2000.

56. Frost, P. J., *Toxic Emotions at Work: How Compassionate Managers Handle Pain and Conflict*, Harvard Business School Press, Cambridge, MA, 2003.

57. Thomas, K., *Intrinsic Motivation at Work: Building Energy and Commitment*, Berrett-Koehler, San Francisco, 2000.

58. Helgesen, S., *Thriving in 24/7: Six Strategies for Taming the New World of Work*, The Free Press, New York, 2001.

59. Vaill, P., *Learning as a Way of Being: Strategies for Survival in a World of Permanent White Water*, Jossey-Bass, San Francisco, 1996.

60. Palus, C.J. and Horth, D.M., *The Leader's Edge: Six Creative Competencies for Navigating Complex Challenges*, Jossey-Bass, San Francisco, 2002.

61. Burns D., *Feeling Good: The New Mood Therapy*, HarperCollins Publishers, Inc., New York, 1999.

62. Langer, E.J., *Well-Being: Mindfulness versus Positive Evaluation*, in: Snyder, C. R. and Lopez, S. J., eds., *Handbook of Positive Psychology*, Oxford University Press, Oxford, 2005, 214-230.

63. Covey, S.R., *Principle-Centered Leadership*, Simon & Schuster Publishing, New York 1991.

64. Maxwell, J., *Developing the Leader Within You*, Thomas Nelson Publishers, Nashville, TN, 1993.

65. Covey, S.R., *The 7 Habits of Highly Effective People*, Simon & Schuster Publishing, New York, 1989.

66. Bloom, N. and Van Reenen, J., Management Practices, Work-Life Balance, and Productivity: A Review of Some Recent Evidence, *Oxford Review of Economic Policy*, 2006, 22(4), 457-482.

67. Carlson, R., *Don't Sweat the Small Stuff at Work*, Hyperion, New York, 1998.

68. Kabat-Zinn, J., *Wherever You Go There You Are: Mindfulness Meditation in Everyday Life*, Hyperion, New York, 1994.

69. Hall, K., *Alter Your Life,* Oak Haven, Clarksville, GA, 2005.

70. Johnson, J. and Erb, D., *EQ in the Workplace*, Learning in Action Technologies, Bellevue, 2003, http://www.learninginaction.com.

71. Kabat-Zinn, J., *Full Catastrophe Living*, Hyperion, New York, 1990.

72. Kabat-Zinn, J., *Coming to Our Senses: Healing Ourselves and the World Through Mindfulness*, Hyperion, New York, 2005.

73. Richardson, C., *Take Time for Your Life*, Broadway Books, New York, 1998.

74. Meyer, A. C., Demotivation: Its Cause and Cure, *Workforce Management*, 1978, 57, 5, 260.

75. Hackman, J. R. and Oldham, G. R., *Work Redesign*, Addison-Wesley, Reading, MA, 1980.

76. Deci, E.L. and Ryan, R.M., *Intrinsic Motivation and Self-Determination in Human Behavior*, Plenum Press, New York, 1985.

77. White, R.W., Motivation Reconsidered: The Concept of Competence, *Psychological Review*, 1959, 66, 297-333.

78. Bandura, A., *Social Learning Theory*, Prentice-Hall, Englewood Cliffs, NJ, 1977.

79. Law, D.W., Exhaustion in University Students and the Effect of Coursework Involvement, *Journal of American College Health*, 2007, 55(4), 239-245.

80. Greenberg, J.S., *Comprehensive Stress Management*, McGraw-Hill, New York, 2008.

81. Mulhern, D., Move! To Model the Way, *Reading for Leading*, November 7, 2005, E-zine by request to: mulhern@danmulhern.com or firstgentleman@MICHIGAN.GOV.

82. Terez, T., The 10 Commandments of a Happy Work Life, Tom Terez Workplace Solutions, Inc. 2007, http://www.BetterWorkplaceNow.com.

83. Snyder, C. R. and Lopez, S. J., eds., *Handbook of Positive Psychology*, Oxford University Press, Oxford, 2005.

84. Fredrickson, B. L., Positive Emotions and Upward Spirals in Organisational Settings, in: Cameron, K., Dutton, J. and Quinn, R., eds., *Positive Organisational Scholarship: Foundations of a New Discipline*, Berrett-Koehler Publishers, Inc., San Francisco, 2003a.

85. Seligman, M. E. P., Positive Psychology, Positive Prevention, and Positive Therapy, in: Snyder, C. R. and Lopez, S. J., eds., *Handbook of Positive Psychology*, Oxford University Press, Oxford, 2005, 3-12.

86. Davidson, R.S., Kabat-Zinn, J., Rosenkranz, M.S., Muller, D., Santorelli, S.F., Urbanowski, F., Harrington, A., Bonus, K. and Sheridan, J.F., Alterations in Brain and Immune System Function Produced by Mindfulness Meditation, *Psychosomatic Medicine*, 2003, 65, 564-570.

87. Folkman, S. and Moskowitz, J.T., Positive Affect and the Other Side of Coping, *American Psychologist*, 2000a, 55(6), 647-654.

88. Folkman, S. and Moskowitz, J.T., Stress, Positive Emotion, and Coping, *Current Directions in Psychological Science*, 2000b, 9(4), 115-118.

89. Fredrickson, B. L.,The Value of Positive Emotions, *American Scientist*, 2003, 91, 330-335.

90. Merriam-Webster, Inc., *The Merriam-Webster Dictionary*, Merriam-Webster, Inc., Springfield, MA, 1997.

91. Haugen, K., Creating Resilient Employees in a Thriving Environment, Presentation Given at the 2007 AWC Health Academy.

92. Mayo Clinic Report, 2000, http://www.mayoclinic.com/health/resilience/MH00078, accessed 10/28/08.

93. American Psychological Association, The Road to Resilience, http:www.helping.apa.org, accessed 10/24/08.

94. Barling, J., Kelloway, D.K. and Frone, M.R., *Handbook of Work Stress*, SAGE Publications, Thousand Oaks, CA, 2005.

95. The Great Place to Work Institute, Inc., http://www.greatplacetowork.com/gptw/index.php, accessed 10/20/08.

96. Dutton, J.E. and Ragins, B.R., *Exploring Positive Relationships at Work: Building a Theoretical and Research Foundation*, Laurence Erlbaum Associates, Inc., Mahwah, NJ, 2006.

97. Anonymous, Culture Conquers (Almost) All - Even in a Retention-Challenge Industry, *HR Focus*, 2008, 85, Oct, 6-7, 9-10.

98. Oksanen, T., Social Capital at Work as a Predictor of Employee Health: Multilevel Evidence from Work Units in Finland, *Social Science and Medicine*, 2008, 66(3), 637-649.

99.   Wallace, H., happiness@work, *body + soul*, March 2008,98-104.

100. Gullo, J. and Voelker, J., Hot Companies: 14 Businesses Go Beyond the Cubicle to Reinvent the Working World (and Better Yet, They're Hiring!), *Seattle Metropolitan*, April 2008, 64-92.

101. Kaye, S. and Kim, I., Time Management: Decide What You Want to Accomplish, How to Get There and What to Do First, *Chemical Engineering*,1998, 105(2),137-140.

ADDITIONAL RESOURCES

Are You a Stress Case? Stress Quiz from LifeScript, http:www.lifescript.com/Quizzes/Personality/Are_You_A_Stress_Case.aspx?, accessed 10/25/08.

BeCanDo Life Coaching, How to Improve Your Life, http://www.becandolifecoaching.com/index.html, accessed 10/26/08. Includes a Stress Coping Strategy Test, A Life Satisfaction Check with graphed results, Is Now the Time to Change self-assessment, and How to Improve Your Life in Four Simple Steps.

Davis, M., Eshelman, E.R. and McKay, M., *The Relaxation & Stress Reduction Workbook,* 6th edn., New Harbinger Publications, Oakland, CA, 2008. A compilation of a wide variety of self-assessment tools and strategies for relaxing and reducing stress.

Job Stress Network. Job Content Questionnaire, http://www.workhealth.org/strain/jsitemsp.html, accessed 10/26/08. Information on job strain and the Job Content Questionnaire., a 42-item research tool to assess job-related stress developed by Robert Karasek, M.D., Ph.D., with two scales of items: one for decision latitude, the second for psychological job demands (copyrighted).

LifePositive: Your Complete Guide to Holistic Living. Stress at Work.,http://www.lifepositive.com/Mind/psychology/stress/stress-at-work.asp, accessed 10/26/08. Definitions, symptoms, and causes of stress; signs, symptoms, and treatment related to job stress; coping skills; Stress Quiz; tips on reducing stress.

Mayo Clinic, Job Satsfaction: Strategies to Make Work More Gratifying, http://www.mayoclinic.com/health/job-satisfaction/WL00051, accessed 10/25/08. Addresses reasons for loss of job satisfaction, the link between work approach and job satisfaction, strategies for improving job satisfaction, and the link between job satisfaction and stress.

Mayo Clinic, Stress Assessment, http://www.mayoclinic.com/health/stress-assessment/SR00029, accessed 10/26/08. Pinpoint your stress level and get tips for managing your stress.

Mayo Clinic, Work-Life Balance: Ways to Restore Harmony and Reduce Stress, http://www.mayonclinic.com/health/work-life-balance/WL00056, accessed 10/25/08. Symptoms of work-life imbalance and tips for restoring harmony and reducing stress.

Paauwerfrully Organized, website of Kathy Paauw, Organizing and Productivity Consultant and Certified Professional Coach, http://www.orgcoach.net/_assessment/worklifebalance.html, accessed 10/26/08. Work/Life Balance Assessment with 22 items on a 4-point Likert scale and 3 open-ended questions. Results are sent out immediately by email. Opportunity for coaching.

TestWell.org, managed by the National Wellness Institute, http://www.natoinalwellness.org/testwell/index.htm, accessed 10/26/08. Offers a self-assessment (the Holistic Lifestyle Questionnaire) focusing on six dimensions of wellness that can be taken from any location in the world with an Internet connection.Assessments and reports can be customized, and individual reports are sent out immediately after taking the assessment. Also includes goal setting and strategy development.

The American Institute of Stress (AIS), Job Stress, http://www.stress.org/job.htm, accessed 10/26/08. Includes information re: stress at work, statistics and quotes, a job stress questionnaire: How Much Job Stress Do You Have?, the 2001 Attitudes in the American Workplace VII Gallup Poll, Working with Stress – a NIOSH educational program and online (streaming) video, and tips for reducing stress.

The Law & Life Journal, Online Publication of the ESQ Development Institute, November 2004 issue. http://www.esqdevelopmentinstitute.com/Newsletters/nov04news.htm, accessed 10/26/08. This issue's focus is Work-Life Balance. Provided are concrete strategies for meeting the demands at work and in your personal life. Includes Defining Your Values & Priorities, the ESQ Life Balance Self-Assessment, a Roadmap to Work/Life Balance, and Ready to Take Action? Opportunities for coaching link.

Wellness Inventory: The Whole Person Assessment Program, http://www.wellnessinventory.net, accessed 10/26/08. Five-step program including assessment, scores, personal wellness action plan, tools to support your wellness action plan, and resources for ongoing wellness.

Work Life Balance Centre, Active Living and Working, http://www.worklifebalancecentreorg/activeliving.php, accessed 10/20/08. Personal work life balance profile, the Balance Wheel, a guide to active living and workload management, and tools/assessments for purchase, such as the Lifestyle Audit.

Work-Life Imbalance, Stress, and Individual and Organisation Intervention Strategies

A Commentary

Jim McKenna
Carnegie Research Institute
Leeds Metropolitan University, Leeds, LS6 3QS, UK
E-mail: J.McKenna@leedsmet.ac.uk

INTRODUCTION

The expansive article of Geithner et al. reminds us that work-life balance *(w-l-b)* is a complex issue. With major financial organisations failing, the ramifications for *w-l-b* remain to be seen; readers may feel sufficiently conflicted about the current situation to avoid even starting to think about working on *w-l-b* now [1]. The uncertainty of the current situation explains our on-going need to understand both sides of this concept - 'work life *balance*' and 'work life *conflict*' – and the many ways in which each might develop.

START FROM SOMEWHERE

By highlighting the many possible routes to achieving *w-l-b*, Geithner et al. emphasise the intriguing relationships between intervention and response. Indeed, recent events in world banking remind us of the need for a clear view of the dominant influences that shape organisations. Often these influences include the respective values of those employees, managers and organisational systems who variously may reject or endorse attending to *w-l-b*. Even our legislators demonstrate some level of conflict around *w-l-b*. They walk the tightrope between ensuring employee welfare and preserving what employers say gives them their competitive 'edge.' In the UK, this results on the one hand with government support for action on workplace stress, but on the other refusing to collaborate with European Union (EU) 48-hour Work Times Directives. Unsurprisingly, The Work Foundation found that most organisations who were not responding to ongoing *w-l-b* issues, justified their decision by focusing solely on establishing the business case for in-building positive approaches [2].

Practitioners appreciate that concerns regarding *w-l-b* are characterised by an unmet endorsement of increased employee autonomy [3-7]. Any such change automatically means redressing the all-important psychological contract between employers and employees, not least because any endorsement can be easily undermined by custom and practice even in well-intentioned settings. Workplace expectations relating to cover for sickness, working at weekends and taking holiday allocations can contribute to the extra working which eventually accumulates to threaten *w-l-b*. One further twist in the *w-l-b* tail is that some recommended and much needed approaches, such as offering flexitime for parents, can transfer a burden to other employees (such as those with no dependents). With a concern to minimise this burden, some carers may even restrict their use of existing services and arrangements.

Employee attempts to establish autonomy at work can even create conflict with managerial approaches based on control and direction. Herein lies another issue for practitioners; workplaces that endorse *w-l-b* are committing to change working practices, which may – even in the short-term – risk worsening the *w-l-b* of the people who champion this move, including Human Resource staff. For this reason, it is important to know how deeply and universally any organisation understands its need for change.

MEANINGS MATTER

The meanings that individuals place on work or home stem, variously, from values relating to attendance, commuting, career perspective, and domestic aspirations, roles and responsibilities and concerns for 'time sovereignty'. Importantly, having choices over these issues influences judgements of how autonomous and trusted employees feel [8]. The case of 'home working' illustrates this well; employees given this choice may see it as an important benefit for themselves and for their organisation, since they may feel that they work better from home on some tasks. Alternatively, less supportive managers may question whether people working from home are working at all or whether their productivity can be compared to those who can be seen at their desks. Deciding on the best course of action regarding individual attendance seems best completed by addressing mutual needs of employees and employers for control, status, connection and challenge.

Different meanings and values also accompany absence and performance. Perceiving organisational over-attention to absence may convey to employees a sense that their behaviour is seen as a wilful undermining of corporate culture, even though it may be explained by, say, providing unexpected care for a dependant. Further, this attention may signal misguided organisational energy since up to 43% of lost days are attributable to as few as 6% of employees [9]. This explains why recent UK government initiatives have shifted employers' attention to long-term absence. Recent data also suggest that more attention should be paid to the predictive nature of absence and to identify those groups with increased health risk and a need for targeted interventions. Among UK employees, major diagnoses for medically certified absences (one or more absence of 7 or more days - over three-years) were associated with increased mortality, excepting those certified for musculoskeletal disease [10]. Another concern is that sickness while working (presenteeism) justifies, but still fails to command, far closer attention. One international review [11] estimated that, on average, 2% of lost productivity costs were attributed to absenteeism compared to 63% for presenteeism.

Attention should also fall on the lost productivity resulting from the inter-employee behaviours that sustain perceptions of exclusion, injustice or inequality.

These behaviours may have their end in employee disengagement which, under the mantra that 'emotions are contagious', ripples outwards to further denude workplace morale. What seems increasingly clear is that as essential resources become less available, individual and collective behaviours assume greater impact. In 2002, disengagement was reported by up to 80% of UK employees (approximately 27 million), at an estimated annual cost to the economy of up to £37.2 billion [12] (equivalent to US$64.8 billion). These data highlight why so many UK employers are seeking positive reform and poses a core question, 'From what *exactly* are these employees disengaging?' Paradoxically, the 20% of employees who are actively engaged may have a lifestyle that, instead of sustaining high quality performance, ends up compromising their w-l-b. The juxtaposition of (few) engaged and (many) disengaged employees inside the same organisation highlights why 'top down' and 'bottom up' approaches are combined within w-l-b policies.

UK data [13] suggest that lost w-l-b is especially common among middle managers, whose effort levels indicate high engagement, but who feel trapped by influences from 'above' and 'below'. Indeed, just as Geithner et al. note that the US may be the 'no vacation nation', in the UK the workday of male and female middle managers has expanded so that they now contribute the equivalent of over 40 unpaid days/year [13]. Among trades union members the 'long-hours culture' affected 12.3% and 12.8% in 2007 and 2008, respectively [14]. Worse, the time dedicated to extra working uses time that they would otherwise dedicate to rest and restoration, including engagement with hobbies or spending more time with families and friends [13].

POSITIVE EMOTIONS ARE IMPORTANT

Increasingly, emotions are seen as central to employee well-being and to the most effective workplace behaviour. Further, *frequent* emotional experiences are now seen as having a greater impact on job satisfaction than peaks and troughs, which highlights the importance of efficient processes. Persistent work life *conflict* is linked to low job and life satisfaction, alcohol misuse, reduced sense of personal accomplishment and depersonalisation [15]. Inasmuch as any conflict may be harmful in itself, the contributing elements each have a negative emotional origin. An important theoretical issue in emotional well-being is that just as it is wrong to conflate the absence of stress with well-being, neither should we conflate positive emotions with negative emotions, since the absence of one does not automatically signal the presence of the other [16].

In this understanding, stress is a strongly negative emotion and work is seen as a major causal agent. In the 2006/07 UK survey of self-reported work-related illness [17] around 530,000 individuals reported experiencing work-related stress illness. Their average time off was 30.2 days/case, accounting for almost one third of illness-related lost days. In 2007 [18] and 2008 [19] 13.6% and 17.1% of employees, respectively, thought their job was either 'very' or 'extremely' stressful. Teachers, nurses, and professional and managerial groups in the public sector reported the greatest proportions of highly stressed workers. Five factors made these issues more common: (i) higher workloads, (ii) more tight work deadlines, (iii) lack of colleague support, (iv) being attacked, and (v) feeling a physical threat.

Refuting the over-attention implicit to micro-management, Geithner et al. note that leading US companies, like IBM, are no longer recording days taken for holidays.

However, for many organisations this requires a level of inter-personal trust that has yet to be established. UK figures for disengagement suggest that emotional dissatisfaction – reciprocated between managers and employees – remains a fundamental problem [13]. This places a high priority on the emotions related to work and to what sociologists describe as the 'feeling rules' [20]. There have been other shifts in 'rules' too, each with obvious emotional impact. For example, in the best modern workplaces, violation rules are increasingly replaced by mutuality practices; over-concerns for consistency have been replaced by attending to specialisation and removing redundant practice.

The bedrock of this emotional perspective is that relationships hold the potential for human development, functioning and change. Workplace studies [21] show that when organisations focus on relationships, they build zest, empower action, build individuals' sense of self-worth, create new understandings and generate a stronger desire to collaborate with strangers. Emotionally-connected language includes words like trust, satisfaction, energy, achievement, fun, creativity, forgiveness, fulfilment, sharing and honesty and these are all housed within the Broaden and Build Theory of Emotions [22, 23].

A central tenet of this theory is that humans are healthiest and perform best when they experience more positive than negative emotions. Positive emotions generate creativity, inventiveness and open-mindedness, all of which enhance problem-solving [24]. These characteristics are as crucial in post-technological workplaces as they are in manual and locally based employment settings. Indeed, the growing prominence of this theory is based on the evidence linking positive emotional states with positive decision-making, learning, motivation and employee engagement [15]. Meanwhile, researchers from USA and UK have combined to operationalize this theory. They showed that average improvements of 21.3% were achieved among employees who focused on positive emotions by identifying and regularly using their personality strengths [25].

Still other theoretical approaches focus on the emotional importance of how employees perceive the workplace. UK data [26-29] confirm that when employees perceive that their workplaces are characterised by 'high effort' plus 'low reward' (which expresses a failed contractual reciprocity in terms of esteem, money and career opportunities, including job security) they elicit recurrent negative emotions and sustained stress responses. These sustained responses can end in serious physical and mental health problems, meaning that these perceptions can be important markers of the need for change. Conversely, the positive emotions evoked by appropriate social rewards promote well-being, health and survival. In an international review of 45 empirical studies [30], the risks of the high effort-low reward environments were accentuated by also perceiving a culture of over-commitment (which may be evidenced by long working hours, not taking holidays and seemingly endless workloads).

RESPONDING IN THE WORKPLACE

Both internal and external factors determine individual approaches to reducing conflict and restoring balance. Notwithstanding the pre-eminence of data derived from reactive rather than preventive interventions, existing literature shows only limited successes of workplace interventions. This questions return on investment [23] and issues a serious challenge to researchers. Further, there is a lack of empirical evidence about transferring laboratory-derived evidence to the dynamism of working life. Neither can researchers make substantive claims for the relative efficacy of programme content (e.g., whether exercising is any better than, say, relaxation, meditation or diet change, for restoring life balance), or for the impact of sequences of interventions.

Perhaps for these reasons, a more convincing case might be made for changes beginning with the individual [31]. Individualised approaches can reflect the span of perception and personal preferences for tolerance, resistance, avoidance or resolution to capitalise on elements of personal coping style [32-34]. Furthermore, individuals who demonstrate resilience, hardiness, self determination or assertiveness may attach differently to work or home, suggesting distinctive needs [35]. A number of studies now show the specific challenges within especially stressful workplaces [36, 37].

The perception of the workplace is as important as the reality in determining not only the psychological health of the individual, but also of the workplace. Individuals may variously seek either changes in organisational processes and managerial support, or undertake personal avoidance behaviours to manage risk of conflict. This, presumably, reflects how they understand the emergence of any specific problems they may be experiencing or witnessing. Recently, the six Health and Safety Executive (HSE) workplace standards (psychosocial working conditions of Demand, Control, Managerial Support, Peer Support, Role, Relationships and Change) were introduced to help organisations to assess and then improve their psychological healthiness [16-18]. These may be useful in motivating those whose political perspectives may reject the idea that w-l-b should be based on individual behaviour change. They may readily reject offers of gym sessions, or individual coaching, seeing them as 'victimising the victim'. Just as some will achieve better w-l-b through subsidised swimming or access to Indian head massage, others profit from having opportunities to enact changes in company practices and systems.

CONCLUSION

While many UK companies and organisations endorse w-l-b for their employees, establishing effective and sustainable interventions represents an on-going challenge. Not only is there is a need to continue highlighting what individuals can do to help themselves, but also there is an urgent need to consider how whole organisations can be encouraged to make profound and meaningful changes. Although we can point to a strengthening evidence-base that links work-base emotions and experiences to changes in health and well-being, so far it has been insufficiently relevant or convincing to establish committed action in many workplaces.

REFERENCES

1.   Caproni, P.J., Work/Life Balance: You Can't Get There From Here, *Journal of Applied Behavioural Science*, 2004, 40, 208-218

2.   Jones, A., *About Time for Change*, The Work Foundation, 2008.

3.   Bryson, L., Warner-Smith, P., Brown, P. and Fray, L., Managing the Work-Life Roller-Coaster: Private Stress or Public Health Issue? *Social Science and Medicine*, 2007, 65, 1142-1153.

Creating An Environment Where High Performance Is Inevitable and Sustainable: The High Performance Environment Model

Graham Jones[1], Mark Gittins[2], and Lew Hardy[3]

[1]Lane4 Management Group,
10 Wall St, Princeton, NJ 08540, USA,
E-mail: graham.jones@lane4.co.uk
[2]Lane4 Management Group,
St Marks House, Station Rd,
Bourne End, Bucks, SL8 5QF
E-mail: mark.gittins@lane4.co.uk
[3]School of Sport, Health & Exercise Sciences,
University of Wales, Bangor,George Building,
Holyhead Rd, Bangor, Gwynedd, LL57 2PX,
E-mail: l.hardy@bangor.ac.uk

ABSTRACT

This article presents a model of the psychological and social factors within a performance environment which impact upon organisational performance. A review of the organisational and performance psychology literatures was conducted to identify variables associated with sustainable high performance at the individual, group and organisational levels. The resultant variables were conceptualised within the areas of 'leadership', 'performance enablers', 'people', and 'organisational climate' to form the core components of the High Performance Environment (HPE) Model. The model (a) provides researchers, practitioners, and leaders with a view of the key areas to focus on to create and sustain high performance in organisations, and (b) encourages them to consider performance environments holistically, rather than considering specific variables in isolation.

Key words: Attitudes, Competing Values Theory, High Performance Environment Model, Organisational Climate, Performance Enablers, Transformational Leadership

Reviewer: Jim McKenna (Leeds Metropolitan University, UK)

INTRODUCTION

Our combined experience of consulting in the performance arenas of sport, business and the military has led to the conclusion that our impact on helping individuals and teams develop is maximised when we are also able to affect the environment they operate in. The majority of interventions and research in performance psychology has focussed on the individual and the team with the result that the performance environment has often been overlooked or factored out. Business organisations, for example, often attribute their success to having great people, rather than the environment these people perform in. However, people do not perform in a vacuum, and our contention is that the performance environment the organisation creates is just as important as the people performing in it.

Currently, there is no validated model which links the performance environment to high performance. The aim of this article is to address high performance from a contextual viewpoint and to identify the key psychological and social factors which impact upon organisational performance. There are clear benefits of such a model to practitioners in any performance domain. Firstly, the model provides a list of important variables to consider in performance development work. Secondly, the model shows the relationship between these variables. This will encourage practitioners to consider performance environments as a whole, rather than considering specific variables in isolation.

THE HIGH PERFORMANCE ENVIRONMENT (HPE) MODEL

The constructs comprising the HPE Model were identified from a review of the organisational performance literature in which business, sport and military domains figured prominently. The model was specifically developed to be applicable across these performance domains, and as such, transferability between them was an important consideration at all times during the development of the model. The development of the model was a challenging task because of the inherent complexity and number of factors at play and involved a number of iterations. It was important that all of the constructs included had either been shown to be associated with organisational performance, or associated with other factors which have been.

The HPE Model shown in Figure 1 comprises *leadership*, *performance enablers*, and *people* factors, represented within three concentric circles, and organisational climate, represented by four boxes containing achievement, wellbeing, innovation, and internal processes.

In development of the model, high performance was defined as performance which is consistently higher than that of the majority of peer organisations in the same sector, and over a prolonged time period. This definition views high performance as (a) consistent and sustainable, and (b) relative to, and affected by, the performance of other organisations. The latter is important because organisations are often described as 'succeeding or failing on the merits of their actions alone, as if performance was absolute' rather than relative [1, p. 112]. Instead, there are determinants of performance which organisations are not able to control; there are no guaranteed blueprints or formulae for organisational success. The aim of the HPE Model is to detail the predictors of organisational performance, which organisations are able to control and influence.

Leadership sits at the core of the model and is hypothesised to interact with *performance enablers* to impact on the *people* variables. In turn, people's attitudes and behaviours are hypothesised to interact with the organisational climate to impact on organisational performance. In addition to this uni-directional relationship radiating outwards from the centre of the model, we hypothesise that there will also be reciprocal relationships; e.g., follower behaviours influence leader behaviours, as well as various moderating and mediating relationships; e.g., follower attitudes to mediate the relationships between leadership behaviours and follower behaviours.

For the practitioner, the number of potential relationships between variables means that the HPE model should be viewed as a system in which variables operate in feedback loops, rather than in one-way, cause-and-effect relationships. Practitioners should be aware, therefore, that they cannot address a specific variable within the model without also having a wider impact on other variables within the performance environment.

The variables within each of the HPE Model components were identified by means of a systematic review of a number of literatures, that can be loosely termed under 'performance psychology', for variables associated with high performance at the individual, group and organisational levels.

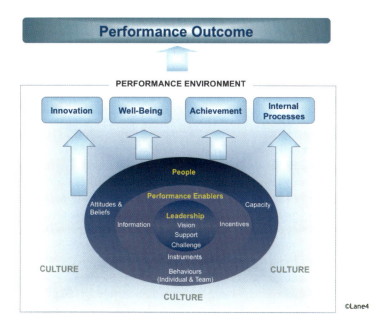

Figure 1. High Performance Environment Model

LEADERSHIP

Leadership has been defined as a process whereby an individual influences a group of individuals to achieve a common goal [2]. The leadership research literature has contrasted two types of leadership - transformational and transactional. Transactional leadership involves gaining compliance through contingent reward and punishment, and management-by-exception. Transformational leadership involves offering followers a purpose that transcends short-term goals and focuses on higher order intrinsic needs, such that followers are motivated to go beyond their self-interest to achieve performance beyond expectations [3].

Within a high performance environment, the authors contend that the role of a leader is to create the conditions in which their followers will excel and fulfil their potential. As such, the goal of leaders in high-performance environments is to minimise the constraints and maximise the supports available. Transformational leadership meets these criteria, with a large body of research demonstrating its effectiveness. This literature suggests that followers of transformational leaders would be likely to report high levels of job satisfaction [4, 5], trust in their leader [6, 7], motivation and empowerment [8], and self-efficacy [9]. Furthermore, they would be likely to feel cohesive as a group [10], and to show high levels of performance individually [11, 12] in their teams [13], and business units [14].

Podsakoff et al. [15] conceptualised transformational leaders as identifying and articulating a vision of the future; being good role models; expecting high levels of performance; promoting co-operation and teamwork toward a common goal; showing respect for their followers and being concerned about their personal feelings and needs; and enhancing their interest in and awareness of problems such that they are able to think about them in new ways. In addition to these six transformational behaviours, Podsakoff et al. [15] included one transactional leadership behaviour - contingent reward - referring to the extent to which leaders reward followers for attaining specified performance levels. These behaviours predicted employees' extra role behaviours; i.e., the extent to which employees went beyond their role requirements for the benefit of the organisation.The effects of these transformational leadership behaviours were mediated by the employee attitudes of job satisfaction, organisational commitment, and trust in and loyalty to the leader.

We hypothesise that Podsakoff et al.'s [15] seven leadership behaviours exert their influence on followers through the provision of three 'macro-behaviours'; specifically, vision, support, and challenge. This representation of transformational leadership as the provision of vision, support, and challenge was first developed as a consultancy model for use in a military setting to simplify transformational leadership theory for section commanders in the early stages of an intervention [16]. We further hypothesise that high levels of all three of vision, support, and challenge are required to create an environment where high performance is inevitable and sustainable. For example, a performance environment in which levels of challenge are high in comparison to levels of support is likely to be stressful and lead to performer burnout. In contrast, high levels of vision and support with low levels of challenge may well be an enjoyable and motivating place to work, but may be too cosy and comfortable for really high levels of performance to occur.

PERFORMANCE ENABLERS

In addition to providing performers with vision, support, and challenge, transformational leadership behaviours also exert their effects through interacting with a number of situational variables [17]. These variables have been investigated in a number of separate streams of research, including job characteristics, substitutes-for-leadership, and the work-design literatures. We have amalgamated these work streams under the heading of 'performance enablers' [18], which we have defined as environmental supports required by people to operate effectively in any performance environment. We have categorised these under 'information', 'instruments', and 'incentives'.

It is widely agreed that individuals need a certain amount of *information* to perform their roles effectively. Performers benefit from clear goals which are specific, appropriately stretching and which they are actively involved in setting, or at least accept [19]. Performers also need information on their role responsibilities, including their scope of responsibilities, the behaviours required to fulfil these responsibilities, and the way in which their role is evaluated, in order to give them a sense of structure in their performance environment [20]. While goals and role clarity provide performers with direction and structure, individuals also benefit both from developmental feedback which helps them to learn, develop, and make improvements [21], and social support, which comprises a variety of resources, such as task-relevant information and praise, which assist them [22].

In addition to the provision of information, people also need to be equipped with the right *instruments* to help them perform their jobs effectively. Within the HPE Model, instruments have been grouped into the *physical* instruments of tools, technology and equipment, *knowledge-related* instruments such as training and development, and the *structural* instruments of communication networks, and the way teams are structured. Whilst some of these variables are not psychosocial, like others in the HPE Model, our contention is that they play an important role in any performance environment.

Finally, the provision of *incentives* ensures that people are motivated to perform to the best of their ability. Self-Determination Theory suggests that a wide variety of motivators can be grouped based on individuals' desire to satisfy their basic psychological needs of competence, autonomy, and relatedness [23]. According to this perspective, leaders need to create a motivational climate in which people feel competent at a given task or activity, have an appropriate level of autonomy to choose how they carry out that activity, and to feel a sense of connectedness to others. These needs can be met through the provision of a number of variables including: motivational feedback in the form of social recognition such as praise, attention and appreciation for good work provided contingently [24], opportunities to further one's career [25], participation in decision-making [26], a high-quality relationship with one's leader [27], and work which is viewed as meaningful in relation to one's own ideals or standards [28]. Monetary reward has been shown to attract, motivate and retain people as well as to positively impact individual [29] and business unit [30] performance. However, if contingent on performance, pay and bonuses can also induce controlled motivation which inhibits the satisfaction of competence, autonomy, and relatedness [31].

PEOPLE

The transformational leadership behaviours and performance enablers described above have been shown to be positively associated with a number of desirable attitudinal and behavioural outcome variables. In the *people* section of the HPE Model, we have grouped these variables under the headings of 'attitudes', 'behaviours', and 'capacity'.

With regard to attitudes, trust in one's leader is one of the main reasons individuals are motivated by transformational leadership to perform beyond expectations [32]. Individuals with high levels of trust in their leader have been shown to perform to a high level and to report higher job satisfaction and organisational commitment [33]. In turn, organisational commitment has been shown to be associated with higher levels of effort at work [34] and increased feelings of comfort and personal competence [35]; whilst job satisfaction has been shown to be positively associated with levels of performance [36]. Also associated with higher levels of performance, is the values fit between individuals and the organisation [37].

In addition to *individual* attitudes, one of the most important characteristics of transformational leadership is that it predicts the collective efficacy of *groups* and *teams* [38]. Collective efficacy reflects the shared beliefs of group members in their group's capabilities [39]. In addition to reporting higher levels of job satisfaction and organisational commitment [40], groups high in collective efficacy are more likely to expend effort on tasks and to show persistence in the face of problems [41], and to perform to high levels in a variety of settings [42].

The attitudinal variables described above play an important role in mediating the relationship between transformational leadership and follower *behaviours*. Specifically, followers of transformational leaders have been shown to go beyond their role requirements for the benefit of the organisation; e.g., helping colleagues from other teams, and participating voluntarily in work groups and meetings across the organisation [43]. In a high performance environment, one would also expect people to demonstrate high levels of engagement with their roles, characterised by high levels of energy, dedication, and absorption in their day-to-day work [44]. Furthermore, one would expect teams to co-operate with each other on tasks, co-ordinate these tasks so that they run smoothly, and communicate effectively. All of these team behaviours have been associated with team effectiveness [45].

While attitudes and behaviour are crucial determinants of performance, organisations need people with sufficient ability or *capacity* to do their job. It is for this reason that organisations invest in the areas of talent assessment and talent management; to ensure that they attract, develop, and retain individuals with the right skills and abilities. Naturally, these skills and abilities include technical skills and knowledge specific to the role. Yet, in addition, there is also literature showing the importance of emotional intelligence- - the ability to perceive, understand, and regulate emotions [46] - and mental toughness [47] - the ability to consistently perform to high standards through times of personal and professional pressure [48].

ORGANISATIONAL CLIMATE

The areas of the HPE Model described above focus on individuals and teams within a performance environment. However, the perception that individuals have of their organisation as a whole - otherwise known as the 'organisational climate' - is also an important predictor of performance [49]. For example, Quinn and Rohrbaugh's Competing Values Theory suggests that organisational performance can be partly explained by the extent to which organisations balance their focus on 4 values, which Quinn and Rohrbaugh originally termed as: 1) a rational goal approach; 2) a human relations approach; 3) an open systems approach; and 4) an internal process approach. To simplify, we have re-labelled these values respectively as: 1) *Achievement* - an emphasis on productivity and goal achievement; 2) *Wellbeing* - an emphasis on the development of people within the organisation; 3) *Innovation* - an emphasis on creativity; and 4) *Internal Processes* - an emphasis on formalisation and internal control of systems and procedures [50]. A research study which followed 67 U.K. manufacturing organisations over a 10-year period found that these four climate factors accounted for a total of 29% of the variation in productivity and 10% in the variation in profitability of the organisations measured [51]. Interestingly, a focus on wellbeing was shown to be the most significant predictor of productivity and profitability.

Competing Values Theory suggests that the four values of achievement, wellbeing, innovation and internal processes compete with each other for focus, therefore providing tensions for organisations to manage. Consequently, one would expect an organisation with an excessive focus on achievement to also have low wellbeing due to burnout. By contrast, an organisation with an excessive focus on internal processes and procedures might report stifled innovation and creativity. Organisations from different industry sectors are also likely to prioritise different values. For example, a pharmaceutical company is likely to focus more on innovation, an investment bank may be very achievement orientated, while a focus on internal processes may be most prevalent in a public sector organisation. Overall, the four values provide a useful framework for the practitioner to explore an organisation's current balance of focus and compare this to their aspired balance of focus. This framework can also be used to set goals within each of the four values, forming a balanced scorecard and a framework for performance management.

DEVELOPING HIGH PERFORMANCE ENVIRONMENTS: APPLYING THE HPE MODEL

The HPE Model has now been applied by Lane4 in the development of teams and organisations, from sectors as diverse as management consulting, aviation, holiday and leisure, legal, IT services, investment banking, engineering and construction, and retail. To supplement the HPE model, a diagnostic has been developed - the HPE Scan - to measure the constructs within the model. The HPE model and scan have been used for a variety of purposes, including the assessment of perceptions of employees involved in mergers and acquisitions, as a framework to develop a people development strategy, to benchmark against competitors, to address under-performance, to understand intra-organisational performance discrepancies, and to demonstrate organisational health in order to secure financial investment.

An example of how the HPE Scan has been used to better understand intra-organisational discrepancies, was Lane4's work with a global car manufacturer. This organisation was concerned with the disparity in performance levels between their UK car dealerships. To develop greater consistency in performance between dealerships, the challenge was for Lane4 to identify the key factors that underpinned their high performing dealerships so that lower performing dealerships could gain greater clarity on how to become high performing.

In this study, 143 dealerships completed the HPE scan, providing 1741 completed scans. Each dealership was then graded 'A', 'B' or 'C' in accordance with how well it scored on the HPE Scan. The data collected was then used to analyse the relationship between dealerships scores on the HPE Scan and their performance on seven Key Performance Indicators. Specifically, the aim was to identify the key predictors of performance for a car dealership.

The results showed that there was a significant relationship between the dealerships' performance environment and their KPI performance; i.e., the dealerships graded 'A' on the HPE Scan were ranked significantly higher on their KPI's than those graded as 'B' dealerships, while 'B' dealerships were ranked significantly higher on their KPI's than 'C' dealerships.

Overall, while the performance environments of Lane4's clients have shown a variety of profiles, a number of themes have emerged. Analysis of the HPE Scan data has shown that several key factors in the HPE Model differentiate high and low performing organisations. Firstly, all of the leadership behaviours included in the model discriminate between the high and low performing organisations except 'high performance expectations'. In explanation, it seems likely that leaders in all organisations insist on the best possible performance from their employees. However, in terms of performance enablers, a few factors have been shown to be key peformance differentiators. These are the extent to which organisations provide employees with autonomy, motivational feedback, advice when things are not going well, and well defined goals. In the 'people' section of the model, high and low performing organisations are differentiated by peoples' dedication to their work, trust in their leader, belief in the organisation's values, and collective efficacy. In summary, these findings provide organisations and organisation development practitioners with key areas of focus in order to maximise performance.

CONCLUSION

This article presents a model of a performance environment where high performance is inevitable and sustainable. For the practitioner, the model can be used to assess the current strengths and weaknesses of any performance environment, and identify strategies for improvement. From a theoretical perspective, the development of this model addresses the criticism that organisational psychology studies have tended to examine either: (a) only how specific aspects of the performance environment influence performance, or (b) a multitude of variables without theoretically linking them together.

Furthermore, the model provides a means of objectively assessing predictors of organisational performance. Indeed, data collected using the HPE Scan from a number of business organisations has demonstrated impressive predictive validity of the model to date. Further work continues to be undertaken to test the structural validity of the model using confirmatory factor analysis.

The HPE Model provides a valuable tool for diagnosing areas of strength and development requirements within organisations. Its holistic perspective enables leaders facing a myriad of seemingly unrelated issues, to piece them together in a way that drives a coordinated approach to developing their whole organisation.

ACKNOWLEDGEMENT

This research was funded by Knowledge Transfer Partnerships (KTP), a government-funded programme to help businesses to improve their competitiveness and productivity through the better use of knowledge, technology and skills that reside within the UK knowledge base. There are over a thousand KTP projects running at any one time; this collaboration between Lane4 Management Group and University of Wales, Bangor won one of nine best project awards in 2007.

Lane4 is a professional services firm working in the fields of organisational change, leadership development, and executive coaching. With a unique heritage drawn from elite sporting and commercial achievement, Lane4 consultants help businesses to excel through the engagement and development of their people. Lane4 has offices in Europe, the US, and Asia Pacific, and works with business and HR leaders to improve organisational performance.

REFERENCES

1. Rosenweig, P.M., *The Halo Effect...and the Eight Other Business Delusions that Deceive Managers*, Free Press, New York, 2007.

2. Northouse, P.G., *Leadership: Theory and Practice*, 3rd edn., Sage Publications Inc, Thousand Oaks, CA, 2004.

3. Bass, B., *Leadership and Performance Beyond Expectations*, The Free Press, New York, 1985.

4. Berson, Y. and Linton, J.D., An Examination of the Relationships Between Leadership Style, Quality, and Employee Satisfaction in R&D Versus Administrative Environments, *R&D Management,* 2005, 35(1), 55-60.

5. Bono, J.E. and Judge, T.A., Core Self-Evaluations: A Review of the Trait and its Role in Job Satisfaction and Job Performance, *European Journal of Personality*, 2003, 17, 5-18.

6. Bass, B. M., *Transformational Leadership: Industry, Military, and Educational Impact*, Erlbaum, Mahwah, NJ, 1998.

7. Nemanich, L.A. and Keller, R.T., Transformational Leadership in an Acquisition: A Field Study of Employees, *The Leadership Quarterly*, 2007, 18, 49-68.

8. Dvir, T., Eden, D., Avolio, B. J. and Shamir, B., Impact of Transformational Leadership on Follower Development and Performance: A Field Experiment, *Academy of Management Journal,* 2002, 45(4), 735-744.

9. Rafferty, A. E. and Griffin, M. A., Dimensions of Transformational Leadership: Conceptual and Empirical Extensions, *The Leadership Quarterly*, 2004, 15, 329-354.

10. Bass, B.M., Avolio, B.J., Jung, D.I. and Berson, Y., Predicting Unit Performance by Assessing Transformational and Transactional Leadership, *Journal of Applied Psychology*, 2003, 88(2), 207-218.

11. Barling, J.,Weber, T. and Kelloway, E.K., Effects of Transformational Leadership Training on Attitudinal and Financial Outcomes: A Field Experiment, *Journal of Applied Psychology*, 1996, 81(6), 827-832.

12. Whittington, J.L., Goodwin, V.L. and Murray, B.,Transformational Leadership, Goal Difficulty, and Job Design: Independent and Interactive Effects on Employee Outcomes, *The Leadership Quarterly,* 2004, 15(5), 593-606.

13. Keller, R.T., Transformational Leadership, Initiating Structure, and Substitutes for Leadership: A Longitudinal Study of Research and Development Project Team Performance, *Journal of Applied Psychology*, 2006, 91(1), 202-10.

14. Howell, J. M. and Avolio, B. J., Transformational Leadership, Transactional Leadership, Locus of Control, and Support for Innovation: Key Predictors of Consolidated Business-Unit Performance, *Journal of Applied Psychology*, 1993, 78, 891-902.

15.   Podsakoff, P. M., MacKenzie, R., H., Moorman, R. H. and Fetter, R., Transformational Leader Behaviours and their Effects on Followers' Trust in Leader, Satisfaction, and Organisational Citizenship Behaviours, *The Leadership Quarterly*, 1990, 1(2) 107-142.

16.   Hardy, L., Arthur, C.A., Jones, G., Shariff, A., Munnoch, K., Isaacs, I. and Allsop, A.J., A Correlational and an Experimental Study Examining the Sub-Components of Transformational Leadership, *The Leadership Quarterly*, In Press.

17.   Podsakoff, P. M., MacKenzie, S. B. and Bommer, W. H., Transformational Leadership Behaviours and their Effects on Followers' Trust in Leader, Satisfaction, and Organisational Citizenship Behaviours, *Journal of Management*, 1996, 22(2), 259-298.

18.   Gilbert, T.F., *Human Competence: Engineering Worthy Performance*, McGraw-Hill, New York, 1978.

19.   Locke, E. A. and Latham, G. P., *A Theory of Goal Setting and Task Performance*, Prentice-Hall, Englewood Cliffs, NJ, 1990.

20.   Beauchamp, M. R., Bray, S. R., Eys, M.A., and Carron, A.V., Role Ambiguity, Role Efficacy, and Role Performance: Multidimensional and Mediational Relationships within Interdependent Sport Teams, *Group Dynamics: Theory, Research, and Practice*, 2002, 6, 229-242.

21.   Zhou, J., When the Presence of Creative Coworkers is Related to Creativity: Role of Supervisor Close Monitoring, Developmental Feedback, and Creative Personality. *Journal of Applied Psychology*, 2003, 88(3), 413–422.

22.   Cutrona, C.E. and Russell, D.W., Type of Social Support and Specific Stress: Toward a Theory of Optimal Matching, in: Sarason, B.R., Sarason, I.G. and Pierce, G.R., eds., *Social Support: An Interactional View*, Wiley, New York, 1990, 319-366.

23.   Deci, E.L. and Ryan, R.M., *Intrinsic Motivation and Self-Determination in Human Behaviour*, Plenum, New York, 1985.

24.   Stajkovic, A. D. and Luthans, F., Behavioral Management and Task Performance in Organizations: Conceptual Background, Meta-Analysis, and Test of Alternative Models, *Personnel Psychology*, 2002, 56, 155–194.

25.   London, M., Relationships Between Career Motivation, Empowerment and Support for Career Development, *Journal of Occupational and Organizational Psychology*, 1993, 66(1), 55-69.

26.   Bakan, I., Suseno, Y., Pinnington, A. and Money, A., The Influence of Financial Participation and Participation in Decision-Making on Employee Job Attitudes, *International Journal of Human Resource Management*, 2004, 15(3), 587-616.

27.   Greguras, G.J. and Ford, J.M., An Examination of the Multidimensionality of Supervisor and Subordinate Perceptions of Leader-Member Exchange, *Journal of Occupational and Organisational Psychology*, 2006, 79, 433-465.

28.   May, D.R., Gilson, R.L. and Harter, L.M., The Psychological Conditions of Meaningfulness, Safety and Availability and the Engagement of the Human Spirit at Work, *Journal of Occupational and Organizational Psychology*, 2004, 77, 11-37.

29.   Stajkovic, A. D. and Luthans, F., A Meta-Analysis of the Effects of Organizational Behavior Modification on Task Performance, 1975–1995, *Academy of Management Journal*, 1997, 40, 1122–1149.

30.   Peterson, S.J. and Luthans, F., The Impact of Financial and Non-Financial Incentives on Business-Unit Outcomes Over Time, *Journal of Applied Psychology*, 2006, 91(1), 156-65.

31.   Deci, E.L., Koestner, R. and Ryan, R.M., A Meta-Analytic Review of Experiments Examining the Effects of Extrinsic Rewards on Intrinsic Motivation, *Psychological Bulletin*, 1999, 125, 627-668.

32.   Yukl, G., An Evaluation of Conceptual Weakness in Transformational and Charismatic Leadership Theories, *The Leadership Quarterly*, 1999, 10, 285–305.

33.   Dirks, K.T. and Ferrin, D.L., Trust in Leadership: Meta-Analytic Findings and Implications for Research and Practice, *Journal of Applied Psychology*, 2002, 87, 611-628.

34. Stroh, L. K. and Reilly, A. H., Loyalty in the Age of Downsizing, *Human Resource Management and Industrial Relations*, 1997, 38(4), 83-88.

35. Allen, N. J. and Meyer, J. P., The Measurement and Antecedents of Affective, Continuance and Normative Commitment to the Organization, *Journal of Occupational Psychology*, 1990, 63, 1-18.

36. Judge, T. A., Thoresen, C. J., Bono, J. E. and Patton, G. K., The Job Satisfaction-Job Performance Relationship: A Qualitative and Quantitative Review, *Psychological Bulletin*, 2001, 127(3), 376-407.

37. Kristof, A., Person-Organization Fit: An Integrative Review of its Conceptualizations, Measurement, and Implications, *Personnel Psychology*, 1996, 49(2), 1-49.

38. Shamir, B., Calculations, Values, and Identities: The Sources of Collectivistic Work Motivation, *Human Relations*, 1990, 43(4), 313-332.

39. Gibson, C. B., The Efficacy Advantage: Factors Related to the Formation of Group Efficacy, *Journal of Applied Social Psychology*, 2003, 33, 2153-2186.

40. Jex, S. M. and Bliese, P. D., Efficacy Beliefs as a Moderator of the Impact of Work-Related Stressors: A Multilevel Study, *Journal of Applied Psychology*, 1999, 84, 349–361.

41. Bandura, A., Exercise of Human Agency Through Collective Efficacy, *Current Directions in Psychological Science*, 2000, *9,* 75-78.

42. Stewart, G. L. and Barrick, M. R., Team Structure and Performance: Assessing the Mediating Role of Intrateam Process and the Moderating Role of Task Type, *Academy of Management Journal*, 2000, 43, 135-148.

43. Podsakoff, P., Ahearne, M. and MacKenzie, S., Organizational Citizenship Behavior and the Quantity and Quality of Work Group Performance, *Journal of Applied Psychology*, 1997, 82(2), 262-270.

44. Schaufeli, W. B., Salanova, M., Gonzales-Roma, V. and Bakker, A. B., The Measurement of Engagement and Burnout: A Two Sample Confirmatory Factor Analytic Approach, *Journal of Happiness Studies*, 2002, 3, 71–92.

45. Campion, M.A., Papper, E.M. and Medsker, G., Relations Between Work Team Characteristics and Effectiveness: A Replication and Extension, *Personnel Psychology*, 1996, 49(2), 429-52.

46. Mayer, J. D., Salovey, P. and Caruso, D. R., Emotional Intelligence: Theory, Findings, and Implications, *Psychological Inquiry*, 2004, 15(3) 197-215 .

47. Jones, J.G. and Moorhouse, A., *Developing Mental Toughness: Gold Medal Strategies for Transforming Your Business Performance*, 2nd edn., Spring Hill, Oxford, 2008.

48. Jones, J. G., Hanton, S. and Connaughton, D., What is This Thing Called Mental Toughness? An Investigation of Elite Performers, *Journal of Applied Sport Psychology*, 2002, 14, 205-218.

49. Denison, D. R., *Corporate Culture and Organisational Effectiveness*, John Wiley and Sons, New York, NY, 1990.

50. Quinn, R. E. and Rohrbaugh, J., A Competing Values Approach to Organisational Effectiveness, *Public Productivity Review,* 1981, 5, 122-140.

51. Patterson, M. G., West, M.A., Lawthom, R. and Nickell, S., *Impact of People Management Practices on Business Performance*, Institute of Personnel and Development, London, 1997.

Creating an Environment Where High Performance is Inevitable and Sustainable: The High Performance Environment Model:

A Commentary

Jim McKenna
Carnegie Research Institute
Leeds Metropolitan University, Leeds, LS6 3QS, UK
E-mail: J.McKenna@leedsmet.ac.uk

INTRODUCTION

For me, environmental and personal factors are broadly inseparable, although I fully endorse identifying factors of the high performance environment. Jones et al. provide an important reference point on which to build new understanding about *what* contributes to high performance; attention now needs to fall on *how* to build them.

Notwithstanding my enthusiasm for this work, my main caveat is that while having the right 'things' in place is important, high performance hinges more on blending things with practices that build appropriate personal meaning (*aka* subjectivity). Indeed, the most recent estimate of UK university research performance [1], which provides a framework for this commentary, afforded research 'environment' a weighting of less than 20% in determining an overall research grading. Indeed, in what amounts to window-dressing, Guest [2] recently noted that work-life balance interventions may be cynically introduced in the knowledge that they can never influence problematic routines and practices. What follows mostly relates to the three concentric circles in the model, described as Leadership, Performance Enablers and People.

Recent publications relating to UK university performance (even allowing for their respective philosophical and methodological shortcomings) help to emphasise four core themes. These reports represent concurrent data that not only spans the sector, but also shows profiles of the respective performance environments across and within UK universities. They are (i) the world's top 200 universities 2008 [3]; (ii) the 2008 UK Research Assessment Exercise (RAE) [1]; and (iii) the 'Stress in Higher Education' report [4], from 9,740 UK university employees in 100+ organisations.

CONSIDER TIME

Any such model needs to consider 'time' [5], whether this means speed, duration, timing and/or sequence. Few leaders of the UK's world-level universities appear to believe that their research infrastructure and reputation was built quickly [6]. Therefore, it is important to consider how long groups have been high performing. Trajectory, which reflects levels and cycles of investment, creates resources and leaves various legacies to allow groups to be in different stages of the high performance cycle [7].

Time-related features contribute to having a high-performance reputation, which may further entice already high performing recruits or those with this potential. Reputation may also increase the chances of being invited to become arbiters of high-performing status, as happened in RAE 2008. Past behaviour evidences and reinforces those values, practices and routines that stay focused on priority issues while being aware, if variably committed to, more systemic or policy-based developments.

Existing data regarding the development of expertise suggests the need for a developmental period of 10,000 hours per person [8]. It is clear that this is not uniformly available across all institutes. This provides an idea of the scale of investments needed by both individuals and organisations. Yet, despite widespread acknowledgement of this rule across the world of specialisation, academics often walk a tightrope to preserve even modest university time allocations for research activity. Therefore, expertise in some environments should be seen as being even more impressive. Worse, individual staff may be motivated to under-report the investments they make to achieve any measure of success. Relying on self-reports of hours spent on research, as is currently the case, will only provide disingenuous and inauthentic evidence about how high performance is achieved.

Institutional knowledge sustains the confidence to persist with core elements of practice, to preserve concentrated attention on research and to withstand the changes in fortune associated with redirection. Crucially, change takes place amid tradition. For others, indicators of maturity or of slow progress may imply resistance to change, lack of modernity or under-investment.

Outside the university, tradition – whether or not the associated reputation reflects 'reality' - may reassure research funders seeking known 'safe hands' to manage their investments; so maybe the rich really do get richer. Irrespective of their origin, positive traditions may remove redundancies [5] and bring efficiencies in daily events, recruitment and retention. In contrast, negative traditions are more likely to continue managing, or even introduce further, rules emphasising violation (see later comments about trust). Importantly, efficiencies are subjectively understood as minimising the individual and collective hassles associated with working with colleagues who do not 'fit', while developing, reinforcing and valuing those who do. Aspirant groups may specifically recruit individuals to generate new norms for performance and who can tolerate their position of non-fit.

It is no surprise, then, that an appropriate time-related research solution is to create more longitudinal models across specific performance scenarios. These designs will also provide practitioners with answers to causality questions; 'Which elements of the environment cause high performance and which are the most important elements?' Other designs could profitably unpick another time-related conundrum; 'Which comes first; performance or the supportive environment?'

REJECT SINGLE FACTOR 'SOLUTIONS'

The proposed model formalises seven core factors in the performance environment. It also hints at some important interactions, which challenges any reliance on single issue solutions. 'Interaction' may be a synonym for 'context', which, obviously, has many subjective interpretations, not least of which is motivational [9], or political, climate. Equally, just as individuals may be either sick or healthy, the same may be true of organisations, due to institutionalised practices and routines. Recent data suggest that it is the average level of daily hassle (which relates most to interactions between Performance Enablers and People), rather than the impact of unusual events, which most influences estimates of job satisfaction.

Appreciating their complexity may lead some high performing university environments to actively counter-balance attention to one area with compensation in others. For example, universities often house both under-performing and high-performing groups. In the 2008 RAE, the university with the highest number of top rated units (n = 18) was based on submissions to 50 to the 67 units of assessment. However, consistent with life in a complex organisation built on different ways of thinking, university staff often disagree about the respective resourcing of teaching and/or research. Indeed, the department with the greatest proportion (95%) of 2008 RAE outputs rated in the highest two quality ranks came from a university that did not feature in the world's top 200. It is unclear which universities might seek high performance in two domains (i.e., teaching and research), when others might regard them as being in competition.

Another complex idea that bears examination is that high performance may be achieved *despite* the work environment. We must address organisational myths and examine what motivates and directs underdogs. The search should be for their really influential factors. Equally, leadership can tire, be inappropriate for, or be irrelevant to high performance. More worryingly it may wilfully misrepresent its own centrality. Study designs, perhaps of a dyadic nature and based on high performing employees, managers and representatives of the constituencies they serve, might resolve these issues.

COMPLEX ORGANISATIONS AND EMERGING CONCEPTS

Another issue questions the legitimacy of describing complex organisations using blanket, anthropomorphising (but individualistic) terms like motivation, character and values. We might also question the validity of summarising the performance of individuals using grouped data. RAE 2008 [1] actively prevented individualising of performance estimates. Further, many academic disciplines, especially those espousing scholarship, thrive on solo academic endeavours. Yet, their success is often dependent on support from non-academics and academics alike, who then go unrewarded. For others, their isolated nature predicated being excluded from the 2008 review.

Just as investments and support may vary across the sector, so too do notions of academic quality and of economic value. In the 2001 RAE, respective subjects had a different economic value; *in the same university* this ranged £23K to £84/person/year of central income. The issue is further complicated by the need to collaborate with academics in other organisations around the world. Unpicking the interplay of these issues seems important.

Handling of unusual, but high, performance is important in every complex organisation. Simonton [10] detailed how US navy ships revolved around three main groups; *leaders* who lead the *followers*, and *non-followers* who completed their tasks while largely disregarding the other two groups. Non-followers focused on their work while followers used time and energy trying to conform and in detecting where conformity was needed. If we can assume that (i) these ideas transfer well, and (ii) a diversified profile of performance is what successful universities will pursue, we should now identify how leaders and followers can facilitate non-followers' creativity, innovation, productivity, motivation and commitment.

In the proposed model, we might anticipate tension between the need for inter-personal trust and the Leadership that might redirect the high performing group. If universities really are little more than small businesses guided by enlightened self-interest, then local-level trust [11] is another crucial subjective notion. Intellectually, trust relates to the *unspoken* psychological contract between the employer and the employee, yet few research-active academics would affiliate more strongly to their university than their research group (which does not obviously employ them). Therefore, academics may have two such contracts. Either way, any contract creates assumptions for employees and employers; this contract influences respective planning, commitment and prediction-making. Further, trust is an element of job control which influences employee health and performance. Low job control combined with high demands and low social support leads to poor employee health [12]. Trust also influences external profile and, with it, the reputation that attracts new high performing staff. Leadership and support styles that influence organisation-wide and/or local-level trust should be distinguished.

There is, therefore, a fundamental need to understand how the different forms of trust – and with them the positive emotions that underpin the constructive and creative thinking that is so central to academic life – are furnished when individuals can anticipate being actively disadvantaged by redirection decisions. Trust and the potential for relational conflict are, then, always bed-fellows. De Vries [13] also relates how an excess of rules indicates a trust disorder, while also noting that trust enhancement provides an antidote to the proliferation of rules and regulations. Figures from the recent stress audit [4] suggest that while mistrust is not universal, it does feature for a sizeable minority of university staff.

Since trust is a reciprocal notion, in their turn, managers may also question why they should invest in academics who recurrently demand academic freedom, but who produce few tangible outcomes. Labelling such individuals as 'disengaged', and then disregarding them, hardly seems appropriate since a single output may be a world-level contribution. Tension revolves around any university that needs to support practices that not only create market share, but that also builds the resumés of aspirant, or already, high performers. Research-active academics know that their resumés must demonstrate personal initiative and independence. Managing these tensions will say much about the sustainability of recent changes in research profile.

FIND THE NEW AND THE REDUNDANT; 'WHAT' AND 'WHO'?

My final point reflects that any model is inevitably limited by the data contributing to it. Universities will increasingly need to address how to best support teams with a diverse cross-cultural composition. This is increasingly the case as research-related recruitment becomes a global feature. We also need to address how changing the gender balance influences the development of high-performance environments.

Along with new constituencies, new ideas are also emerging; organisational justice is but one [14]. The three elements of organisational justice, interaction, procedure and distribution, could all be considered in the current model. This seems highly relevant to 'resource-poor' public organisations. Recent figures suggest that this designation applies to many UK universities; most hold fewer than 60 days worth of cash assets [15]. Further, annual 'profits' of less than 2% have only been achieved by withholding investments in reserves. Yet, as further confirmation of the segregation within the sector, few of the UK's world-class universities would be widely seen as resource-poor. In this context, new frameworks and ideas that might be important in securing the mission of most universities include the positive psychological notions of flourishing, languishing, resilience, curiosity and learned optimism [16].

We should also consider willingness to act *outwards* to influence those whom the organisation serves. For example, do high performing groups dispose of 'redundant' customer groups in favour of others? Further, how do high performing units handle overly demanding, or even abusive, clients? If they do, their attention antennae (for Performance Enablers and People) are both outward *and* inward.

It remains to be clarified how and when attention shifts from and between these respective elements and which core questions furnish the most valuable decision-making. Inwardly, loyalty, trust, group coherence and process efficiency also seem important in optimising decisions about making investments, such as talent development programmes. They also influence judgements about return on investments, which relate to estimates of pre-existing skills and resources within the organisation. These should be considered in subsequent model-making. Interestingly, the single university that met government standards for working-life quality was also a high RAE performer.

The UK houses four of the top 10 and eight of the top 50 world's universities [3], which indicates high performance. However, despite this independently assessed status, only one of over 100 universities met government standards for working-life quality [4]. Nearly half of university respondents scored their average level of stress as 'high' or 'very high'. Subjective estimates of 'change fatigue' provide another individualised experience of the UK public sector. The impact of innovation – positive but imposed developments can be made ineffective, ineffective options may be imposed to emphasise power and authority – may also be an issue. Since the same stressor can be seen as either harmful or a mark of positive adaptation to the immediate environment, this reminds us of the need to consider both the benefits and the human costs of high performance within universities.

CONCLUSION

The commentary builds on the model proposed by Jones et al. It considers important issues to guide practitioners and researchers. Based on concurrent data and estimates of performance, UK universities are presented as complex and segmented organisations – both individually and across the sector. However, the subjective relevance of these values, practices and routines to the daily lives of university high performers remains unclear. The commentary also addresses the tensions and unresolved issues that seem to be operating across the UK university sector and that may need to be addressed to help more units to perform well.

REFERENCES

1. RAE 2008: The Results, 18 December 2008, *www.rae.ac.uk.*

2. Guest, D.E., Perspectives on the Study of Work-Life Balance, *Social Sciences Information,* 2002, 41, 255-79.

3. Times Higher Education Supplement, The World's Top 200 Universities, 9 October 2007, www.timeshighereducation.co.uk.

4. Court, S. and Kinman, G., *Stress in Higher Education*, University and College Union, London, 2008.

5. Latham, G.P., *Work Motivation; History, Theory, Research and Practice*, Sage, Thousand Oaks, CA, 2007.

6. World Beaters: But What Makes These Universities Special? 9 October 2007, *www.timehighereducation.co.uk*

7. Locke, E.A. and Latham, G.P., *A Theory of Goal-Setting and Task Performance*, Prentice Hall, Englewood Cliffs, NJ, 1990.

8. Ericsson, K.A., Krampe, R.T. and Tesch-Römer, C., The Role of Deliberate Practice in the Acquisition of Expert Performance, *Psychological Review*, 1993, 100(3), 363-406.

9. Dweck, C., *Mindset: The New Psychology of Success*, Random House, New York, 2006.

10. Simonton, B., *Leading People to be Highly Motivated and Committed*, Simonton Associates, Sun City, FL, 1999.

11. Galford, R. and Seibold Drapeau, A., The Enemies of Trust, in: *Harvard Business Review on Building Personal and Organizational Resilience*, Harvard Business School Press, Cambridge, MA, 2003, 155-174.

12. Karasek, R.A., Job Demands, Job Decision Latitude and Mental Strain: Implications for Job Redesign, *Administrative Science Quarterly,* 1979, 24, 285-308.

13. de Vries M.F.R.K., High Performance Teams: Lessons from the Pygmies, *Organisational Dynamics,* Winter 1999, 66-76.

14. Kivimäki, M., Elovaino, M., Vahtera, J. and Ferrie, J.E., Organisational Justice and Health of Employees: Prospective Cohort Study, *Occupational and Environmental Medicine,* 2003, 60, 27-34.

15. Richardson, H., Universities 'May Face Deficit', *http://news.bbc.co.uk/go/pr/fr/-/1/hi/education/7773034.stm.*

16. Paterson, C., *A Primer in Positive Psychology*, Oxford University Press, Oxford, 2006.

Higher Education, Personal Development & Coaching

Paul Dowson and Simon Robinson
School of Applied Global Ethics
Leeds Metropolitan University, The Grange,
Beckett Park Campus, Headingley, LS6 3QS, UK
E-mail: P.A.Dowson@Leedsmet.ac.uk

ABSTRACT

This article argues that life-coaching is directly relevant to higher education as a whole. Having looked at one example of coaching practice and its underlying values, the article notes a symmetry with views of higher education that focus on personal development. These suggest that the learning experience itself contributes to that development, focused in critical conversation. This in turn requires a suitable learning environment, most obviously found in the tutorial system, which itself has similarities with coaching. Given the demise of the tutorial system the article suggests that an obvious place to explore the use of coaching approaches is in personal development modules. The rationale and values of such modules are set out and two examples, around life planning and the development of personal and professional responsibility, are presented. The article concludes that such developments can then link in to the wider curriculum.

Key words: Employability, LifePlan, Personal Development Planning, Responsible Engagement, Values

INTRODUCTION

The term coaching has always been used in education, largely in a narrow, individualistic and instrumentalist way. The student hires a tutor who will 'coach' him with the specific aim of passing a particular exam. This is target led and says little, if anything, about the nature of the learning involved, or the relevance of that learning to practice. In recent decades the concept of coaching has developed, beyond narrow instrumentalism, to ideas such as life coaching. At the same time, within the traditional areas of coaching, such as sport there has been an increased concern for

Reviewers: Ronald Barnett (Institute of Education, University of London, UK)
Darryl Tippens (Pepperdine University, USA)

more holistic perspectives that take the activity beyond simply enabling the player to win. This article will suggest that these developments in coaching make the concept and activity relevant to higher education as a whole. Having looked at one example of coaching practice and the underlying values, we will then note the symmetry with three views of learning and the context of learning related to higher education. The first, that of Ronald Barnett, focuses on the nature of a higher form of learning that is practiced in higher education. The second, set out by Michael Oakeshott, argues for student-centred critical conversation as a means of enabling higher learning. The third, from Parker Palmer, argues for the importance of a holistic environment for such learning. Such a framework is applicable to all teaching, and is perhaps most successfully practised in the tutorial system. This system is perhaps the closest to the idea and practice of coaching, with small numbers involved, and the development of values, skills and virtues centred in the immediate relationship.

The article then notes that massification and post modernity have created major obstacles to such an approach to higher education. One area, however, that provides an opportunity for reconnecting with this approach is through the Government's concern for employability, expressed in the development of personal development planning. We note the tensions in the term employability, between simple occupational utility and a more reflective view of personal development that links to life planning. The article will then focus on two examples of personal development modules that embody this deeper sense, providing a bridge between coaching and higher education.

COACHING

It would be easy to think of coaching, both sport and life coaching, as being value neutral, with a very narrow purpose and modus operandi. Jennifer Rogers, however, points to six underlying principles [1, p. 7-8]:

   #1 – The client is resourceful
   #2 – The coach's role is to 'spring loose' the client's resourcefulness
   #3 – Coaching addresses the whole person – past, present and future
   #4 – The client sets the agenda
   #5 – The coach and the client are equals
   #6 – Coaching is about change and action

Beneath these principles are an implicit set of values that take coaching, in whatever context, beyond a narrow view. First, the client is given respect, as someone who already possesses resources, involving skills, experience, virtues and the like. This is close to Carl Rogers' unconditional positive regard [2]. Second, the task of coaching is to enable the client to use those talents to the full. This involves enabling the client to reflect on his or her resources. The core of this is about reflection on practice, not least because resources are embodied, and therefore only known to the person, in practice. This involves awareness and appreciation of those resources, leading the client into an awareness of identity, or some aspect of her identity. Third, the client reflects on the whole person. It is difficult to do that without the client looking at her social and physical environment. In other words, the whole person involves the person in relationships over time. The time context inevitably provides a sense of the person being an agent over time, and as articulating her narrative, and, with that, any sense of purpose.

The fourth principle inevitably follows from that, focusing on the autonomy of the client in her planning. Setting an agenda is not simply a utilitarian task. It arises out of views about vision, mission, and purpose, of the person or of the group to which the person belongs. This further develops the person's identity, but also develops agency and personal responsibility. The fifth principle focuses more on equal respect than upon strict equality. In one sense, this might be better thought of as mutuality, enabling free and open critical exchange. Mutuality does not have to be symmetrical. Mutuality in turn sets up reciprocal accountability. This sense of responsibility to the other sets up a strong motivational aspect of coaching. Mutuality is often expressed in terms of coaching conversation. Finally, coaching involves change and action. This is partly about how purpose and values are embodied in action, and thus about integrity, but also about a broader sense of responsibility for action, in relation to a project and people involved in the project. The latter is sometimes referred to as moral liability [3]. All of this is focused in development and change, and thus continued reflection.

The function of the coach then is to enable the focused development of the client. In Jennifer Rogers' words:

> The coach works with clients to achieve speedy, increased and sustainable effectiveness in their lives and careers through focused learning. The coach's sole aim is to work with the client to achieve all of the client's potential – as defined by the client. [1, p. 7]

The client herself takes responsibility for her development, supported by the coach. By implication, the coach enables or empowers the client to decide her purpose and aims. However, the development of the person is not individualistic. It occurs within and in response to a social and physical environment, and thus is increasingly seen in terms of transpersonal psychology. Sir John Whitmore sees 'transpersonal coaching' as an 'empowering process' that focuses on core values and relationships that in turn fuel the person's strengths and creativity [4]. Increasingly, this is focused in life planning.

HIGHER EDUCATION

Such a view of coaching has much in common with the project of higher education. The work of Barnett, Oakeshott and Palmer suggests that the nature of higher education itself involves personal development and we will briefly examine each of their views.

Ronald Barnett lists the general aims of higher education as follows [5, p. xx]:

- The pursuit of truth and objective knowledge
- Research
- Liberal education
- Institutional autonomy

- Academic freedom
- A neutral and open forum for debate
- Rationality
- The development of the student's critical abilities
- The development of the student's autonomy
- The student's character formation
- Providing a critical centre within society
- Preserving society's intellectual culture

At the level of the institution, this sets the bar very high, with nothing less than contributing to a civilized society, not least through preserving intellectual culture and providing social critique. At the level of the student experience of learning, he looks to the development of higher-order thinking that involves "analysis, evaluation, criticism and even imagination" [5, p. 85]. This level of thinking transcends the simple acquisition of work-centred skills, developing an awareness of a wider context and the capacity to learn about learning, thus taking responsibility for learning. Like the person-centred view of coaching, Barnett views higher education as, in essence, emancipatory and holistic. It liberates the student from a narrow, purely utilitarian view, of both academic discipline and work, enabling personal development.

Philosophers such as John White [6] critique Barnett on liberal grounds; namely, that any student should choose whether they want to be developed, and that academic disciplines are value-free. Barnett argues the very activity of learning in higher education, involves holistic engagement, and enables students to develop personally. Philosophy and sociology are important tools in this reflection, both empowering the student and enabling self-understanding. Increasingly, this is reinforced by the work of academic disciplines that are associated with the professions. Engineering, for example, is looking to develop not simply the applied ethics of the professional [7] but the identity of the profession and the underlying philosophies of engineering [8]. Nevertheless, Barnett's message is that this higher-order thinking is not confined to the professions. Hence, he refers to masters of several different academic disciplines who have supported this vision, including John Newman, Aldous Huxley, John Mill, Karl Jaspers and Frank Leavis.

Central to Michael Oakeshott's vision for higher education is that it should provide a place where conversation is explicitly given priority [9, p. 11]. The distinctive mark of a university, he argues, is a place where the undergraduate "has the opportunity of education in conversation with his teachers, his fellows and himself, and where he is not encouraged to confuse education with training for a profession" [9, p. 101]. For Oakeshott, this conversation is an "unrehearsed intellectual adventure" [9, p. 13] and has several dimensions. Firstly, it is about making available to young adults resources found beyond current thinking, feelings, images and skills and informing their conversation with literary, philosophical, artistic and scientific expressions of (European) civilization. Oakeshott argues that this constitutes something that more closely approximates the *whole* of their inheritance [9, p. 48-49]. Secondly, it is about helping young adults see that the pursuit of learning is not a race pitting students against one another in competition for the best place and the highest achievement [9, p. 98]. Conversation is about joint-discovery and exploration. Thirdly, the reflective process of conversing with oneself Oakeshott regards as the chief advantage to be gained from education [9, p. 133]. This critical conversation sets up both an environment in which persons can respectfully challenge, and be challenged. It enables learning and development of articulation and reflection on one's own thinking and practice, and critical reflection on the thinking of others. Fourthly, the critical conversation enables one to develop the capacity to handle plurality, many different voices, and by extension to manage ambiguity in the self and others.

Like Barnett, then, Oakshott sees the student learning about life and developing as a person through the practice of her discipline - but with critical conversation at the core. Like Barnett, and the view of coaching outlined above, Oakshott sees the student as taking responsibility for his or learning, in this case through the practice of conversation. Like coaching based in mutuality, Oakshott offers the mutuality of conversation. Conversation, however, extends some of Barnett's ideas into the realm of cross-cultural dialogue and this is picked up effectively by Jonathan Sacks, and particularly so in the new context of the "clash of civilizations", after Samuel Huntingdon [10]. Conversation for Sacks is central to his call for a "dignity of difference". It is not mere debate, but a disciplined act of communicating and listening. It is respectful, engaged, and reciprocal and calls forth our greatest powers of empathy and understanding [11, p. 83-84]. Conversation is a bridge in a society of strangers and for Sacks the greatest single antidote to violence [11, p. 2]. Through it, we make ourselves open to the stories of others, which may profoundly conflict with our own [11, p. 23]. Through better listening, we may hear for the first time something that will help us face the dilemmas that confront us [11, p. 19].

Parker Palmer's book *The Courage to Teach* [12] approaches some of these issues from the perspective of teaching and as its title suggests is aimed at teachers. There are a number of instructive dimensions to Palmer's thinking that provide timely input to higher education teaching and learning. The first of these highlights the importance of what is termed elsewhere a 'holistic approach'. Teaching for Palmer should involve walking three important paths: the intellectual, the emotional and the spiritual. All three are required for wholeness and are the basis of education at its best. Inclusion of the *emotional* is needed to appreciate the way our students and we ourselves feel as we teach and learn – feelings Palmer says that can "either enlarge or diminish the exchange between us" [12, p. 5]. By *spiritual,* Palmer means the "diverse ways we answer the heart's longing to be connected with the largeness of life" [12, p. 5]. It involves the development of consciousness and significant life meaning related to community and practice.

Palmer argues for a new diagnosis of our students' inward condition, one combining greater perception about their needs, less absorption in the teacher's role, and more open to creative modes of teaching [12, p. 43]. For Palmer, student stories are every bit as significant as the scholarly texts we assign to them, as is the process of helping students to build bridges between the academic and their own lives [12, p. 71]. The heart of Palmer's book, however, is his instruction as to how to build a creative space for learning. This consists of holding together a set of six paradoxical guidelines as follows [12, p. 76-80]:

1. The space should be both bounded and open
2. The space should be both hospitable and charged
3. The space should invite both the voice of the individual and the voice of the group
4. The space should both honour 'little' stories of those involved and the 'big' stories of the disciplines and tradition
5. The space should both support solitude and surround it with the resources of community
6. The space should welcome both silence and speech

We will enlarge on the meaning of these paradoxes in the context of commenting on the design of the Responsible Engagement programme. In summary, Palmer focuses on providing a context and framework for learning that values:

(i) Holistic learning, critical reflection through conversation, and learner autonomy; all of which can all have a positive effect on the personal development of the student.

ii) The dynamic experience of critical conversation that enables the person to practice a wide range of skills and virtues. These include: empathy (the capacity to listen to the whole person, both the explicit words and the tone of the words); the capacity to challenge with respect; awareness and appreciation of the other; the capacity to assess rational arguments; the capacity to work together in both searching for the truth and in response to that truth; the capacity to connect responsibility in theory, value and practice. The latter takes the intellectual experience into practice not least through the association of the professions, and their training, with higher education.

In all this, Palmer still focuses on the learning involved in the disciplines and on how the student can be most effectively engaged in that learning.

For all these writers, the experience of learning in higher education is not developed to act as an instrument to improve personal development and thus employability. On the contrary, all of them argue that personal development is central to the very nature of higher learning. So, for instance, effective critical conversation happens to enable effective learning. Effective learning has to be able to handle a plurality of voices, seeing how they differ, judging their value, and working with them or challenging them. All these learning skills have direct occupational utility. Even where such learning is focused on the abstract, it is not to the exclusion of practice. All of this resonates with the values and practice of coaching outlined above, including the importance of personal development, autonomy, responsibility, accountability, holism, integrative thinking and creativity.

THE CONTEMPORARY SOCIAL CONTEXT

There are many aspects of the contemporary social scene that militate against the focus of personal development in higher education. There is not the space to cover all of these adequately in this article, thus we will simply offer a few examples.

First, higher education is faced by the experience of so-called massification - the increase in student numbers. Richard Tawney [13] saw education as a kingdom of ideas in which all can participate. He would have been delighted by the great improvement in access to higher education, but appalled by the way in which the numbers of students make it seemingly impossible to provide the access to the depth of that kingdom through conversation, holistic reflection, and so on. The obvious place for such conversation, the tutorial, is increasingly under attack, precisely because of student numbers.

Second, Zygmunt Bauman argues that society has moved into late or "liquid modernity" [14, p. 163]. The spirit of the age and the emerging generation that embodies that spirit are more fluid in their ways, more prone to change shape than to hold to a fixed identity, more challenged than former generations to be flexible rather than settled or defined. One of his most telling observations is the primacy of the 'now', over the future or even the past. The reason for this being:

> …in a world in which the future is at best dim and misty but more likely full of risks and dangers, setting distant goals, surrendering private interest in order to increase group power and sacrificing the present in the name of a future bliss does not seem an attractive, nor for that matter sensible, proposition [14, p. 163].

All this takes individuals away from a focus on identity and purpose, which would demand reflection on narrative of the past, present and future.

Third, Knud Illeris argues that in late modernity there has been a practically limitless proliferation (or at least presentation) of choices [15, p. 7]. The choices on offer in the areas of education, work, consumption, relationships, leisure and lifestyle are much greater than ever before and are as Illeris argues "inexorably concentrated in the years of youth" [15, p. 7]. Most young adults respond to choices on offer through a 'search process' of trial of error:

> They try out the one thing after the other with respect to absolutely everything such as friendships, relationships, sexuality, alcohol, drugs, interests, activities, competitions, sports, music, education, types of holidays, and ways of living, and they move around globally either on the Internet and through the media, or directly by travelling. [16, quoted in 15, p. 15]

The main challenge in this new situation is that there is a continuous struggle for identity. Connecting with Bauman's liquid theme, individuals in late modernity, he states, are 'drowning' in the struggle, on the one hand, to establish a core identity and, on the other hand, to retain extreme flexibility [15, p.13-14]. External pressures such as the explosion of the compensatory, including compensatory consumption and compensatory satisfactions, the fragmentation of the nuclear family and the intensification of work, as cited by Zeihe and Stubenrauch [16, quoted in 15, p. 11]] only add to the struggle. In all this, there is little space for the meaning of the values and purpose behind choice or the creative possibilities that result form such individualistic choosing.

Fourth, Sacks notes the effects of globalization. This is characterised by a series of institutions including the market, the media, multi-national corporations and the Internet [11, p. 20]. This has created an environment of systemic change [11, p. 71] where constant flux and uncertainty challenge what Alvin Toffler calls "personal stability zones", once reflected in permanent homes, permanent relationships and permanent jobs [17, cited by 11, p. 70-71]. When the world out there changes faster than the world within, including our mental and emotional responses, this creates extreme anxiety [17, cited by 11, p. 70-71]. People do not easily adapt to significant change, nor to addressing personal development.

In such a social context, made worse by pressures of the economy and the focus on managerial targets, there are real dangers for any higher form of learning. First, learning can easily be instrumentalised, with a focus purely on occupational utility. Second, learning can lose its holistic perspective, with stress on skills and concepts. Third, the relational aspect of learning, building up the mutuality of conversation, can easily be replaced by the commodification of learning.

In that light, we argue that one of the most important developments of the past decade is around the introduction of modules for personal development planning (PDP).

PERSONAL DEVELOPMENT PLANNING (PDP) AND EMPLOYABILITY

PDP is bound up with higher education's adoption of a Progress File now being introduced across all levels of higher education. The progress file provides students with a transcript recording of their learning and achievement as well as a means by which students can further their personal development. PDP is usually defined as "a structured and supported process undertaken by an individual to reflect upon their own learning, performance and/or achievement and to plan for their personal, educational and career development" [18]. Hence, PDP explicitly and systematically focuses on personal development.

PDP seeks to empower the students to take responsibility for their learning, connecting the learning with the wider curriculum and connecting that to their focused planning for the employment and life-long learning. In turn, this connects learning skills to employment skills. PDP calls upon personal development tutors and career professionals to support the process whereby students take responsibility for their own development. This has caused teaching and guidance staff to change from instruction-centred approaches and in the direction of empowering and listening approaches.

The PDP practitioner then seeks to empower their students to develop key outcomes that closely resonate with the values of coaching and higher learning, summarised as follows:

- Identifying what people want
- Setting development goals
- Maximizing positive attributes and skills
- Addressing unhelpful patterns and behaviours
- Equipping with tools and techniques
- Providing a support structure

There are, of course, differences. A coach will normally work with highly motivated persons or teams. For the PDP leader, some students may have little motivation to work through the issues. This may be because employment is not an immediate concern, or even because there is little sense of the purpose of higher education or their role in it, other than a vague assent to myths about the need for a degree to gain employment. Nonetheless, the focus is there for reflection on present narrative and purpose, and for planning for the future that relates to practice.

At the heart of PDP is the concept of employability, which is easily seen as exclusively about occupational utility. Hence, employers suggest that a number of qualities and task-centred skills go to make up employability, including: effective learning skills, self-awareness, the capacity for networking, negotiation skills, transferable skills, self-confidence, interpersonal skills, team-working skills, taking responsibility, the capacity to make decisions, and the capacity to cope with uncertainty [19, p. 5]. However, learning skills are directly related to these other skills. Hence, for instance, it is difficult to see how learning can be advanced without team-work, social support and negotiation. Equally, self-awareness and the awareness of the social environment are important in developing learning and research. Hence, it is argued that employability needs a broader definition that links directly to the experience of learning and of self-development. Yorke and Knight [20, p. 5], for instance, offer four interrelated components of employability:

Understanding. This is intentionally differentiated from knowledge, signifying a deeper awareness of data and its contextual meaning.

Skills. This term refers to skills in context and practice, and therefore implies the capacity to use skills appropriately.

Efficacy beliefs, self theories and personal qualities. The connection of these to a sense of underlying purpose and value enables the student to feel that it is possible to make a difference in work. They also influence how the person will perform in work.

Metacognition. This involves self-awareness, the capacity to learn through reflective practice, the capacity to reflect on learning itself, and so learn how to learn, and the capacity to regulate the self.

It is striking how close these ideas are to the broadly transpersonal views of coaching and to the idea higher learning. Bluckert [21], for instance, stresses the importance of awareness and responsibility and the building of self-belief. All of these enable and enrich choice, hence:

> As people become more aware of their assumptions, belief systems, attitudes and behavioural patterns they move into a position of choice, to stay with them or to change. [21, p. 5]

The coach seeks to enable the client to develop such reflection and thus believe in and trust herself and others. Employability, then, is a complex idea about how these four components can influence life-long learning, life-long performance and personal development [21, p. 5]. It is evidenced in the "application of a mixture of personal qualities and beliefs, understandings, skilful practices, and the ability to reflect productively on experience" [22, p. 11]. John Stephenson's earlier concept of "capability" exhibits a number of similarities to employability. In brief, capability is characterised by confidence in one's ability to [23, p. 2]:

- Take effective and appropriate action
- Explain what one is seeking to achieve
- Live and work effectively with others
- Continue to learn from experiences.

Employability is about what makes for successful employment and is thus very much about maximising good consequences for the individual and society. It is also intrinsically a good, and therefore not value-free. It involves [24]:

- *Reflectivity*, including the capacity to reflect holistically and to learn.
- *Responsibility*, involving the capacity to identify and articulate self beliefs, and be responsible for these beliefs and their development.
- *Connectivity*, involving the ability to make connections between: experiences over time; the self and its core communities, including work; and the social and physical environment outside such communities.
- *Innovativity*, the capacity to both handle new challenges and create new opportunities. This recognises risk and initiative as an inevitable part of the work experience, summed up partly in the idea of entrepreneurship.

The goals of this view of employability, coaching and higher learning are strikingly similar. Personal development is tied to an effective learning experience that enables the growth in confidence, and values the learning process in itself. We have argued that all this should be true of any learning experience. By implication, didactic approaches that do not engage in a holistic way work against such development.

However, PDP is a particularly relevant area where personal development, academic learning and employability can come together most effectively. The danger is that even this area falls prey to non-engaged teaching or to focus purely on skills. In the following two examples, we suggest ways in which these connections can be made in PDP, and in which the person-centred coaching approach can contribute to the higher forms of learning. The first is through LifePlan courses, and the second through the Responsible Engagement modules.

LIFEPLAN

LifePlan is a short course in Life & Career Management developed by Paul Dowson of Leeds Metropolitan University. It is particularly suitable for adults (either young or older) at a life or career crossroads. Generally, however, it provides a training in the ways of PDP and helps individuals to take responsibility for their own futures. In perhaps its most successful format, it consists of five sessions of 150 minutes. At the end of the short course, participants have produced a personal development plan and examined a number of central life and career themes.

LifePlan was launched in 2006 as part of the *Yorkshire Forward* funded *Graduates Yorkshire* project. The initial motivation was to develop a course which could be used by higher education careers services as a strategy for income generation and regional retention. The target audience were graduates of all ages attracted to completing a short-course in life and career planning. In 2007, LifePlan was 'rolled out' across the Yorkshire region. Six universities participated in the programme, including Leeds Metropolitan University, University of Bradford, University of Huddersfield,

University of Sheffield, Sheffield Hallam University, and York St John University. The learning outcomes for LifePlan are as follows:

- Construct a personal development plan (PDP)
- Produce a verified strengths and weaknesses profile
- Use the journey metaphor to plot adult and career development
- Evaluate balance across life's domains
- Map and analyse personal and social support network
- Approach self-presentation more confidently
- Specify career fitness issues

What makes LifePlan innovative is how it combines a number of distinctive features as listed below:

Holistic. LifePlan puts life and career planning/management together. Adults are increasingly concerned about how best to fit together their work lives and their lives beyond work.

Journey Perspective. Using Law's model [25] of two guiding metaphors, LifePlan underlines the view that one's life and career path should be seen as a journey of discovery and development involving other people and different places and not as a straight line route-way, like a 100-metres sprint where competition reigns and collaboration plays no part.

Group-Based. Bringing together a group of adults to share experiences and their stories is central to the richness of LifePlan, which seeks to serve the individual and at the same time encourage a community perspective.

Facilitated. The LifePlan Tutor acts as facilitator and coach, nurturing a democratic group dynamic and encouraging participants to positively contribute to the course.

Identity Focused. The LifePlan has its own distinctive identity including an attractive logo and a range of materials, including original illustrations which set LifePlan apart both visually and in terms of its content.

Reflection Centred. LifePlan seeks to assist participants in becoming reflective practitioners. This is incorporated as part of the learning process.

More details of the LifePlan programme can be found in Robinson et al. [26]. It is relevant here, however, to summarise the learning that has been gained from the development of LifePlan and to go on to review the Responsible Engagement programme in relation to Palmer's [12] six paradoxical guidelines. These sections are particularly relevant to the development of PDP curricula.

The major findings from developing and delivering LifePlan were presented in a session at the Association of Graduate Careers Advisory Services (AGCAS) Heads of Service Conference in Harrogate (Yorkshire, UK) in 2008. Six major findings were recorded as follows:

A Branded Experience. The contemporary social experience faces us with more choices than former generations, reflecting sophisticated marketing associated with global capitalism, 'presented' via advertising, the media and the internet. Higher education institutions are discovering that it is not sufficient to offer excellent courses and facilities, but that these must be presented to students in an environment where higher education institutions compete for student attention and student selection as consumers. To gain student attention, engage them and retain them requires higher education institutions to offer curricula which capture their imaginations and minimize the distractions.

Resource Intensity of Genuine Intervention. One of the consequences of offering a holistic course encompassing what Palmer identifies as the intellectual, emotional and spiritual does not allow for tutor detachment, nor an unrealistic minimal contact teaching approach of imparting information without any reference to the wider personal development needs of the students. This implies a 'resource intensity' not only on the part of the tutor who should be prepared to offer more of herself or himself than a well-crafted session plan and accompanying PowerPoint, but also making room within the teaching sessions to allow for the specific developmental needs of the students.

Significance of the Group. The resources for learning are not only to be found in competent tutors, but in the students themselves; not only as individuals, but particularly through their interaction as a group. Building on Bauman's point that liquid modernity induces a state or sense of 'drowning', supported by Illeris' contention that the proliferation of choice causes extreme anxiety, connecting with others who share the same challenges, who are able to voice shared experiences and explore possible solutions assumes great significance.

Facilitators Only. Clearly, this challenges the expectations and sometimes the personal style, if not the personal needs of teachers. A tutor-as-facilitator must be reconciled to not being the main focus of the session. Like a good coach as highlighted by Rogers [1], the teacher makes the needs of the students central. A balance needs to be found between providing information, and facilitating discussion. For most teachers, this involves creating more space for interaction and student stories than they may be accustomed to providing. Palmer's point about stories being as prominent as the course text is relevant here.

The Confidence Component. Concepts are important, but that which is relationally centred is every bit as significant as helpful theory and rich information. Participants often join personal development programmes lacking confidence in themselves and in their abilities. There is no quick fix to the kinds of issues that inhibit personal interaction, public communication and authentic-self relating; however, creating an environment where students can gain confidence in these areas is intrinsic to personal development. Coaching skills are useful to help students feel better about themselves and their abilities.

The Planning Lag. Surprisingly, one of the most challenging issues is helping students to be more deliberate about PDP – about defining aims and dividing these into objectives. Most students are either not accustomed to action planning, or they action plan in a reactive way that falls short of the strategic approach that would benefit them. Planning for one's personal, educational and career development is far too wide and complex an exercise to be left to chance or instinct.

RESPONSIBLE ENGAGEMENT

In 2007, Paul Dowson and Simon Robinson developed a new programme in Personal Development Planning entitled *'Responsible Engagement'*. The programme consists of one module at each level of the undergraduate and Masters courses offered by the School of Applied Global Ethics (SAGE) at Leeds Metropolitan University. The programme introduces students to the concept of progressive responsibility, starting in the first year with their responsibility to themselves as students; progressing in the second year to professional responsibility and responsibility toward others; and culminating in the third year and at Masters level with the contemporary challenge of global responsibility. The programme facilitates the moral development of cohorts of young adults transitioning to assuming greater leadership responsibility in wider society.

In addition to the notion of progressive responsibility, the programme reflects Leeds Metropolitan University's commitment to connect a number of key cognate areas including: ethics, citizenship, employability, enterprise, internationalisation, volunteering and global responsibility. The programme was launched at level 1 in October 2008. The *'Student Engagement'* module seeks to build upon the findings and success of LifePlan and incorporates three major elements.

THE UNIVERSITY STORY

Students will be introduced to the *Leeds Met Story* through small group information gathering. This will help the students to understand how the organisational narrative of the University interplays with and contributes to individual narratives. Our story interrelates with the stories of others who have shared experiences with us and with the organisations - including educational, employers and third sector organisations - we have invested our lives in.

HIGHER WAYS OF OPERATING

Through a number of sessions entitled *A Higher Way of Operating,* students gain an understanding of what higher education and ultimately 'graduateness' is all about. Higher education institutions are places where meaningful conversation is explicitly given priority. Students are introduced to reflection and reflective practice, the notion of the professional student and the skills and virtues they may want to develop for the employment market and for their futures.

LIFEPLAN

In the *LifePlan HE* (Higher Education) element of the module, students are introduced to a number of subjects and skills that will be foundational to their study and personal development at University, all of them overlapping with the content of the LifePlan short-course. These include self-awareness, life-balance, personal planning, self-presentation, and working collaboratively.

At level 2, Responsible Engagement will change its focus from Student Engagement to *Professional Engagement* and include a focus on the development of professional and community related skills. The subject matter to be addressed will include: citizenship; values definition and differentiation; world view articulation and mapping; diversity and opportunity awareness; and conflict resolution. At level 2, undergraduates in SAGE commit to a three week block - or the equivalent of three weeks - of volunteering as part of an accredited *Voluntary Work Placement* module. The Professional Engagement module will support this experience and dovetail with the volunteering module. This accords with Leeds Metropolitan University's emphasis on the value of volunteering in terms of the personal and professional development of its students and staff.

At level 3 and at Masters level, Responsible Engagement will change its focus again to responsible *Global Engagement* and combine this with an emphasis on the development of leadership skills. This module will build on the successful development of the *Living as a Global Citizen* and *Working as a Global Citizen* modules delivered to SAGE undergraduates and postgraduates in 2006-7 & 2007-8. Topics will include: globalisation and global issues; global citizenship; sustainability; and environmental issues. Helping students to engage with a rapidly changing and globalising world is considered central to both their personal and career development.

In terms of its pedagogical design the Responsible Engagement programme, building on the learning and experience of the LifePlan programme, will seek to follow Palmer's six paradoxical guidelines to build into the teaching and learning space:

1. The space should be both bounded and open. A good learning space for Palmer is one which embodies both openness and boundaries. Within boundaries created by remaining focussed on the subject-matter at hand, students are free and welcomed to speak. Palmer states: "If boundaries remind us that our journey has a destination, openness reminds us that there are many ways to reach that end" [12, p. 77]. This calls upon the tutor to be prepared to forego a preferred or anticipated route and allow the students freedom in finding paths which can still take them to the destination bounded by the session. The *Student Engagement* module as stated earlier involves students in exploring why they came to university and what in their view is the purpose and justification for higher education. The learning space must allow here for students not simply to be told why they are at university or how they may have fallen short in their understanding of the greater significance of universities. Instead, there is an opportunity to express and to hear what exactly was in the minds and hearts of students as they ventured to university and to discover the richness and limitations of their views about the purpose of higher education. These will of course be profoundly reflective of the time in which they are living and from a research perspective should be most enlightening.

2. The space should be both hospitable and charged. A learning space should be inviting, open, safe, trustworthy and free. The learning place, Palmer argues, should offer places to rest, places to find nourishment for those who feel overexposed, and places to seek shelter [12, p. 78]. Hospitality for Palmer also involves receiving one another, the mix of who we are, welcoming and forming ideas; all with openness and care [27, p. 74]. At the same time the space must be 'charged' meaning students need to feel something of the risks inherent in pursuing matters of depth associated with life matters and the human soul. Built into the Student Engagement module is a session dedicated to the students evaluating their experience of participating in the module. This forms the last of the 12 sessions and in Semester 1 of the undergraduate programme and conveniently takes place just prior to the Christmas break.

Hospitality will include creating an informal atmosphere, but this will be supported by providing the students with lunch to accompany the evaluation. A story circle supported by individual storyboards that will be brought to the evaluation will be the approach adopted to elicit the rich qualitative data. A story circle differs from a focus group in being far more open-ended with the facilitator being careful to encourage the group to bring up what they wish and for a free and spontaneous conversation to emerge. This session illustrates Palmer's paradox of hospitality combined with 'charged' conversation.

3. The space should invite both the voice of the individual and the voice of the group. Palmer argues that "only when people can speak their minds does education have a chance to happen" [12, p. 78]. This includes not only expressing ideas that work and are well received, but also those that do not work so well for others. It includes wide-ranging emotions, confusions, ignorance and prejudice. These all constitute the voice of the individual. The paradox is that there is also a voice of the group, something the group is saying and the tutor's responsibility involves listening for this message and summarising it from time to time so the group can hear what is being said and change its collective mind if it so wishes to. In addition to the story circle evaluation mentioned above, where the group is encouraged to find and express its voice, the way the Student Engagement module is assessed also seeks to allow for voice of the group. Two out of the five assessed components include team presentations (one of them being video recorded). The remaining three components place emphasis on individual expression, but in all cases the group dynamic will have helped shape these individual items.

4. The space should both honour 'little' stories of those involved and the 'big' stories of the disciplines and tradition. Palmer speaks of creating a space where both the stories of individual participants and stories that are universal in scope can be heard. If only 'little stories' are heard, then this becomes narcissistic. If combined with the big stories that are archetypal in their depth, however, personal tales are contextualised and become more meaningful – the two work well together [12, p. 79]. Student Engagement is seeking to develop narrative tools and approaches in terms of its pedagogy. Indeed it has attracted funding from the Higher Education Careers Service Unit (HECSU) to develop a distinctive narrative-based approach involving the key input of Bill Law, a leading theorist in careers thinking.

5. The space should both support solitude and surround it with the resources of community. Learning demands both solitude and community. A degree of solitude promotes reflection and space is needed to think our own thoughts. At the same time the community resource of 'dialogical exchange' as Palmer terms it, permits us to air ignorance, test ideas, challenge biases and expand our knowledge [12, p. 79]. This notion of solitude is critical to the reflective processes at work in a quality personal development module. The focus at level 1 of the Responsible Engagement programme is very much on the student as an individual and content on self-awareness is built on at levels 2 and 3 which push out to a greater sense of the significance of other and making a difference in terms of global responsibility. A measure of solitude is necessary when completing self assessments, introducing such things as reflection and reflective practice, strengths and weakness profiling, personality type and learning styles. At the same time, without the community dimension the module might become too pensive and introspective and in danger of not encouraging forms of extraversion that participants will either be drawn to, or to some degree should be encouraged toward from a developmental perspective.

6. The space should welcome both silence and speech. It is easy to edge out silence and always prioritize speech. Some tutors even fear the component of silence which can make for an over concentrated 'filling' with words of the learning space. "In authentic education", Palmer argues, "silence is treated as a trustworthy matrix for the inner work students must do, a medium for learning of the deepest sort" [12, p. 80]. For many teachers, this matrix which Palmer speaks of is largely uncharted territory.

We cannot point to any structure in the Student Engagement module as constituting an expression of Palmer's matrix of silence. This has more to do with process of teaching and the tutor's ability in the situation of teaching to welcome a degree of silence in a discussion or a conversation involving students. There is a time to speak and a time to remain silent. Every tutor and indeed every individual from a personal development perspective learns this, often slowly.

CONCLUSION

Coaching and learning in higher education are closely related. What connects them is a focus on personal development, and on the skills and capacities that are involved in that development. The more that stress is put on this connection, the more coaching can be accepted as an important part of higher education. This points to the development of a culture of coaching in community; one that enables holistic learning, links into employability and enterprise, and enables the development of responsibility and identity through reflection on purpose. Importantly, this also links into underlying values, not least because appreciation of such values, and hence appreciation of how any enterprise links to the social context, enables more effective learning. What links the two is the core experience of higher forms of learning which have personal development at their centre. We have suggested that one way of beginning to reassert the connections between personal development and learning is through work in PDP. The danger of this approach is that it might simply leave all responsibility for this purely to PDP tutors. Hence, the work of PDP has to be connected to the wider curriculum. The advantage is that PDP can most effectively make connections between work and learning, and by extension connect the experience of learning in higher education to the wider experience of life long learning, expressed in the values and practice of coaching. Hence, PDP, focused in the spirit and practice of rigorous conversational coaching can actively support Barnett's vision for the whole of the curriculum in higher education.

REFERENCES

1.   Rogers, J., *Coaching Skills: A Handbook*, Open University Press, Buckingham, UK, 2004.

2.   Rogers, C., *The Freedom to Learn*, 2nd edn., Charless E. Merrill, Columbus, 1983.

3.   McKenny, G.P., Responsibility, in: Meilander, G. and Werpehowski, W., eds., *The Oxford Handbook of Theological Ethics,* Oxford University Press, Oxford, 2005, 237-253.

4.   Sparrow, S., Transpersonally Speaking, *Training and Coaching Today*, 2007, September, 22-23.

5.   Barnett, R., *The Idea of Higher Education*, Open University Press, Buckingham, UK, 1990.

6.   White, J., Philosophy and the Aim of Higher Education, *Studies in Higher Education*, 1997, 22 (1), 7-19.

7. Robinson, S., Dixon, R., Preece, C. and Moodley, K. *Engineering, Business and Professional Ethics*, Butterworth-Heinneman, London, 2007.

8. Royal Academy of Engineering, http://www.raeng.org.uk/news/releases/shownews.htm?NewsID=470

9. Oakeshott, M.J., *The Voice of Liberal Learning* (T. Fuller, ed.), Yale University, New Haven, CT, 1989.

10. Huntingdon, S., *The Clash of Civilizations and the Remaking of World Order*, Simon & Schuster, New York,1996.

11. Sacks, J., *The Dignity of Difference: How to Avoid the Clash of Civilizations,*, Continuum International Publishing Group, London, 2002.

12. Palmer, P. J., *The Courage to Teach: Exploring the Inner Landscape of a Teacher's Life*, Jossey-Bass, San Francisco, 2007.

13. Tawney, R. H., *Equality*, Allen and Unwin, London, 1931/1964.

14. Bauman, Z., *Liquid Modernity*, Polity Press, Malden, MA, 2000.

15. Illeris, K., *Learning, Identity and Self-Orientation in Youth* [Online], http://www.ruc.dk/upload/application/pdf/4d9f1787/youth.pdf

16. Zeihe, T. and Stubenrauch, H., *Plädoyer für ungewöhnliches Lernen* Rowohlt, Reinbek, Germany 1982.

17. Toffler, A., *Future Shock,* Pan, London, 1971.

18. Quality Assurance Agency, http://www.qaa.ac.uk/academicinfrastructure/progressFiles/guidelines/progfile2001.asp.

19. Yorke, M. and Knight, P., *Employability: Judging and Communicating Achievements*, Learning and Teaching Support Network, York, 2004a.

20. Yorke, M. and Knight, P., *Embedding Employability in the Curriculum*, Learning and Teaching Support Network, York, 2004b.

21. Bluckert, P., *Psychological Dimensions of Executive Coaching*, Open University Press, Maidenhead, UK, 2006.

22. Yorke, M., *Employability in Higher Education*, Learning and Teaching Support Network, York, 2004.

23. Stephenson, J., The Concept of Capability and its Importance in Higher Education, in: Stephenson, J. and Yorke, M., eds., *Capability and Quality in Higher Education*, Kogan Page, London, 1998, 1-13.

24. Robinson, S., *Ethics and Employability*, Higher Education Academy, York, 2005.

25. Law, B., *Narratives for Well-Being*, http://www.hihohiho.com, 2008, 35-37.

26. Robinson, S., Dowson, P. and Price, A., Ethics, Enterprise and Employability: Towards an Integrated Curriculum, *Discourse: Learning and Teaching in Philosophical and Religious Studies*, 2008, 7, 2, 121-156.

27. Palmer, P. J., *To Know as We are Known: Education as a Spiritual Journey,* Harper, San Francisco, 1993.

Stepping Out of the Box:
How Stories Can Inspire Growth, Development, and Change

David Carless[1] and Kitrina Douglas[2]
[1]Carnegie Faculty of Sport and Education
Leeds Metropolitan University, Leeds, LS6 3QS, UK
E-mail: D.Carless@leedsmet.ac.uk
[2]Department of Exercise Nutrition and Health Sciences
University of Bristol, Tyndall Avenue, Bristol BS8 1TP, UK
Email: k.douglas@bristol.ac.uk

ABSTRACT

In this article we explore, on the basis of our research in elite sport, the way that certain culturally prominent stories shape and constrain lives, actions, and identities in ways that threaten development, individuality, well-being, and creativity. Next, we consider how alternative kinds of stories can act as maps or scripts which permit – and even encourage – individuals to step outside normative behaviours and beliefs in ways that promise growth, development, and change. Finally, we draw some parallels between the worlds of sport and business on the basis of narrative theory. These parallels, we suggest, offer an alternative way of providing education and development opportunities to promote not only enhanced performance and creative thinking but also long term-well being and development.

Key words: Elite Sport, Narrative, Personal Development, Story

INTRODUCTION

In his book of short stories, *Tales of the Night*, Peter Hoeg [1] tells a story within a story about a woman on trial for an undisclosed crime. During the trial she alights on the notion that all those involved in the case – judge, jury, prosecution, defence, along with the public audience – are mechanical dummies. Terrified at this thought, she decides to test it out by diverging further and further from the due processes of law and order until, finally, she lures the trial participants into an unfamiliar area where they are no longer on their guard. Stepping gingerly from the dock, she finds all the

Reviewer: Ross Anderson (University of Melbourne, Australia)

participants – including the judge – to be frozen in time, staring blankly into space. Inspecting the motionless beings in the court-room she finds that each person has a key hole – complete with large key with which to wind them up – in their back. Aghast, she realises that all these people are little more than clockwork models following a preordained plan of action, behaviour and thought until, some day, the key stops turning and their time runs out. Doubting herself for a moment, she reaches behind her to her own back to check for a keyhole: she is relieved to find none there. Over time, she comes to the horrifying realisation that she is the *only* person without a key – she is alone and unique in the world and faced with the choice of whether to continue in her individuality or resume her place on the court-room stage among all the clockwork people.

In this article we would like to explore, on the basis of our research in elite sport, the way that particular kinds of stories can act a little like the 'key in the back' of Peter Hoeg's clockwork characters. We begin by considering how certain culturally prominent stories can come to shape and constrain lives, actions, and identities in ways that threaten development, individuality, well-being, and creativity. Next, we consider how *alternative* kinds of stories can act as maps or scripts which permit – and even encourage – individuals to step outside normative 'clockwork' behaviours and beliefs in ways that promise growth, development, and change. Finally, we draw some parallels between the worlds of sport and business on the basis of narrative theory. These parallels, we suggest, offer an alternative way of providing education and development opportunities to promote not only enhanced performance and creative thinking but also long term-well being and development.

HOW STORIES SHAPE BEHAVIOUR

To what extent is our behaviour autonomous and independent, the outcome of 'free choice'? Traditional approaches to psychology, such as behavioural and experimental psychology, have tended to treat the person as an autonomous bounded self; that is, contained within a biological body which has little or no connection to the world outside. Within this conception, the causes of a person's behaviour are considered to lie within that person's *body* – or, more specifically, the brain – which is biologically separate and distinct from other people, the surrounding environment, and the effects of culture. Thus, these approaches have assumed that it is possible to understand what a person does by studying that individual in isolation. In behavioural and experimental psychology this often takes the form of studying thought processes and cognitions as evidenced by, for example, biochemical changes in the brain. This approach has been critiqued [see, for example, 2] on the basis that, by focussing solely or primarily on the brain, it neglects to consider the complex ways in which behaviour and thinking is affected by the social and cultural world outside the individual. When socio-cultural factors are considered in addition to individual psychology, human behaviour can be understood to be a result of complex and subtle processes that involve delicate symbiotic interactions between the individual and their socio-cultural environment. In this light, what we do, think, and feel cannot be reduced to autonomous, disconnected brain activity. Instead, we suggest that behaviour needs to be understood as an interaction between individual agency and autonomy within some very real limits and constraints imposed by the individual's socio-cultural setting.

But how can we gain access to and understanding of these complex psychosocial processes? One route, which we employ in our research, is through an awareness of narrative theory. Narrative theory holds that, "people are guided to act in certain ways, and not others, on the basis of the projections, expectations, and memories derived from a multiplicity but ultimately limited repertoire of available social, public, and cultural narratives" [3, p. 614]. In this way, narratives – in the form of socially available stories which are told and retold within a particular culture – come to act as a map or template for our own behaviour and identity. As McLeod [4, p. 27] observes, "The stories that, for the most part, construct our lives are 'out there', they exist before we are born and continue after we die." From this perspective, it is possible to appreciate that socially accepted scripts – which stipulate, for example, 'the way things are done round here' – can come to shape and constrain an individual's actions in the world.

This is not to say, however, that our behaviour and identity is *entirely* the result of pre-existing culturally available narrative scripts; that it is entirely beyond personal control, as is perhaps the case for Hoeg's clockwork characters. Instead, we hold the view that to function effectively in a society or culture, the individual must *negotiate* a degree of alignment between the culturally available narratives which surround them and their own unique life experiences. From this perspective, in McLeod's [4, p. 27] terms: "The task of being a person in a culture involves creating a satisfactory-enough alignment between individual experience and 'the story of which I find myself a part.'" Narrative theorists hold that this task is achieved through creating and sharing stories of one's own life which involves a "shaping or ordering of past experience" as a way of "understanding one's own and others' actions, of organising events and objects into a meaningful whole, and of connecting and seeing the consequences of actions over time" [5, p. 656]. Research suggests this task is necessary and important because success is associated with personal development and adaptation while failure can lead to stagnation and mental health problems [2, 4, 6].

Certain narratives within a particular culture are so powerful that they come to shape many people's personal stories. At these times, one particular story can become dominant, to be seen as *the only possible* story within a particular context. This dominance in itself is a problem because not everybody's experience follows the dominant story's plotline. For example, in Western medicine, Frank [7] has shown how one particular narrative – a *restitution* narrative which follows the plot yesterday I was healthy, today I'm sick, but tomorrow I'll be healthy again – has come to influence many people's personal illness stories and expectations. This is not necessarily a problem *provided that* the individual's experiences align with or 'fit' the plot of the restitution narrative – in short, the person returns to health. Not all people, however, *do* successfully return to health: some remain unwell, some experience permanent disability or impairment, and some die. In this regard, the narrow and prescriptive terms of the dominant restitution narrative, Frank suggests, can deny such individuals alternative ways by which to story their lives. An inability to create and share a personal story which 'fits' both one's own concrete experience *and* the culture within which one is immersed ultimately threatens psychological well-being and personal development [2, 4].

Significantly, it is not just the storyteller who is immersed in the dominant narrative – narratives also provide a template for *others* to follow. In medical settings this might include family, friends, doctors, and so on. Frank [7] shows how family members as well as the medical profession, through collectively expecting the 'cure' which is implicit in the restitution narrative, may find it impossible to 'hear' or accept an alternative story. These others, perhaps inadvertently, will often attempt steer the ill person back to the restitution story – to 'never give up' and to expect a 'cure' – even when restitution is impossible. The result is psychological tensions and/or trauma for the individual concerned and, for some perhaps, the denial of an opportunity to die with dignity or say goodbye in a way that is in keeping with their personal life story [see 7 for more on this].

NARRATIVES IN SPORT

We have used the premises of narrative theory to explore the kinds of stories that circulate within elite sport culture. Through life history interviews with nine highly successful women professional golfers [8], we have identified a dominant narrative type which permeates sport culture. We describe this as a *performance narrative* [9]. As we have argued elsewhere [9-13], this narrative dominates elite sport culture to the extent that it has come to be seen by many as *the only way* to achieve success in sport. In performance stories, performance-related concerns appear to infuse all areas of the storyteller's life and the storyteller illustrates a single-minded dedication to sport performance often to the exclusion of all other areas of life and self. The story provides illustrations of how and why, for some athletes, 'sport is life and life is sport' and the storyteller demonstrates how personal beliefs align with the dominant cultural storyline with comments such as, "I think for all of us, it (sport) becomes our whole life." The plot of the narrative shows the fragile nature of self-worth when it comes to be dependent on sport performance, and how a glorified self and overriding athletic identity can become problematic during periods of poor performance, injury, and when the storyteller contemplates retirement.

Dominant narratives, such as the performance narrative, tend to act as a script or a map for others' lives. Through 'modeling' a particular course of action or behaviour they may help an individual navigate their way in life. However, as we previously noted, the very fact that a singular narrative has become *dominant* implies that a certain plotline (replete with particular values and perspectives) is the *only possible* plotline. This becomes a significant problem, in Richardson's [14, p. 213] terms, "if the available narrative is limiting or at odds with the actual life" because "peoples' lives end up being limited and textually disenfranchised." By using the word "limiting", Richardson suggests that the dominant narrative can come to deny or prevent alternative plotlines being pursued or even appreciated as possible. Thus, a person's life possibilities are constrained. We suggest that this process has been clearly evidenced in sport: the narrowly prescribed values and beliefs inherent in the performance narrative have come to limit and restrict the expectations of athletes, coaches, parents, the media, and the public concerning what is required to *be* an elite athlete. To combat this imbalance, Sparkes [15] calls for alternative narratives to be made publicly available so that they might offer a reservoir of storylines to guide different courses of behaviour, facilitate alternative identities, and broaden future horizons.

One alternative story, which we have identified in our research, we call a *discovery narrative*. For us – as well as for the students, coaches, athletes, and psychologists who have listened to the story – the discovery narrative explicitly challenges the core assumptions that characterize performance stories. Because our point is that stories provide a *unique* way to present and consider alternative ways of living and being, we now provide an example story which we invite the reader to consider in the light of the previously described performance narrative. We provide here excerpts from a previously published story [9, p. 21-22] which is presented in the words of one highly successful professional tournament golfer. We think it provides a brief illustration of an alternative story which contravenes and challenges the dominant narrative in sport.

A Discovery Narrative: "Golf was a conduit to be in different worlds"
When I was a kid in my mind it was not important to be the first or the second or the third. The important thing was to have a good time. When I was an amateur and I started to be good and to win - about fifteen, sixteen, seventeen - it was good, but it was not that important. It was nice because you go away for a week or for four days, you are in another world, it's a trip. It is like "Oh that's nice!" So you are going to see new people, discover new towns, new food, the hotel, you know, a different bed! Everything is very exciting. As a kid my mother was saying "Kandy, she doesn't know how to walk! Always running!" I was always running. I love to be in the air. I love to be outside. I love to swim in the sea. I love to run. I am very active. That's why I love to bicycle always. Every kind of something you could do outside - I hated always to be inside.

If I was working in golf and I was good in golf I could have the opportunity to discover more, and to discover was interesting for me. So, because I wanted to discover, in my mind it was logical that I had to work at golf, to be good. I was outside, which was nice for me, and it makes me discover. Winning, yes, it was important, but it was not the only thing. It was not, I have to win, only winning, winning. No. I spent a lot of time *playing*. So winning was a personal satisfaction like, I did my homework, I have a good note, okay? … The day I played badly, or the tournaments I played badly, it was not like, I am not good enough or I am bad. No, I have less money. It was part of the job. For me it was "Well, I am pro." I don't know, if you are a butcher you have to cut meat. I know people were expecting, the press, people, but in my mind golf was not a priority, 'you have to play well because they expect and have an image.' No, golf was important because it was money and education for my daughter. I never felt better because I won a tournament. I felt fantastic when I had my baby – the best moment in my life was when I gave birth …

A lot of players think "What shall I do later on?" I don't have that problem. When I finish and I retire I will play golf for my pleasure but I won't work in golf. I want to learn to play the guitar. I want to learn Russian. I want to learn to restore antiques because I love wood, the smell, colour, I love it. I love gardening. I'll have a big garden. I want a dog. I want to go and bicycle with my dog and I want to do many things and I want to travel. And my boyfriend is the same. We want to travel and discover the countries we don't know because we don't know the food, we don't know… It's like "Oh my goodness!" I want to have time to do all these things.

THE POTENTIAL OF SHARING ALTERNATIVE STORIES

Through sharing alternative stories – such as the preceding discovery story – in educational, coaching, and consultancy settings we have learnt that stories can provide unique learning opportunities which stimulate individuals to grow, develop, and rethink aspects of their lives. For example, one 26-year old male responded to the discovery story in this way: "[I was] surprised by the lack of competitiveness and how her motivation overcomes this." Being surprised by a story – through becoming aware of a previously unconsidered alternative – can be an important first step towards change through opening the door to an awareness of new possibilities. As one individual remarked simply after hearing the discovery story, "I never considered that."

For some people, presenting an individual's experience in story form seems to stimulate an alternative perspective on what were previously taken for granted values. One professional coach (female, 48), for example, expressed reservations about the performance story despite this orientation being generally accepted in sport culture: "I feel very sad that this person's self-esteem is so linked to her performance. She needs to have much more balance in life. She needs to find other interests now so she can ease into retirement. It could be very painful." In contrast, the same coach responded to the discovery story in this way: "Much healthier attitude to golf and life. Sounds like she'd be a really interesting person and good companion." While the values and perspectives inherent in the discovery story are typically surprising to those in sport, a storied form of communication often seemed to prompt a positive appreciation of this alternative. One coach (male, 31) described it as, "A healthy approach to competitive golf" while another (male, 34) responded, "An attitude that I can relate in some ways to and find very refreshing that golf is not the be all and end all." Another still (male, 32) wrote: "Sounds a more balanced person, multi-sided, much more contented, knows what she wants, has experienced ups and downs but can separate golf, love, life and children into what seems to be a fairly balanced and varied life, very level headed."

Changes such as these are made possible because a story which articulates alternative ways of living, being, and thinking can free an individual from the constraints of a dominant story which articulates a singular 'way we do things round here.' For example, the discovery storyteller above explicitly *resists* cultural pressures to conform to the singular expectations of the dominant performance narrative. In telling her story, she simultaneously proves an alternative to be possible *and* sustains a personal narrative which aligns more closely with her own experiences. Thus, her story provides not only an alternative script for her own life, but also a map for others to follow which demonstrates a different way for an elite athlete to be, live, and think. In what follows, we would like to specifically consider the ways in which *storied* forms of communication – as opposed to other ways of communicating – can come to stimulate and facilitate these kinds of changes.

HOW STORIES FACILITATE DEVELOPMENT AND CHANGE

An important step if change and growth is to occur, is for the individual to become open to alternatives. The preceding story achieves this aim by providing an alternative which helps individuals in sport become sufficiently 'open' to be able to experience change and growth. According to Frank:

> Those who accept an invitation into the storytelling relation open themselves to seeing (and feeling and hearing) life differently than they normally do. Listening is not so much a willing suspension of disbelief as a willing acceptance of different beliefs and of lives in which these beliefs make sense … Those who have accepted the invitation to the story may not choose to remain in the world of the story, but if the story works, then life in their worlds will seem different after they return there. [16, p. 361]

In this excerpt, Frank makes the point that stories can be an effective way to create an opening which provides insights into another's life. Through personal reflective processes, these insights into *another's life* can subsequently lead to new perspectives on *one's own* life.

Gergen and Gergen [17] suggest that stories are particularly suited to this task, because a good story "eliminates the tendency to argue against a point of view" as "it is socially difficult and even rude to directly challenge or undermine a personal life story (p. 116)." Rather than stating opinion or view, a good story *shows* someone's personal lived experience unfolding. In this way, the listener is taken into the unfamiliar experience of another's world where the listener is, to some extent, a stranger. As Gergen and Gergen suggest, it is difficult – as a stranger – to challenge what another person knows of their own experience; the experience is what it is and, at some level, demands to be accepted as such. This has been the case when we have used the discovery story in coaching and consultancy: because the story tells of one woman's personal lived experience, those who hear the story are obliged to accept it as possible. Critical to the success of this process therefore is the story's ability to effectively *evoke* the other's lived experience – feelings, sights, sounds, smells – in ways that are convincing and believable. Stories which *tell about* the life or lives through abstract details or statements – as opposed to *show* the life unfolding through detailed description and evocation – are less likely to be effective in encouraging acceptance or consideration of alternative beliefs and values.

A second issue relates to the way that good stories are, to some degree at least, 'open' in terms of the way in which they may be interpreted. This quality differentiates storied forms of communication that privilege statements of fact or propositional knowledge which leave little room for questions. Through our research into the uses of stories in coach education settings [10], we documented how many coaches responded to the previously presented discovery narrative by asking questions. Questioning is important because it indicates that a degree of personal reflection on the story has taken place and suggests that the coaches took the stories seriously and had begun to consider the possible implications of each story. Thus, by retaining a degree of openness or ambiguity, stories can and do serve as an excellent stimulus for group discussion and personal reflection. In this light, one of the particular benefits of stories is that they permit or encourage new understandings of topics or issues that may not be amenable to being communicated in a resolved and 'nailed down' manner. Thus, as we have noted elsewhere, "stories stand in contrast to more scientific forms of knowing which are ill-suited to communicating multiple perspectives, ambiguities, and uncertainties" [10, p. 43]. It may very well be these kinds of multiple perspectives, ambiguities, and uncertainties are central characteristics of 'real world' and applied knowledge.

A third point we would like to make relates to the way that a story can allow a particular incident or event to be explored in greater detail than might otherwise be possible. This might be an event which would not normally be spoken about or an incident at risk of being overlooked. One example in the discovery story is the storyteller's discussion of the ways in which her role as a mother was overlooked by many in sport who chose to focus on her role as a professional golfer. In this way, stories can facilitate a "focus on the hidden margins of sporting life which occur in many sporting contexts but are rarely talked about" [18, p. 248]. Story forms can allow these moments to be held in 'freeze-frame' or 'replayed' for closer inspection and consideration. An opportunity to reflect upon and reconsider happenings is an important component of learning and development because, as Freeman [19] puts it, "human existence frequently involves a *delay,* or 'postponement,' of insight into its affairs: realizations, narrative connections, are made after-the-fact, when the dust has settled. The result is that we are frequently *late* in our own understanding of things (p. 136)". Thus, as we have previously observed, "through replaying or freezing events which in 'real life' scenarios may occur 'in a blur'" [10, p. 45] we get a second chance to develop understanding. This provides an opportunity for the coach or consultant to consider 'hidden' tensions – such as the difficulties a mother may face when leaving her child to go to work – in order to prevent these difficulties impacting performance or well-being.

A final point concerns the ways in which storied forms of communication may help to bring "a moral compass back into the reader's (and the writer's) life" [20, p. 118]. If stories are able to achieve this goal, then it is likely to be because a good story encourages the listener or reader to *incorporate* the story – of another's experience – within their own experience in some way. Coaches, for example, sometimes responded to the discovery narrative in this way when they described an emotional reaction to the story. As we have previously observed: "Particularly noticeable in these kinds of responses were expressions of empathy with the storyteller and a sense of identification with the events, motives, or orientations associated with a particular story type. [10, p. 42]" In taking this step, coaches opened the possibility for a valuable learning opportunity through a reconsideration of previously taken for granted assumptions. For example, one coach's candid statement that, "I would attempt to it all differently if I had my time again" provided a chance for the group to enter into discussion of the kinds of factors and experiences which led to this realization. Through discussing the group's responses to a performance story and a discovery story, we were able to reflect on the ethics of encouraging sport performance at the expense of other areas of life and consider the ways in which we, as coaches and educators, might perpetuate a damaging performance focus among those with whom we work:

> In other sport-related work we have observed how stories have the potential to: introduce a moral dimension to the events, somehow recasting in a negative light events which are accepted within sporting culture ... Insults which are

acceptable in sport, like the football coach in the park yesterday shouting "Come on girls!" to a group of male sportspeople implying they are not putting in enough effort to be "real men," through a different angle of observation, come to be seen as unacceptable. [18, p. 250]

This kind of moral repositioning can prompt – in any domain – a personal reflective process which has the potential to lead to new understandings and perspectives on ethical and moral issues. These kinds of insights are, oftentimes we suggest, unlikely through factual and propositional communication forms. As Frank [16] observes, at this point in time gaining more knowledge may be less important than developing a clearer sense of value. In his words, "the old faith was that more facts and better theories would render ethical dilemmas moot; the new realization is that knowledge only increases the density of ethical dilemmas." From this perspective, "Deciding what to do about what we know requires having an ethical standpoint" [16, p. 363]. In our experience, storied forms of communication – in written or verbal form – have been the most effective method to stimulate these kinds of development and we believe they have much to offer in a broad range of coaching and consultancy settings.

CONCLUSION

Gergen and Gergen [17] provide a commentary on the ways in which work involving narrative – in both theory and in practice – has begun to contribute to 'real world' environments including organizational transformation and conflict reduction. In the context of organizational transformation, Gergen and Gergen note:

> In both the case of metaphor and narrative, one of the chief ideas is that such tropes are significant to participants in centering the meaning of the organization. For example, if the shared understanding of the organization is as a "machine," this metaphor emphasizes efficiency and the impersonal character of workers as the "cogs" in the machine; a "family" metaphor can foster images of convivial action and dedication to a mission, as well as "family feuds" and patriarchal power. [17, p. 114]

These authors also highlight the practice of *appreciative inquiry* (AI), which they suggest is now used internationally. Providing an alternative to 'problem solving' approaches, AI assists an organization to focus on its positive core values through the production and collection of personal narratives – or stories – from group members. Positive themes – such as times when an individual experienced success, discovery or joy – are identified in the stories which are then used to inform the development of the organization. According to Gergen and Gergen: "Besides being very effective in creating change, the AI process is one that typically builds enthusiasm and commitment among the participants." [17, p. 115]

We would like to conclude by reinforcing two points which we see as central to the possibilities and potential of using story and narrative in business and consulting contexts. First, the use of stories is premised upon the understanding that – despite what culture, organizations, or individuals might say – there are always alternative ways to 'do' and to 'be'. These alternatives are important because, in addition to offering hope for the future for some individuals, they show that people are rarely, if ever, 'fixed' in terms of their identities and horizons: we can and we do have potential to change our stories and our lives. If individuals are to be provided with opportunities to story their lives and their work differently, it is first necessary to offer stories which show alternatives to be possible. Merely becoming aware of these alternatives can widen an individual's options in terms of both identity development and life horizons.

The second point relates to the ways particular narratives tend to be privileged in particular socio-cultural environments. In sport, performance-type stories are currently dominant and alternative stories are routinely silenced. We ask: Does a similar dynamic exist in business, education, healthcare, politics and, perhaps, in Western society at large? Is our culture currently demonstrating an imbalance towards stories which privilege the kinds of values communicated by athletes who tell performance stories? If so, we suggest that coaches and consultants might wish to reflect on the implications of this imbalance through becoming aware of the ways their current practice and dialogue may serve to silence or impede alternative stories. Sharing alternative stories, in our experience, tends to invite and support *further* alternative stories which better fit some people's experiences. One possible outcome of this process is enhanced psychological well-being; another is more open and trusting relationships between individuals. Both of these outcomes, we suggest, are good for the long term development of any organization.

ACKNOWLEDGMENTS
We thank the women who have made our research possible by sharing with us the stories of their lives. We also thank Ross Anderson for his informed and constructive response to an earlier version of this article.

REFERENCES
1   Hoeg, P., *Tales of the Night*, The Harvill Press, London, 1997.

2   Crossley, M., *Introducing Narrative Psychology: Self, Trauma and the Construction of Meaning*, Open University Press, Buckingham, UK, 2000.

3   Somers, M., The Narrative Construction of Identity: A Relational and Network Approach, *Theory and Society*, 23, 605-649, 1994.

4   McLeod, J., *Narrative and Psychotherapy*, Sage, London, 1997.

5   Chase, S., Narrative Inquiry: Multiple Lenses, Approaches, Voices, in: Denzin, N. and Lincoln, Y., eds., *The Handbook of Qualitative Research*, Sage, Thousand Oaks, CA, 2005, 651-679.

6   McAdams, D., *The Stories We Live By*, The Guilford Press, New York, NY, 1993.

7   Frank, A. W., *The Wounded Storyteller*, University of Chicago Press, Chicago, 1995.

8   Douglas, K., *What's the Drive in Golf? Motivation and Persistence in Women Professional Tournament Golfers*, Doctoral Dissertation, University of Bristol, 2004.

9   Douglas, K. and Carless, D., Performance, Discovery, and Relational Narratives Among Women Professional Tournament Golfers, *Women in Sport and Physical Activity Journal*, 2006, 15(2), 14-27.

10   Douglas, K. and Carless, D., Using Stories in Coach Education, *International Journal of Sports Science and Coaching*, 2008, 3(1), 33-49.

11   Douglas, K. and Carless, D., Training or Education? Negotiating a Fuzzy Line Between What "We" Want and What "They" Might Need, *Annual Review of Golf Coaching*, 2008, 1-13.

12   Douglas, K. and Carless, D., Abandoning the Performance Narrative: Two Women's Stories of Transition from Professional Golf, *Journal of Applied Sport Psychology,* In Press.

13   Carless, D. and Douglas, K. "We Haven't Got a Seat on the Bus for You" or "All the Seats are Mine": Narratives and Career Transition in Professional Golf, *Qualitative Research in Sport and Exercise*, 2009, 1(1), 51-66.

14   Richardson, L., Narrative and Sociology, in: Van Mannen, J., ed., *Representation in Ethnography,* Sage, Thousand Oaks, CA, 1995, 198-222.

15   Sparkes, A. C., Bodies, Narratives, Selves, and Autobiography: The Example of Lance Armstrong, *Journal of Sport and Social Issues*, 2004, 28, 397-428.

16   Frank, A.W., Standpoint of Storyteller, *Qualitative Health Research,* 2000, 10(3), 354-365.

17   Gergen, M. and Gergen, K., Narratives in Action, *Narrative Inquiry,* 2006, 16(1), 112-121.

18   Douglas, K. and Carless, D., The Team Are Off: Getting Inside Women's Experiences in Professional Sport, *Aethlon: The Journal of Sport Literature, 2008, XXV:I,* 241-251.

19   Freeman, M., Life "On Holiday"? In Defence of Big Stories, *Narrative Inquiry,* 2006, 16(1), 131-138.

20   Denzin, N., *Performance Ethnography*, Sage, Thousand Oaks, CA, 2003.

Critical Effort and Leadership in Specialised Virtual Networks

Kurt April[1, 2], Victor Katoma[1] and Kai Peters[2]
[1]UCT Graduate School of Business
University of Cape Town
Private Bag X3, Rondesbosch 7701, RSA
E-mail: aprilkur@gsb.uct.ac.za
[2]Ashridge
Berkhamsted, Hertfordshire, HP4 1NS, UK
E-mail: Kai.Peters@ashridge.org.uk

ABSTRACT

Leadership has been defined in various ways with some scholars strongly suggesting that it is a calling or something driven by a trait [1], which is expressed through personal values, integrity and certain qualities [2-5]. Leadership in virtual networks, however, is more of an earned recognition. This article argues that leadership in these virtual networks is about character-building.

We approach this study by reviewing the literature around character-building, which we then model as discretionary effort (DE), a construct of expectancy, instrumentality, valence and self-affirmation, which explains the extra effort spent beyond the work-role requirement. Additionally, we review the coaching literature, which, when applied to our DE model, provides a path along which DE can be encouraged.

We investigate whether work leverage earned through DE is shaped by process-oriented factors such as 'experience'. 'Gender' and 'profession' are also investigated as other added influencer factors. The study is based on professional networks with a data sample of 1548 managers and specialists in different sectors. Results reveal that process-oriented variables, such as 'experience', significantly explain the variability in the DE build-up process. DE levels are also observed to be different between sectors. 'Gender' did not have any effect on the results, either at unit or inter-unit relations, in clusters of employees who are either virtually-located or co-located.

Key words: Coaching, Expectancy, Instrumentality, Professional Networks, Self-Affirmation, Valence, Virtual Networks

Reviewers: Niki Panteli (University of Bath, UK)
Stacey Connaughton (Purdue University, USA)

INTRODUCTION

The main aim of this paper is to discuss the factors influencing discretionary effort (DE)[1] and its relationship to leadership in professional and virtual networks. We suggest that the issues surrounding DE are separable from those governing leadership generally, which are manifested through other artefacts like organisational citizenship behaviour and stewardship.

Thus, instead of focussing on leadership characteristics, which tend to be complex constructs, in order to explain and develop performance in professional and virtual networks, DE may be the construct which can serve this function more simply.

Measuring the real impact this approach may provide, must, we believe, take context into account. Specialised networks have specific characteristics that require redefined leadership roles. Virtual network leadership[2], manifested through the desire to generate DE, requires an ability to influence indirectly. In this paper, the two terms of leadership and DE are thus used interchangeably when looking at the unsolicited effort especially at the networking level, and the behavioural variables involved. An alternative would be to state this concept as the discretionary leadership effort (clearly decoupling the concept from the traditional view, i.e., organisational positions of authority).

Although, initially, DE is based upon individuals, the application of multiple-level modelling in this study indicates that researching team or sector DE is possible. From this perspective, rather than conceptualising a team's entire leadership status, it seems sensible to discuss a team's total discretionary force. The DE constructs, which are illustrated later in this paper, provide substantive response variables, with little or no ambiguity. The statistical inference, or modelling strategies, adopted support the measurement of DE, and are thus used to model leadership development more broadly.

The content of the research is subdivided into four sections. First, we discuss professional and virtual networks, focusing on leadership and DE. Second, we review the coaching literature to consider whether coaching specifically for DE in virtual networks is plausible. Third, we explain how we measure DE overall and the underlying variables used. Fourth, we implement multi-level modelling using LISREL. This approach is taken because of the layered nature of the information gathered, taking employees in virtual and co-located work environments into account.

The data was collected from a sample of 1548 employees in different sectors including education, engineering, mining, finance, and retail industries. Respondents were either virtually located and/or co-located.

---

[1] We define discretionary effort (DE) as an individual's free choice, in which intrinsic motivation is operationalised, and which emanates from the individual's desire to engage in, or to bring to bear his/her already full engagement to, an activity or activities because s/he enjoys, is interested in, and/or is committed to, the activity.

[2] Virtual teams or networks can be described as those that work on projects with interdependent tasks and common objectives. Their interaction wholly or solely takes place through the use of some kind of technology; be it computer, telephone, video, etc. In this context, virtual network leadership in turn can be defined as the set of competences, approaches and outlook needed to lead such teams effectively, in a way that allows them to develop, learn and operate to their best ability.

RESEARCH CONTEXT

Professional and virtual networks are informal teams that arise because individuals need to learn and share knowledge. They can be defined as communities of practice (COP) [6], to describe an activity system where individuals that are united in action and meaning can collectively share ideas and find solutions. Professional networks include public ones such as LinkedIn or the Linux COP. These networks also exist within complex organisations where geographic dispersion creates virtual teams with similar characteristics.

The purpose of this study is to survey the factors that influence people in exercising DE within professional and virtual networks. Our main concern in this study is with virtual teams. Virtual teams can easily involve global membership, such as in Shell International and Novartis. Traditional DE researchers have targeted co-located teams, but the rapid emergence of virtual teams attracts debate about how DE is affected by this geographic dispersion.

Creating cohesive teams is critical for organisational success. Cohesive teamwork drives competitiveness [7], with such mobilized action also driving innovation [8]. This is especially necessary in the global knowledge economy where the focus is on knowledge and service, such as in Ernst & Young, Edwardian Hotels and Standard Chartered Bank. Mullins [9] notes that while teamwork is important to any organisation, it is particularly significant in a service industry where there is a direct affect on customer satisfaction.

Secondly, other vital business strategies, such as knowledge management which have been linked to organisational performance [10-12] are also highly reliant upon professional and virtual networks. These virtual networks are also redefining work configurations and shift the employee-employer relationship. A virtual worker now can be a contingent or contract employee who is self-employed and has no dominant organisational affiliation, but has temporary relationships with multiple organisations. These electronically-connected contractors are part of the move from the traditional command-and-control organisational unit, to one based on the work of individuals.

What is not clearly known, however, is the nature, direction and magnitude of the influence these teams of individuals have on DE, and hence the extent of the business value they create. This is mainly because very little research has been conducted on DE in professional network environments. When these networks extend beyond co-location to virtual professional networks, there is even less research available. In both instances, the way network members relate and exercise DE is dependent on team leadership. Intuitively, it seems fair to suggest that networks of professionals are less likely to flourish in a command-and-control environment than in a non-threatening and supportive environment. This suggests that influencing is more important than commanding, and we thus seek to measure leadership influence and understand how leadership roles are perceived and should be executed in these virtual conditions.

LEADERSHIP IN PROFESSIONAL NETWORKS

Recent studies on organisational team leadership have pointed out that the use of teams can foster productivity, result in optimal use of resources and improve innovation and creativity [13-15]. Different researchers note, however, that a major challenge lies in identifying the factors that make teams more practical and effective [16], as team leadership is complex and premised on multiple social dimensions, and is not well understood [17-19]. Murphy [20] suggested that, irrespective of work location, there are always situational needs that demand certain knowledge, skill and abilities. Consequently, leadership attitudes have to be developed flexibly.

In professional and virtual networks, face-to-face interactions are uncommon and membership is often based on interests and needs. Unless leadership is effective and appropriately administered in these specialised networks, the rapidly changing work landscape will gradually and easily disconnect network members from their team leaders. Such contingent or situation-based leadership is a challenge, especially for charismatic leadership, since contingent leadership is context-oriented where the leader has to fit in with particular situations rather than being driven purely by a more uni-dimensional charisma [21-24].

In virtual networks, DE and leadership are not as obvious as they may have been perceived in traditional settings. Virtual professional networks tend to be shaped by many more factors that are naturally dynamic, and require continuous interpretation. Some of these factors are technology-inherent, since communication technologies continue to evolve, but others are social elements such as trust, a sense of belonging and perceived leadership support; especially where members have never physically met. Sproull and Kiesler [7] posit that performance, as the key measure of team dynamics, is related to team composition, trust and cohesiveness. Team members contribute readily if there is a need for knowledge or help, but they also want some form of control over their own intellectual property. Bollen and Hoyle [25] suggest that perceived cohesiveness is based on an individual's sense of belonging to a particular group, and his or her feelings of moral association to that membership. Self-efficacy, emanating from an internal locus of control [26], is another attribute important to virtual network success.

As the work landscape changes, professional and virtual team members' needs also change. Team leaders thus need to learn to analyse situations rapidly depending on what is required [27]. Zaccaro, Rittman and Marks [28] note that leaders must use discretion in altering their approach to managing virtual networks, due to the communications challenges that virtual teams present. Leadership therefore can be viewed as mediation and coordination [27], and as the creation of inclusive environments [29]. When a leader meets the necessary behaviour of the circumstance, the fulfilment of the team's desires are likely to be met [30].

DEVELOPING LEADERSHIP IN PROFESSIONAL NETWORKS
Morgan [31], among others, suggests that managers require increasing skill and competence in dealing with change. Research has indicated that a failure to manage change successfully leads to stress and negative attitudes. [32-34] Mumford, Zaccaro, Harding and Marks [35] note that leaders develop competencies over time through exposure to increasing difficulty and complex long-term problems, as they ascend an organisational hierarchy.

Numerous authors [36-39] indicate that while traditional classroom education, based on the transfer of knowledge, is suitable where technical skills are required, coaching is more suitable as issues become more complex. Helping individuals develop their skills at advanced levels of organisational hierarchy requires thoughtful engagement with multiple, people-centred issues. De Haan [40] posits that coaching encourages and facilitates the self-development of the coachee within the coachee's own network of relationships, which closely mirrors the professional and virtual network situation.

De Haan [40] suggests a valuable typology of the intellectual sources of coaching traditions, which he classifies into four categories: *person-focused coaching*, based on Kline [41] among others, focuses on facilitating the coachee with encouragement and understanding; *insight-focused coaching* [42] based on greater distance, seeks to explore unmentioned issues; *problem-focused coaching* [43, 44] makes concrete suggestions on ways in which problems can be tackled; and *solution-focused coaching* [45, 46], which is similar to problem-focused coaching, but searches for solutions to challenges rather than trying to deconstruct problems.

All of these coaching traditions have precedents in various strands of psychology, with many relying on psychotherapy and De Haan [40] spends considerable effort in relating the psychotherapy evidence-base to the modern coaching construct, in order to intuit the efficacy of each specific approach. Coaching is clearly shown to benefit the development of individuals as they grapple with the challenges facing them, especially as issues involve relationships rather than technical challenges.

While De Haan [40], and the various studies he cites, can be seen to provide an indication that coaching could be considered an appropriate methodology to deal with relationship issues which are virtual rather than co-located, issues of virtual teams are not specifically mentioned. Caulat [47] is one of very few authors who have specifically investigated the development of virtual teams in order to raise levels of trust. She notes that knowing how to develop and maintain high performing virtual teams has become a critical competitive advantage. Her research indicates that by coaching virtual team leaders, using a methodology closely aligned to De Haan's [40], problem-focused coaching yields considerable benefits.

Caulat [47] indicates that since there is such a dearth of information on managing in virtual teams, certain transferred insights are beneficial. She suggests that in order to better understand how to 'contract' the rules of the virtual team, we should begin with our understanding of informality in live face-to-face meetings. Of interest then, would be how we perceive and understand large degrees of informality and spontaneity. Spending sufficient time in such a setting, research shows, creates trust and intimacy. Furthermore, she claims that we could learn from communication theory – for instance, orderly discussions were shown to facilitate the defence of individual's positions (debate) and the closing off of individuals to learn from others' perspectives, as opposed to dialogue, in which judgement is suspended, positions are lightly held and individuals open themselves up to learn from others. In this way, her research has debunked some of the common perceptions regarding, for instance, teleconferencing, where it is believed that good order should be maintained and only one person should speak at a time. Caulat [47] has shown such behaviour to actually be counterproductive to involvement and engagement.

Additionally, in a virtual environment, one cannot see others in the traditional sense, one must therefore become sensitized to the messages being sent through tone of voice, speed of delivery and intonation during a teleconference; visual cues from a videoconference; reading between the lines in all of the above situations as well as with e-mail/electronic exchanges. A further suggestion is to learn to live with silences, which can seem tremendously long in an audio environment.

Even at this level of insight, virtual team development remains within the general leadership realm. By applying our DE model, we believe that coaching and specifically virtual team coaching, can be made more efficient and effective.

METHOD
THE INTRICACIES OF DISCRETIONARY EFFORT (DE)

In this section, we introduce and investigate the details of DE to highlight the relationship between DE and leadership. At the basic level, DE can be described as the act of doing more for the organisation, without necessarily receiving extra pay for extra effort. DE is the voluntary level of performance above that which is required for the team member to maintain their employment. In certain cases, highly motivated, innate character may be evident in individuals. The challenge, however, is in understanding how to create an environment in which others want to willingly offer their DE to the team and/or organisation, and how to encourage the exercise of DE in an optimal manner for other individuals who are in a position to calculate whether they will, or will not, contribute any extra effort.

The process of DE builds from a rational mental analysis of motivational variables that are defined by expectations. When people join work, they come with expectations that must be fulfilled for them to be motivated. Expectations are necessary for gauging the value we pin on work and are also the channels to best performance. Well-tested motivational variables are expectancy, instrumentality and valence [48]. Self-affirmation [49] is another important variable, particularly in virtual teams, and was included in this study because it has not been fully explored in relation to DE.

The variables that we have identified, and tested for, within this professional network context are therefore expectancy, instrumentality, valence and self-affirmation. When these are combined, these variables produce a cohesive force known as expectancy force, or usually called DE.

Expectancy   This is a belief based on the principle that an effort is likely to lead to an anticipated performance outcome [50, 51]. It is a probability that a certain goal can be attained by making a particular attempt. Expectancy is therefore mostly guided by an individual's experience, by self-efficacy (confidence), and by the perceived difficulty of the task in question. While self-efficacy is influenced by skill and work level-appropriate competencies, perceived difficulty is determined by goal-setting. When goals are too high, expectations are likely to be low [52]. To avert the problem of low expectations caused by too high goals, employees should possess some sort of perceived control over the task output requirements, so that the ability to achieve that goal is within reach.

Instrumentality   This is a probability based on the belief that, by attaining performance expectations, a greater reward awaits [50, 52]. Rewards can be in terms of pay rises, recognition and/or sense of accomplishment. Instrumentality is, nonetheless, likely to be low if it is not sufficiently differentiated. For example, if a company gives the same bonuses to everyone, regardless of performance levels, then instrumentality would be low.

Valence   This is the value an individual places on the reward [50, 51]. Usually, this is a function of an individual's needs, goals, values and sources of motivation. Valence has also been described as the perceived emotional-orientation people develop towards the outcome or reward [52]. Valence is associated with high positive and negative outcome perceptions in a situation, and therefore can be defined as consequential.

Self-Affirmation   This is based on the understanding that, following a particular performance or engagement, an individual will achieve something such as a skill that builds and protects the image of self-worth [53]. Affirmation of self is further described as something that provides an individual with the abilities to adapt to change [54]. Rather than perceiving self-affirmation as a response to threatening events, it can be seen as a process of reinforcement, or enhancement, for future challenges. Others look at physiological factors, and changes in behaviour, that arise from threatening experiences [55, 56]. The process of enhancement can also emanate from contrasting mental models, in order to assess and develop ideas concisely. Examples of self-affirmation thus include positive comparisons of expectancy with peers, and whether expectancy is meaningful and is evaluated positively in the workplace. It would also depend on whether the self is seen to have the capacity for efficacious action.

Expectancy, Instrumentality and Self-Affirmation are therefore attitudes or cognitive leanings that an individual perceives [52, 57]. They are based on the likelihood that an effort would lead to performance, and performance would lead to reward (desired outcome). Consequently, they can be assigned a value domain of $[0,1]$ while *Valence* may range from -1 to +1 $[-1,1]$. This makes valence deterministic of the stability of the expectancy processes. A negative valence would entail a negative DE. Results that place valence in the range of $[0,1]$ are henceforth important, and of much interest in this study.

Expectancy and Instrumentality have also been noted as perceptions that are influenced by an individual's experiences (learning theory), observations of others (social learning theory), and self-perception [51]. This paper also tests these assumptions, and investigates what role self-affirmation plays with these viewpoints. These behavioural variables are attitudes. They are not just individually-formed, but arise out of interaction with others. Attitudes, in some sense, are defined as providing a state of readiness to respond in a particular way [58]. Katz [51] further suggests that motives and attitudes are interlinked, and are functions of the following:

1. *Knowledge* – with a good knowledge-base, employees attain grounds to provide a basis for interpretation and classification of new information. Well-natured attitudes provide the necessary openness and the base of knowledge, and the framework from which new information can be placed and enriched.

2. *Expressiveness* – attitudes are one form of conveying expressions. They allow employees to show the values they hold to their affinity-tribe and peers, thereby expressing their self-concept.

3. *Instrumentalism* – long-held path-dependent attitudes maximize rewards and minimize sanctions. Such historicity of attitudes towards an object, or

other people, can thus be helpful because of past positive or negative experience. It can be deduced that behaviours or knowledge that resulted in the satisfaction of needs are therefore more likely to culminate in a favourable attitude for the future.

4.   *Ego-Defensiveness* – attitudes can also be held if they are seen to protect one's image or ego. Such attitudes are helpful in protecting one's ego from undesirable truth or reality [59].

RESEARCH QUESTIONS

In addition to measuring for expectancy, instrumentality, valence and self-affirmation, the study looks at a number of *influencer variables*. Earlier on in the literature review, 'experience' was noted by a number of authors [27, 28] as an important factor.

We therefore control for experience with the hypothesis that there is a correlation between 'experience' and how employees come to learn and master how to use DE in professional networks (H_1).

Additionally, the study included profession and gender as influencer variables because we believe that while individuals may be the direct objects on which DE can be measured, profession may in certain cases be a strong influencer. For example, professions such as financial [60], retail and education industries may yield more DE because of, for instance, the close interface between financial organisations and their clients.

Gender was also investigated as an influencer variable due to suggested differences in both DE and communication skills [61]. In separate studies using multivariate-ordered logistic regression models controlling for individual abilities, household and family responsibilities and workplace characteristics, no gender differences were self-reported for DE in the USA. In the UK, however, women reported greater DE than men [61]. This lack of clarity both about gender and about the specific professional work environments led us to control for the hypotheses that there is a correlation between 'gender' and DE variation in professional networks (H_2) and there is a difference in DE between organisations (H_3).

DATA COLLECTION

For this study, data was collected through the use of a questionnaire. The questionnaire was designed to assist respondents in thinking through the critical behaviours in 10 key areas for effectively engaging in, utilizing and creating conducive, value-adding, professional network relationships. The questionnaire (Appendix 1) addressed the expectancy issues (our definitions) listed below:

- *Effort-Performance Expectancy* (EP): Belief that desired levels of performance are possible, given the resources, competencies and skills s/he possesses.
- *Interpersonal-Performance Expectancy* (IP): Belief that one is seen to be assisting, and developing, others.
- *Effort-Learning Expectancy* (EL): Belief that expended personal effort will have future, value-adding learning benefits.

- *Leading-Visibility Expectancy* (LV): Belief that one is seen to be in step with new trends and the cutting-edge, and acknowledged as being knowledgeable and practicing at the forefront.
- *Network-Performance Expectancy* (NP): Belief that you or your colleagues are committed to the goals and objectives of the network.
- *Internal-Recognition Expectancy* (IR): Belief that one will be recognized (with little or no financial rewards), both within the network and the greater organisation, for the contribution s/he has made.
- *Mutual-Reciprocity Expectancy* (MR): returning directly, or indirectly, aid, resources and/or friendship offered by another network member.
- *Individual-Network Learning Expectancy* (NL): Belief that one's own personal learning, knowledge and insights are of value, and can contribute, to the network's learning.
- *Performance-Outcome Expectancy* (PO): Belief that what one's doing will lead to certain outcomes.
- *Team-Sustainability Expectancy* (TS): Belief that you are focused on sustaining the network, and its future.

Organisations, we believe, that cultivate these expectancy behaviours will begin to meet employees' personal expectancies, leading to the meeting of workplace goals that will lead to the employee offering his/her DE. The four variables underlying DE (expectancy, instrumentality, valence and self-affirmation) are developed from the 10 items above.

The questionnaire was sent out through e-mails, fax and the web-based survey software system at http://www.questionpro.com. Parts of the data were collected from managers on a leadership course at the Graduate School of Business (University of Cape Town). Responses were subsequently collected on the database in a spreadsheet format, and thereafter exported to SPSS. The internal consistency of the measurement yielded a Cronbach's alpha of 0.84, indicating that the responses and the items on the questionnaire were appropriate and sufficient to the study. After the initial analysis and further screening, the data was finally exported to LISREL for modelling.

RESULTS
MULTI-LEVEL MODELLING
In the process of investigating the aforementioned variables, multi-level data analysis was used. This was prompted by the clustered nature of the data, since multi-level data arise when units are nested in clusters [62, 63]. Students in a class and employees in a particular department or group are some of the examples. The latter is interpreted as follows: employees form or work in units because of location or work interests and these units form clusters which are teams or departments. In this study, employees were clustered into units within virtually and or co-located workspaces. Departments were further nested into sectors such as education, finance and retail. In this case, sectors are super or higher clusters, in what is reviewed as a *level three structure*. Employees fall in the first cluster called the *micro-level*, departments in the second called the *macro-level,* and sectors are the last level in the hierarchy. Units tend to

share the same cluster influence. For instance, employees in the same unit (team) could be led by one leader and therefore influenced by that same leadership and, to some extent, share similar work experience. However, not all information in the clusters is usually present, as it is not feasible to account for all cluster-specific influences as covariates in the analysis. This creates what is called cluster-level unobserved heterogeneity [64]. Because of unobserved heterogeneity, not all relations between the variables in the units are therefore determined. Specific response variables, namely, expectancy, instrumentality, valence and self-affirmation, are therefore measured on these clusters, and the variability in the response recorded.

Usually, units in clusters tend to lie in particular areas around some means that are different from the overall group variable means. This creates inter-unit dependence or intra-cluster correlations [65, 66]. In order to explain unobserved heterogeneity error ($m_{ij} + e_{ij}$) values are included in the measurement equations of the response variables, as shown in Equation 1 later on.

MULTI-LEVEL ANALYSIS RELEVANCE
Multi-level analysis is very useful for data that shows complex patterns of variability. Mostly, it is the variability focused in nested sources of data, and the social context on individual behaviours [67].

Specifically this data set had nested information, such as employees in different locations, who were either co-located or virtual. And, apart from localities, these employees belonged to professional networks and further sectors. There is variability between employees' responses to DE actions, and also between the groups they belong to, by location and by profession. In this study, the primary objective was to identify some of the factors that lead to this variability and tackle the following questions:

1. Do variables such as 'experience', 'education', 'age', and 'gender' contribute to variability in the processes of generating DE?
2. Does 'profession' contribute to this variability in the clusters, at the individual level?
3. Are there some differences in DE between organisations, and what should be done to improve DE if differences do exist?

In the diagram below, given as an example, there are 11 clusters with units clustering around means indicated by horizontal bars. The response in this case measures expectancy, instrumentality, valence and self-affirmation. Employee units are represented by the white and dark circles according to whether they are virtually or co-located, respectively, and are clustered around the mean (horizontal bars).

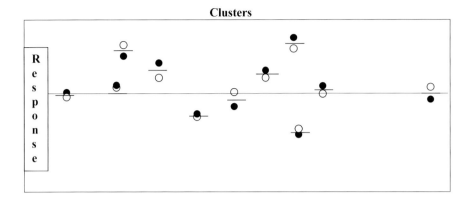

Figure 1. Clusters Around Mean Values

The final model is specified as:

$$Y_{ij} = \beta_o + \beta_1 \text{Experience}_{ij} + \beta_2 \text{Profession}_{ij} + m_{ij} + e_{ij} \quad\quad\text{1.}$$

j is the index for the groups (j= 1,...........,N)

i is the index for the individuals within the groups (i = 1,...........nj)

Characteristics of the data set (n = 1548) are shown below:

Table 1. The Sectors and Percentage of the Respondents in Each Particular Sector

Sector	%
Education	4%
Engineering	5%
Financial	25%
FMCG	3%
ICT	15%
Medical	4%
Mining	15%
NGO	3%
Petroleum	13%
Retail	4%
Support	6%
Media	0%
Consulting	0%
Transport	3%
Grand Total	100%

Table 2. The Distribution of the Age Groups of the Respondents

Age Group	%
<30	20%
31-35	25%
36-40	21%
41-45	19%
46-50	9%
>50	4%
Not given	2%
Grand Total	100%

Table 3. Seniority of the Respondents

Position	%
CEO	1%
Director	17%
Lecturer	0%
Manager	65%
Not given	1%
Section Head	2%
Specialist	14%
Grand Total	100%

Table 4. Qualification Levels of the Respondents in the Six Selected Sectors

Lower Qualification refers to the Matric in the South African education system which is the equivalent of the senior secondary school general certificate.

		Qualification				
		Lower Qualification	Secondary School	Bachelors Degree	Masters Degree	Doctoral Degree
Sector	Education	4.1%	19.2%	32.9%	23.3%	17.8%
	Engineering	7.1%	18.9%	52.0%	18.9%	0.0%
	Finance	7.4%	6.0%	59.5%	23.3%	0.9%
	ICT	15.4%	13.7%	46.9%	15.4%	2.9%
	Mining	4.3%	24.3%	55.7%	12.9%	1.4%
	Retail	40.3%	15.6%	28.6%	7.8%	0.0%

Table 5. Highest Qualification Obtained by the Respondents

Highest Qualification	%
Doctoral Degree	3%
Masters Degree	17%
Bachelors Degree	49%
Secondary School Diploma	19%
Lower Secondary School Qualification (Matric)	11%
Not Given	1%
Grand Total	100%

In terms of qualifications, Table 5 shows that the majority had Bachelors degrees (49%), followed by Secondary School Graduates at 19%. Masters degrees were at 17%, a Lesser Secondary School Qualification at 11%, and a Doctorate Degree at 3%.

Females constituted 36%, while males 64% of the total sample survey.

CROSS-SECTOR SAMPLING

Sampling from across sectors or organisations increases the test of predictive accuracy of DE [68]. For clarity, a few sectors were later identified as important in illustrating how DE is evolving. These were Education, Mining, Retail, ICT, Finance and Engineering. The selection of these sectors was simply based on how independent, or distinct, these were between each other, and from the rest. Secondly, these sectors had a large number of respondents as compared to the rest, and had formed distinct clusters according to the location of employees, whether these were co-located or virtually-located. Thirdly, there is little literature on DE in sectors. We did find some motivation and performance literature relating to these six sectors, that to some extent confirmed our findings (for example, the Engineering sector was much lower in DE as compared to the Retail industry). The point is that while at *micro-level* (employee-level) DE is very much influenced by 'experience' in these networks, this may not be so at the *macro-level* (sector-level) level.

The computer output for the three PRELIS multi-level programs are summarised in Table 6, for the variance decomposition of the response variable, *Expectancy*. Model 1 provides a baseline – models 2 and 3 help determine if additional variables help in reducing the amount of variability in Expectancy variables. It is evident from the deviance chi-square value (Deviance -2LL) of 4625.31, that additional variables are needed to reduce the variability in Expectancy. Model 2 with Experience added, reduces substantially the unexplained variability in Expectancy (chi-square difference = 2943.60, df = 1). Model 3, with Profession added, did not significantly reduce the amount of unexplained variability in Expectancy (chi-square difference = 1.1, df = 1). Therefore, Expectancy is statistically significantly explained by Experience fixed variables.

The computer output for the three PRELIS multi-level programs are summarised in Table 7, for the variance decomposition of the response variable, *Instrumentality*. It is evident from the deviance chi-square (Deviance-2LL) value of 5413.28, that additional variables are needed to reduce the variability in Instrumentality. Model 2 with Experience added, substantially reduces the unexplained variability in

Table 6. Results of the *Expectancy Response Variable* in the Models
(df = 1, p = 0.05)

Multi-Level Model Fixed Factors	Model 1 Intercept Only	Model 2 Intercept + Experience	Model 3 Intercept + Experience + Profession
Intercept only (β_o)	4.08 (0.02)	4.00 (0.013)	4.00 (0.034)
Experience (β_1)		0.0058 (0.0013)	0.0058
Experience(β_2)			0.0011
Level 1 error Variance (μ_{ij})	0.122	0.008	0.01
Level 2 error Variance ($e_{ij.}$)	0.25	0.01	0.008
Deviance(-2LL)[3]	4625.31	1681.71	1680.70
Df	3	4	5
Chi-square Difference (df = 1)		2943.60	1.1

Instrumentality (chi-square difference = 177.30, df = 1). Model 3, with Profession added, did not significantly further reduce the amount of unexplained variability in Instrumentality (chi-square difference = 0.0, df = 1). Therefore, Instrumentality is statistically significantly explained by the Experience fixed variables.

The computer output for the three PRELIS multi-level programs is summarised in Table 8, for the variance decomposition of the response variable, *Valence*. The results from the deviance chi-square value (Deviance-2LL) of 4755.19 show that additional variables are needed to reduce the variability in the Valence response variable. Model 2, with Experience added, substantially reduces the unexplained variability in Valence (chi-square difference = 1551.91, df = 1). Model 3, with Profession added, did not significantly further reduce the amount of unexplained variability in Expectancy (chi-square difference = 0.11, df = 1). Therefore, Valence is statistically significantly explained by the Experience fixed variables.

---

[3] Deviance – instead of finding the best fitting line, by traditionally minimizing the squared residuals (as one does with ordinary least squares (OLS) regression), we have used a different approach with logistic–maximum likelihood (ML). ML is a way of finding the smallest possible deviance between the observed and predicted values (almost like finding the best fitting line) using calculus (derivatives specifically). With ML, the computer uses different iterations in which it tries different solutions, until it gets the smallest possible deviance or best fit. Once it has found the best solution, it provides a final value for the deviance, which is usually referred to as "negative two log likelihood". This deviance statistic is referred to as "-2LL" by some researchers. A log "likelihood" is a probability, specifically the probability that the observed values of the dependent may be predicted from the observed values of the independents (and is the basis for tests of a logistic model). Because -2LL has approximately a chi-square distribution, -2LL can be used for assessing the significance of logistic regression, analogous to the use of the sum of the squared errors in OLS regression (and is therefore referred to as deviance chi-square by some, D_M).

Table 7. Results of the *Instrumentality Response Variable* and the Models (df = 1, p = 0.05)

Multi-Level Model Fixed Factors	Model 1 Intercept Only	Model 2 Intercept + Experience	Model 3 Intercept + Experience + Profession
Intercept only (β_o)	6.653 (0.046)	6.651 (0.082)	6.644 (0.046)
Experience (β_1)		-0.00048 (0.0013)	-0.0045
Experience(β_2)			0.0011
Level 1 error Variance (μ_{ij})	0.122	0.149	0.122
Level 2 error Variance ($e_{ij.}$)	0.149	0.122	1.149
Deviance(-2LL)	5413.28	5235.98	5235.98
Df	3	4	5
Chi-square Difference (df = 1)		177.30	0.000

Table 8. Results of the *Valence Response Variable* and the Results of the Multi-Level Analysis Models (df = 1, p = 0.05)

Multi-Level Model Fixed Factors	Model 1 Intercept Only	Model 2 Intercept + Experience	Model 3 Intercept + Experience + Profession
Intercept only (β_o)	2.58 (0.021)	2.529 (0.03)	2.50 (0.05)
Experience (β_1)		0.0048 (0.0013)	0.00493
Experience(β_2)			0.00151
Level 1 error Variance (μ_{ij})	0.27	-0.02892	0.285
Level 2 error Variance ($e_{ij.}$)	0.033	0.045	0.0447
Deviance(-2LL)	4755.19	3203.48	3203.27
Df	3	4	5
Chi-square Difference (df = 1)		1551.91	0.11

Table 9. Results of the *Self-Affirmation Response Variable* and the Results of the Multi-Level Models (df = 1, p = 0.05)

Multi-Level Model Fixed Factors	Model 1 Intercept Only	Model 2 Intercept + Experience	Model 3 Intercept + Experience + Profession
Intercept only (β_o)	5.977 (0.046)	6.03 (0.081)	4.00 (0.034)
Experience (β_1)		-0.0049 (0.005)	-0.00483
Experience (β_2)			0.00628
Level 1 error Variance (μ_{ij})	0.123	0.1233	0.1234
Level 2 error Variance $(e_{ij.})$	0.21	0.21	1.21
ICC			
Deviance(-2LL)	5426.47	5249.59	5248.95
Df	3	4	5
Chi-square Difference (df = 1)		176.88	0.000

The computer output for the three PRELIS multi-level programs is summarised in Table 9, for the variance decomposition of the response variable, *Self-Affirmation*. There is enough evidence, given by the deviance chi-square value (Deviance-2LL) of 5426.47, that more variables should be added in the equation to reduce the variability in the Self-Affirmation response variable. The addition of the Experience fixed-variable significantly reduced the deviance chi-square value by 176.88. On the other hand, the addition of the Profession fixed-variable did not significantly reduce the variability in the response variable Self-Affirmation (just a difference of 0.36).

Apart from Profession, we also tested other variables such as Gender and Position to check whether they affected the variability in the response variable, but none of them showed this to be the case.

DISCUSSION
FINDINGS AT THE MICRO AND MACRO LEVEL
'Work experience' showed high variability influence in the way employees responded to all the four attributes of DE, namely expectancy, instrumentality, valence and self-affirmation at the *micro-level* (i.e., at the basic network level). We also tested other personal attributes such as 'age' and 'gender' and the results suggested that these do not reduce variability in the DE process. We suspect that 'experience' has high influence, because individuals have significant knowledge and high inter-sector relationships, which are critical in virtual environments.

Although at the micro-level employees' attitudes towards discretionary effects, such as valence, were much influenced by their experience in a particular work environment, the results were a bit different at the sector-level (*macro level*). The results in the four tables showing the models, suggest that 'profession' did not influence the levels of valence, expectancy, instrumentality and self-affirmation perspectives within the networks.

Tests for DE without the cluster-level analysis revealed slightly different results. For example, the average work experience for the Engineering sector and Retail was about 13 years, yet Retail showed higher expectancy, instrumentality and ultimately higher DE than did Engineering. The strongest point in the Engineering sector, as compared to the rest of the five sectors, was valence.

Retail was, on average, the sector with highest levels of DE, followed by Education and then Mining. This was very interesting, for one would have anticipated Retail to have the lowest DE as it had the highest number of managers with lesser academic qualifications. In a roundabout way, 'educational levels' can be shown to not necessarily determine DE, but to be a powerful influencing factor. This can be tested in further investigations and studies.

At the *macro-level*, the retail industry (Table 10) generally was high on expectancy, instrumentality, and self-affirmation and ultimately DE. This was followed by mining, and then education. In terms of 'experience', self-efficacy and perceived difficulty play important roles. This could be as a result of the fact that employees in the retail industry are more oriented to providing grounds for the stated expectancy variables.   Finance and ICT were in the middle, while engineering was generally last on both DE and on the expectancy outcomes. An interesting and opposite result was that valence was highest on the engineering category, and lowest on the education and retail sectors. This could possibly be because engineers are more concerned with rewards, such as bonuses. The structure of engineering firms could also be a contributing factor to the high valence values. Project managers may be very certain that they will get rewards on the completion of specific large-scale projects. It is therefore much easier to be certain of a result in engineering than in service-oriented, human-centred industries such as retail, which are highly fragmented and unpredictable.

The high values in sectors such as education, retail and mining could also be attributable to short- and long-term training. For instance, education was the field with the most highly-experienced employees. This was followed by engineering, then retail, ICT and finance in that order. A further potential explanation of the disparities could be associated with management hierarchies; for example, retailers generally have flatter management hierarchies compared to fields such as engineering, with steep organisational structures.

Table 10. Results of Scoring Recorded at the Macro-Level of the Specified Industry

Sector	DE	Expectancy	Instrumentality	Valence	Affirmation
Mining	0.887	4.0507	6.7841	2.5194	6.4136
Finance	0.838	4.0298	6.7791	2.5978	5.9165
Engineering	0.759	4.0295	6.5192	4.495	5.8658
Education	0.87	4.14	6.93	2.37	6.37
Retail	0.888	4.1635	6.8118	2.49	6.1953
ICT	0.8228	4.0879	6.4771	2.754	5.603

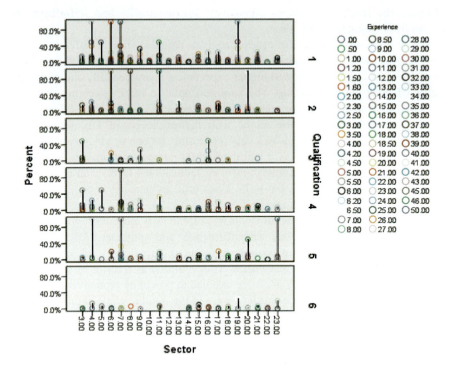

Figure 2. Sectors, Qualifications and the Percentage (Skill Levels of the Industries)

Some sectors had very few employees, and also were very much in line with other sectors. Therefore, most of the sectors were merged so that we only had six sectors to represent the entire population. Engineering is represented by 4, Finance by 7, retail by 20, Mining by 17, education by 3 and ICT by 11.

The level of qualification can be seen in Table 12. It can be deduced that retail employees respond well to experience and self-efficacy variables of expectancy. This could be as a result of training, and the more direct nature of their tasks. Goal-setting and control of tasks are also part of expectancy understanding and measure, which also scored highest for retail employees.

A TECHNICAL NOTE

It is common practice in social research with two-level data to integrate the micro-level data to the macro-unit. This is usually done by averaging the results of each and every macro-unit. However, in cases where the research refers to details that are more implicit at the micro-level, this can result in gross errors. One of such errors would be a shift in meaning [69]. A variable that is considered at *macro-level* refers to the macro unit, not directly to the micro-unit. The firm's average of a rating of employees on performance, for example, may not be used as an index for an individual performance. This variable refers to the firm, not directly to the employees.

Table 12. Level of Qualification: Frequencies of the Respondents

		Positions (excluding missing variable)		
		Frequency	**Percent**	**Valid Percent**	**Cumulative Percent**
Valid	1 (CEO)	72	2.0	5.4	5.4
	2 (Director)	212	5.8	15.9	21.3
	3 (Lecturer)	1	.0	.1	21.4
	4 (Manager)	673	18.6	50.6	72.0
	6 (Section Head)	69	1.9	5.2	77.2
	7 (Specialists)	302	8.3	22.7	99.8
	8 (Not given)	2	.1	.2	100.0
	Total	1331	36.7	100.0	

Furthermore, averaging may neglect the original data-structure, especially when analysis of some form of covariance is considered. A correlation between *macro-level* variables cannot be used to make assertions about correlations concerning *micro-level* relations. Because of these factors, we embarked on investigating DE variables at both *micro-* and *macro-levels.*

CONCLUSION

The global knowledge economy has led to the development of increasingly complex professional and virtual networks. These networks have generated social and technological characteristics that need careful planning.

In our study, we have researched discretionary effort (DE) based on expectancy, instrumentality, valence and self-affirmation within these professional and virtual networks. We have shown that while each factor is important on its own, a combined construct of DE provides further differentiation between organisations and performance. We have shown that DE is particularly important in newly emerging professional and virtual networks.

We suggest that organisations conduct a DE audit and use that as a basis for development. We have gone on to posit that developing the attitudinal factors described as DE can be addressed through coaching, as coaching focuses on behaviours rather than on knowledge accumulation. Coaching explicitly for the specific DE attributes is suggested as a methodology which supercedes more general behavioural coaching. Further research to specifically link performance with the development of DE attributes is suggested.

We have also noted that Profession is an important factor concerning DE. Research by Hicks [70] in the hotel industry (which in this study was part of Retail) confirms our finding that Profession is significant. Similarly, Gellerman [71] notes that, of the many different occupational groups identified in his research on motivation, scientists (inclusive of engineers) emerged as the most strongly oriented as motivation seekers. This could, in part, explain our finding that engineers were lowest on expectancy, instrumentality and self-affirmation responses, but highest on valence. While Experience is equally significant in our findings, we note that Gender is not an important influencing variable.

Finally, our research could be extended by examining dynamic models of newcomer processes and effects [72]. For instance, newcomer trust evolution, as well as newcomer credibility evolution, over time in an established professional network, would potentially have effects on both the newcomer's and established members' DE. It would be interesting to note the consequences on team performance of such time-based changes, starting from initial levels (without newcomer introduction), to newcomer introduction, and finally to full credibility and trust establishment. Additionally, it may be interesting to research locus of control effects in relation to DE, and potential ego altering in relation network development.

REFERENCES

1.   Jago, A.G., Leadership: Perspectives in Theory and Research, *Management Science*, 1982, 28(3), 315-336.

2.   Seijts, G.H. and Kilgour, D., Principled Leadership: Taking the Hard Right, *Ivey Business Journal*, 2007, May/June, http://www.iveybusinessjournal.com/article.asp?intArticle_ID=688, accessed 13th August 2007.

3.   Giberson, T.R., Resick, C.J. and Dickson, M.W., Embedding Leader Characteristics: An Examination of Homogeneity of Personality and Values in Organizations, *Journal of Applied Psychology*, 2005, 90(5), 1002-1010.

4.   Tourigny, L., Dougan, W.L., Washbush, J. and Clements, C., Explaining Executive Integrity: Governance, Charisma, Personality and Agency, *Management Decision*, 2003, 41(10), 1035-1049.

5.   Mirvis, P., Executive Development Through Consciousness-Raising Experiences, *Academy of Management Learning & Education*, 2008, 7(2), 173-188.

6.   Wenger, E., *Communities of Practice: Learning, Meaning and Identity*, Cambridge University Press, Cambridge, MA, 1998.

7.   Sproull, L. and Kiesler, S., *Connections: New Ways of Working in the Networked Organization*, MIT Press, Cambridge, MA, 1991.

8.   Prahalad, C.K. and Ramaswamy, V., The New Frontier of Experience Innovation, *MIT Sloan Management Review*, 2003, 44(4), 12-18.

9.   Mullins, L.J., *Managing People in the Hospitality Industry*, Addison-Wesley Longman, Harlow, 1998.

10.   Baldwin, T.T., Bedell, M.D. and Johnson, J.L., The Social Networks in a Team-Based MBA Program: Effects on Student Satisfaction and Performance, *Academy of Management Journal*, 1997, 40, 1369-1397.

11.   Gorelick, C., Milton, N. and April, K., *Performance Through Learning: Knowledge Management in Practice*, Butterworth-Heinemann, Burlington, MA, 2004.

12.   Mehra, A., Kilduff, M., and Brass, D.J., The Social Networks of High and Low Self-Monitors: Implications for Workplace Performance, *Administrative Science Quarterly*, 2001, 46, 121-146.

13.   Parker, G.M., *Team Players and Teamwork*, Jossey Bass, San Francisco, 1990.

14.   Ensley, M.D., Pearson, A. and Pearce, C.L., Top Management Team Process, Shared Leadership, and New Venture Performance: A Theoretical Model and Research Agenda, *Human Resource Management Review*, 2003, 136, 1-18.

15.   Day, D.V., Gronn, P. and Salas, E., Leadership Capacity in Teams, *The Leadership Quarterly*, 2004, 15, 857-880.

16.   Ilgen, D.R., Major, D.A., Hollenbeck, J.R. and Sego, D.J., Team Research in the 1990's, in: Chemers, M.M. and Ayman, R., eds., *Leadership Theory and Research: Perspectives and Directives*, Academic Press, San Diego, CA, 1993, 245-270.

17. Bass, B.M., *Bass and Stogdill's Handbook of Leadership: A Survey of Theory and Research*, Free Press, New York, 1990.

18. Bryman, A., *Charismatic and Leadership in Organizations*, Sage, London, 1992.

19. Gardner, J.W., *On Leadership*, Free Press, New York, 1990.

20. Murphy, A.J., A Study of the Leadership Process, *American Sociological Review*, 1941, 6, 674-687.

21. Blanchard, K., Zigarmi, D. and Nelson, R., Situational Leadership after 25 Years: A Retrospective, *Journal of Leadership Studies*, 1993, 1(1), 22-36.

22. Blanchard, K., Zigarmi, P. and Zigarmi, D., *Leadership and the One Minute Manager: Increasing Effectiveness Through Situational Leadership*, William Morrow, New York, 1985.

23. Hersey, P. and Blanchard, K.H., *Management of Organizational Behaviour: Utilizing Human Resources*, 3rd edn., Prentice Hall, Englewood Cliffs, NJ, 1977.

24. Hersey, P. and Blanchard, K.H., *Management of Organizational Behaviour: Utilizing Human Resources*, 5th edn., Prentice Hall, Englewood Cliffs, NJ, 1988.

25. Bollen, K.A. and Hoyle, R.H., Perceived Cohesion: A Conceptual and Empirical Examination, *Social Forces*, 1990, 69(2), 479-584.

26. Rotter, J.B., Generalized Expectancies for Internal versus External Control of Reinforcement, *Psychological Monographs: General and Applied*, 1966, 80(1 Whole No. 609), 1-28.

27. Barge, J.K., Leadership Skills and the Dialectics of Leadership in Group Decision Making, in: Hirokawa, R.Y. and Poole, M.S., eds., *Communication and Group Decision-Making*, 2nd edn., Sage, Thousand Oaks, CA, 1996, 301-342.

28. Zaccaro, S.J., Rittman, A.L. and Marks, M.A., Team Leadership, *The Leadership Quarterly*, 2001, 12, 451-483.

29. April, K. and Shockley, M., eds., *Diversity: New Realities in a Changing World*, Palgrave Macmillan, Basingstoke, 2007.

30. Drecksel, G.L., Leadership Research: Some Issues, *Communication Yearbook*, 1991, 14, 535-546.

31. Morgan, G., Emerging Waves and Challenges: The Need for New Competencies and Mindsets, in: Henry, J., ed., *Creative Management*, Sage, Newbury Park, CA, 1991, 283-293.

32. Richmond, A. and Skitmore, M., Stress and Coping: A Study of Project Managers in a Large ICT Organization, *Project Management Journal*, 2006, 37(5), 5-16.

33. Cartwright, S. and Cooper, C.L., *The Psychological Impact of Merger and Acquisitions on the Individual*, Paper presented at the British Psychological Society Occupation Psychology Conference, Liverpool, UK, 1992.

34. Spender, J.C., Exploring Uncertainty and Emotion in the Knowledge-Based Theory of the Firm, *Information Technology & People*, 2003, 16(3), 266-288.

35. Mumford, M.D., Zaccaro, S.J., Connelly. M.S. and Marks, M.A., Leadership Skills: Conclusions and Future Directions, *The Leadership Quarterly*, 2000, 1, 155-170.

36. Wexley, K.N. and Baldwin, T.T., Management Development, *1986 Yearly Review of Management of the Journal of Management*, 1986, 12(2), 277-294.

37. Baldwin, T.T. and Patgett, M.Y., Management Development: A Review and Commentary, in: Cooper, C.L. and Robertson, I.T., eds., *Key Reviews in Management Psychology*, Wiley, New York, 1994, 270-320.

38. Peters, B.K.G., The Four Stages of Management Education, *Biz Ed – Journal of AACSB International*, 2006(May/June), 36-40.

39. Peters, B.K.G., National and International Developments in Leadership and Management Development, in: Mumford, A., Gold, J. and Thorpe, R., eds., *Handbook of Management Development*, 5th edn., Gower, London, 2009.

40.   De Haan, E., *Relational Coaching: Journeys Towards Mastering One-to-One Learning*, Wiley, London, 2008.

41.   Kline, N., *Time to Think: Listening to Ignite the Human Mind*, Cassell, London, 1999.

42.   Brunning, H., *Executive Coaching: A Systems-Psychodynamic Perspective*, Karnac, London, 2006.

43.   Whitmore, J., *Coaching for Performance: GROWing People, Performance and Purpose*, Nicholas Brealey, London, 1992.

44.   Skiffington, S. and Zeus, P., *Behavioral Coaching*, McGraw-Hill Professional, New York, 2003.

45.   Green, J. and Grant, A.M., *Solution-Focused Coaching*, Momentum Press, London, 2003.

46.   Pemberton, C., *Coaching to Performance*, Butterworth-Heinemann, Oxford, 2006.

47.   Caulat, G., Virtual Leadership, *The Ashridge Journal*, 2006, Autumn, 6-11.

48.   Mitchell, T.R., Expectancy-Value Models in Organization Psychology, in: Feather, N.T., ed., *Expectations and Actions: Expectancy-Value Models in Psychology*, Lawrence Erlbaun Associates, Hillsdale, N.J, 1982, 293-312.

49.   Steele, C.M., The Psychology of Self-Affirmation: Sustaining the Integrity of the Self, in: Berkowitz, L., ed., *Advances in Experimental Social Psychology*, Academic Press, New York, 1988, 21, 261-302.

50.   Vroom, V., *Work and Motivation*, Wiley, New York, 1964.

51.   Katz, D., The Motivational Basis of Organizational Behavior, *Behavior Science*, 1964, 9, 131-146.

52.   Scholl,   R.W.,   *Motivational   Processes   –   Expectancy   Theory*,   2002, http://www.cba.uri.edu/Scholl/Notes/Motivation_Expectancy.html, accessed 2nd August 2008.

53.   Mruk, C., *Self-Esteem: Research, Theory and Practice*, Free Association Books (Springer), London, 1999.

54.   Howard, A., Positive and Negative Emotional Attractors and Intentional Change, *Journal of Management Development*, 2006, 25(7), 657-670.

55.   Meirick, P.C., Self-Enhancement Motivation as a Third Variable in the Relationship between First- and Third-Person Effects, *International Journal of Public Opinion Research*, 2005, 17(4), 473-483.

56.   Langner, E.E., Cognitive Dissonance: A Motive for Self-Affirmation or Self-Consistency?, *Dissertation Abstracts International*, Section B: The Sciences and Engineering, 1997, Vol. 57(9-B).

57.   April, K. and Smit, E., Diverse Discretionary Effort in Workplace Networks, in: Özbilgin, M.F. and Syed, J., eds., *Diversity in Asia*, Edward Elgar, London, 2009.

58.   Ribeaux, P. and Poppleston, S.E., *Psychology and Work*, Macmillan, Basingstoke, 1978.

59.   Katz, D., The Functional Approach to the Study of Attitudes, *Public Opinion Quarterly*, 1960, 21, 163-204.

60.   Fai, F., A Structural Decomposition Analysis of Technological Opportunity, Corporate Survival and Leadership, *Industrial and Corporate Change*, 2007, 16(6), 1069-1103.

61.   Kmec, J.A. and Gorman, E.H., *Gender and Self-Reported Discretionary Work Effort*, Sheraton Boston and the Boston Marriot Copley Place, Boston, MA, 2008, 7-31.

62.   Hox, J.J., *Applied Multilevel Analysis*, TT-Publikaties, Amsterdam, 1994.

63.   Longford, N.T., *Random Coefficient Models*, Oxford University Press, New York, 1993.

64.   Bryk, A.S. and Raudenbush, S.W., *Hierarchical Linear Models, Applications and Data Analysis Methods*, Sage Publications, Newbury Park, CA, 1992.

65.   Goldstein, H., *Multilevel Statistical Models*, 2nd edn., Edward Arnod, London, 1995.

66.   Kreft, I.G.G. and De Leeuw, J., *Introducing Multilevel Modelling*, Sage Publications, London, 1998.

67.   Robinson, W.S., Ecological Correlations and the Behavior of Individuals, *American Sociological Review*, 1950, 15, 351-357.

68.   Budhwar, P.S. and Sparrow, P.R., Developing Levels of Strategic Integration and Devolvement of Human Resource Management in India, *International Journal of Human Resource Management*, 1997, 8(4), 476-494.

69.   Huttner, H.J.M., Contextual Analyses, in: Albinski, M., ed., *Onderzoekstypen in de Socologie*, Van Gorcum, Assen, 1981, 262-288.

70.   Hicks, L., Excluded Women: How Can This Happen in the Hotel World?, *The Service Industries Journal*, 1990, 10(2), 348-363.

71.   Gellerman, S.W., *Motivation and Productivity*, Amacom Books, New York, 1963.

72.   Chan, D. and Schmitt, N., Inter-Individual Differences in Intra-Individual Changes in Proactivity in during Organizational Entry: A Latent Growth Modeling Approach to Understanding Newcomer Adaptation, *Journal of Applied Psychology*, 2000, 85, 190-210.

APPENDIX 1: PROFESSIONAL NETWORK
EXPECTANCY QUESTIONNAIRE
Self-Assessment Tool for Expectancies within Professional Networks

The following self-assessment tool is designed to assist you in thinking through critical behaviours in 10 key areas for effectively engaging in, utilising, and creating conducive, value-adding, professional network relationships. Through self-reflection, the tool highlights areas for personal growth, and raises personal awareness with regard to working through a professional network. It will also assist the researchers in establishing a baseline against which to measure future development and success of employees and managers such as yourselves, and gain understanding of the enhancing and mediating effects of expectancies in professional network performance and learning.

INDUSTRY	CURRENT AGE	GENDER	NATIONALITY	ETHNICITY

HIGHEST ORGANISATIONAL POSITION	YEARS WORK EXPERIENCE	CURRENT & PRIOR QUALIFICATIONS

circle YES / NO	circle YES / NO	circle YES / NO	CL%	V%
CO-LOCATED WORK EXCLUSIVELY	VIRTUAL WORK EXCLUSIVELY	MIX OF CO-LOCATED & VIRTUAL WORK	APPROX. % MIX	

This questionnaire is designed so as to help you to reflect on your own experiences in your professional network (possibly team) in the workplace, i.e., the people you draw on, work with and count on, to complete your work successfully. Expectancy refers to a person's strength of belief and conviction about whether or not what they set out to do on a personal level is achievable, and desirable, on a workplace level, of their effort and productivity. Underpinning this expectancy is the fact that people have different expectations and levels of confidence about what they are capable of doing. Desire and expectation are interwoven, and only mitigated by workplace issues and openness to their expectations, as well as personal self-esteem and self-confidence issues.

1. EFFORT-PERFORMANCE EXPECTANCY
*Network member (you) believes that desired levels of performance are possible,
given the resources, competencies and skills s/he possesses*

SPECIFIC RESPONSES   (1-5)

1a	Am confident in my skills and competencies, and therefore show courage and sense of purpose to stand up for what I believe, in pushing for the desired levels of performance
1b	When appropriate, honestly acknowledge to my network when I am unable to contribute significantly or am "lost" (i.e., don't fully know what I am doing nor do I know what to do next)
1c	Believe that, with some effort, I am capable of learning the required amount, and at the required pace, in order to work competently in all workplace eventualities and situations
1d	Believe that my network members will match my effort in ensuring our shared success in overcoming challenging tasks/projects or navigating areas not previously ventured into
1e	For any given workplace scenario/situation, posses both the required technical and organisational skills to perform well
1f	Comments or further insights on the impact of this expectancy on your self-esteem and productivity:

2. INTERPERSONAL-PERFORMANCE EXPECTANCY
*Network member (you) believes that s/he is seen to be assisting,
and developing, others*

SPECIFIC RESPONSES   (1-5)

2a	Is seen, by organisational employees as well as other stakeholders, to be treating network members, as well as their inputs and perspectives, with respect and dignity
2b	Provide network members with the necessary development, and resources, to play meaning roles in something that is quite significant to the network, and/or organisation
2c	Allow for the expression of emotion as it relates to the performance and under-performance of network members, without allowing it to impact negatively on others or the organisation
2d	Insist on, and am known to insist on, the same high standards of cooperation as I personally demonstrate in my dealings with my network members
2e	Proactively seek out opportunities to assist network members in challenging projects, or help them to do something extra, beyond the minimal requirements of workplace performance
2f	Comments or further insights on the impact of this expectancy on your self-esteem and productivity:

3. EFFORT-LEARNING EXPECTANCY
You believe that expended personal effort will have future, value-adding learning benefits

	SPECIFIC RESPONSES	**(1-5)**
3a	Make use of all the available communication tools (newsletters, Intranet, Internet, articles in business press, papers in academic journals, workshops, etc.) to raise personal awareness	
3b	Seek to involve myself in activities that exposes me to knowledge and learning, that could eventually aid my future career(s), inside my current organisation, or outside of it	
3c	Proactively seek to create and shape a performance support & shared-learning context (environment) for network members, in order that I may gain from their knowledge & insight	
3d	Expend my personal energy and effort only in those things/processes/projects that currently has personal learning benefit for me, or will have in the future	
3e	Tailor my effort and contribution expenditure to match the amount of learning I receive in return from my network members	
3f	Comments or further insights on the impact of this expectancy on your self-esteem and productivity:	

4. LEADING-VISIBILITY EXPECTANCY
You are seen to be in step with new trends and the cutting-edge, and acknowledged as being knowledgeable and practicing at the forefront

	SPECIFIC RESPONSES	**(1-5)**
4a	Purposefully explore unconventional ideas and different approaches that could eventually (currently, or in the future) be important for my network to know	
4b	Actively seek to ensure the transference of my knowledge and insights across, and outside my, discipline boundaries (both within and outside of the organisation)	
4c	Regularly subject my ideas to scrutiny from non-network members (i.e., present at conferences, publish in international peer-reviewed journals, write books, etc.)	
4d	Regularly feed back new and different information and knowledge to my network members (information and knowledge that they may not have come across)	
4e	Seek out, and participate in, cutting-edge research projects (both within the organisation and outside)	
4f	Comments or further insights on the impact of this expectancy on your self-esteem and productivity:	

5. NETWORK-PERFORMANCE EXPECTANCY
Network member (you) believes that his/her colleagues are committed to the goals and objectives of the network

SPECIFIC RESPONSES (1-5)

5a	Monitor whether all network members contribute to shaping organisational policy, work practices and learning processes to promote network effectiveness
5b	Assess the reliability and dependability of individual network members (e.g., whether they attended all face-to-face meetings, completed tasks and projects on time, etc.)
5c	Regularly elicit accurate and constructive feedback from network members regarding their understanding or misunderstanding of important knowledge relating to our network's work
5d	Identify barriers that sometimes hinder the self-determination and self-motivation of my network members in achieving the network's goals
5e	Monitor whether individual network members proactively seek project engagements, and periods of projects, that suit (are aligned to) their personal team styles
5f	Comments or further insights on the impact of this expectancy on your self-esteem and productivity:

6. INTERNAL-RECOGNITION EXPECTANCY
Network member (you) believes that s/he will be recognised (with little or no financial rewards), both within the network and the greater organisation, for the contribution s/he has made

SPECIFIC RESPONSES (1-5)

6a	Am satisfied with the amount of recognition I receive, from my network members and general organisation, for contributing to my network-, and organisational success
6b	Prefer non-financial rewards over financial rewards
6c	Look for alignment (connections and gaps) between the feedback I get, and the team or organisation recognition programs being used
6d	My preference is for specific recognition and feedback concerning my contribution (not general platitudes and global statements)
6e	Prefer feedback and recognition from my other network members, than from the other organisational members and general stakeholders (non-network members)
6f	Comments or further insights on the impact of this expectancy on your self-esteem and productivity:

7. MUTUAL-RECIPROCITY EXPECTANCY
Network members returning directly, or indirectly, aid, resources and/or friendship offered by another network member

	SPECIFIC RESPONSES	**(1-5)**
7a	Feel pressured to enforce equal sharing of resources and aid (by myself, and others) within acceptable time frames	
7b	Mobilise opposition against would-be dominant individual's, who do not appear to share the same, underlying intent and values of the network (e.g., public complaint, ridicule, ignoring)	
7c	Consistently work at, and seek through the eliciting of their viewpoints and perspectives, the integration and alignment of my work goals with the goals of reciprocal members	
7d	Continuously seek to improve network processes and communication to achieve more effective network cooperation and higher levels of reciprocity among network members	
7e	Share reputation and successes of network members with other networks (not necessarily organisational stakeholders or related to organisational outcomes)	
7f	Comments or further insights on the impact of this expectancy on your self-esteem and productivity:	

8. INDIVIDUAL-NETWORK LEARNING EXPECTANCY
Network member believes that his or her own personal learning, knowledge and insights are of value, and can contribute, to the network's learning

	SPECIFIC RESPONSES	**(1-5)**
8a	Proactively assists network members to stay informed of industry/sector developments (e.g., access to, and sharing of, professional periodicals, making them aware of conferences, etc.)	
8b	Put aside specific time slots/periods for sharing, informally and formally, personal knowledge and insights with other network members	
8c	Provide accurate and constructive feedback to my network members regarding their understanding or misunderstanding of important knowledge relating to our network's work	
8d	Confidently and consistently, where knowledgeable, state positions and ideas on issues that I believe are important for my network to know	
8e	Seek to pull knowledgeable people, and sources of learning and knowledge, into my network (who/that do not yet have informal, or formal, membership of my network)	
8f	Comments or further insights on the impact of this expectancy on your self-esteem and productivity:	

9. PERFORMANCE-OUTCOME EXPECTANCY
Network member (you) believes that what s/he is doing will lead to certain outcomes

	SPECIFIC RESPONSES	**(1-5)**
9a	Establish measurement criteria, using quantitative- and qualitative measures, of the impact effect of my network's contribution to an organisational goal(s)	
9b	Ensure that my network members' personal goals and needs are aligned with the desired organisational outcome(s), and therefore their needs are gratified when achieved	
9c	Periodically highlight and celebrate my network members' behaviours and actions that appear to be aiding the achievement of the desired organisational outcomes	
9d	Personally play a pivotal role in consistently ensuring the achievement of desired organisational outcomes (i.e., I am needed and valuable to organisational success)	
9e	Often draw on my intuitive sense and faith in believing that desired organisational outcomes will be achieved, even when it does not look possible to others.	
9f	Comments or further insights on the impact of this expectancy on your self-esteem and productivity:	

10. TEAM-SUSTAINABILITY EXPECTANCY
Network member (you) focused on sustaining the network, and its future

	SPECIFIC RESPONSES	**(1-5)**
10a	In consultation with stakeholders of my network's contribution (not network members), build a coherent set of both achievable, and stretch, long-term goals for the professional network	
10b	Set time aside for regular feedback and honest disclosure from my network members, to ascertain their perspectives on possible hindrances that could impact the network's future	
10c	Consistently demonstrate high levels of respect for my network members in conversations and dealings with other non-members (in & out of the presence of my network members)	
10d	Provide consistent protection for my network members, and their work, through my authority, influence and persuasion of stakeholders (non-members) of my network's contribution	
10e	Build a broad base of support, for my network, among key stakeholders by identifying and positioning ideas to satisfy their needs, interests and concerns.	
10f	Comments or further insights on the impact of this expectancy on your self-esteem and productivity:	

Sport Coaches' Informal Learning from Business and Military Discourse

Mike Voight
Department of Physical Education and Human Performance
Central Connecticut State University
1615 Stanley Street, New Britain, CT 06050
E-mail: voightmir@ccsu.edu

ABSTRACT

What is it about books, documentaries, and/or interviews from business, military, and sport leaders that intrigue us, especially for those of us who coach, teach, or consult? What do we derive from these written or spoken words? How do we use stories and quotations in our work? These questions are discussed and attention given to the results from an exploratory study with a sample of coaches and consultants in sport regarding their use of resources from the military and business leaders.

Key words: Informal Learning, Motivational Quotations, Stories

INTRODUCTION

I have derived many lessons from books and documentaries about successful leaders from the world of sport, business, and the armed forces. From an early age, when I realized that coaching and teaching was my passion, I began collecting books from famous coaches, beginning with my favorite, Vince Lombardi, then Pat Riley, Rick Pitino, Bob Knight, and Scotty Bowman. As the years rolled on, I moved from one sport to another, adding famous athletes to my collection as well, including Larry Bird, Magic Johnson, and Pelé, and even a former baseball commissioner, Bowie Kuhn (who would later show his graciousness to give of his time to be a guest-speaker at a sportspersonship-ethics program I ran for the student-athletes at Jacksonville University in the early 1990s). It was not until graduate school that books from leaders in the business world and the military struck my interest, most notably Sun Tzu II's *The Art of War* [1], books written about Jack Welch and his work at General Electric [2, 3], and a host of academics and business consultants who have covered leadership, job satisfaction, teamwork, and motivational issues in their writings [e.g., 4-6].

Reviewer: David Whitaker (Performance Consultants, UK)

Even now, I find it difficult to pass on a recent release from a top coach, business leader or military leader. Recently, for example, I purchased former General Electric CEO Jack Welch's new book, *Winning*. What is it about these books, documentaries, and/or interviews that intrigue us, especially for those of us who coach, teach, or consult? What do we derive from these written or spoken words? How do we use these stories and lessons? Are these lessons inspiring enough to change us, our behaviors, or our practices? Finally, why do we love to recite, memorize, and use quotations from business and military leaders? What do we get out of them and how do we use them?

TRANSFER OF LEARNING

Although the focus of this particular article is the impact that professionals from business and the military play in the learning of lessons applicable to coaching, I realize the important role that top coaches play in educating, inspiring, and motivating the workforce. Due to this symbiotic relationship, the title of this article should include the expression "vice versa.". For example, while watching the 2008 NBA finals which included old rivals LA Lakers and the Boston Celtics, one of the announcers said that despite all the successes that Ervin "Magic" Johnson had on the basketball court as a player, it pales in comparison to the successes he has had in the business world. Johnson cited his experiences as an athlete and coach as a critical prerequisite for what he was to face in the world of business when asked in a follow-up interview about his business acumen. Another example comes from Pat Riley's *The Winner Within* [7], when Riley was asked by Walt Disney Company CEO Michael Eisner's to speak to his animators during his first days at Disney:

> Eisner is a sport-loving guy and a true Showtime Warrior. He calls himself and his group of managers and co-executives "Team Disney." What did Eisner bring to Disney? Like many teams in business, the animators needed a good cheerleader to help them rejuvenate and reinvent the team, so Eisner took the quality people that were already there, added a few draft choices, and created a new enthusiasm.
> Basically, they inundated the team with one concept: Excellence at everything you do. [7, p. 262]

Pat Williams from the NBA's Orlando Magic shared some studies on what the top CEO's do so the rest of us could apply them to our chosen field of endeavor [8]. For example, it was found that thirteen hundred senior executives on a survey reported that integrity was the most important human quality necessary for success in business and teams, and that seventy-one percent placed this quality at the top of the list for leaders. He also quoted a study on top executives which found that they "spend eighty percent of their time communicating; specifically, forty-five percent listening, thirty percent speaking, sixteen percent reading, and nine percent writing" [8, p. 45]. Moreover, after interviewing coaches and executives from business and sport, he identified six qualities that he believes effective leaders must possess: vision, communication skills, people skills, character, competence, and boldness. Williams also authored a book that applied the wizardry and artistic domination of one Michael

Jordan to be used by those in the business world to achieve their own level of success (see [9]).

I have yet to meet a coach who has not picked up a 'few things' from other coaches, especially those who have achieved a lot of success at their respective level. This was never more apparent to me than when I was visiting the White House in 2004 with the USC football and volleyball teams after their NCAA championship victories. The USC Head Football Coach, Pete Carroll, was outwardly excited to meet and talk with Anson Dorrance, the very successful women's soccer coach at UNC Chapel Hill, who wrote a book entitled *Training Soccer Champions* [10] that Coach Carroll found such a valuable read. He then sought out another coach visiting President Bush that day, Jerry Yeagley, who was retiring as the all-time winningest coach in men's soccer history with six national titles with the Indiana Hoosier men's soccer team. Lou Holtz, former Notre Dame football coach and winner of the 1998 national championship, sums this point up nicely: "The only things that are going to change you from where you are today to where you are going to be five years from now are the people you meet and the books you read" [11, p. 51].

Business, military, and sport are institutions very different in terms of organizational structure, financial parameters, scope of responsibilities, and global significance, but they are alike in many aspects, such as importance placed on leadership, motivation, team building, and communication. For example, Pat Williams who is both a sport and business leader as Executive Vice President of the NBA's Orlando Magic, stresses the importance of teamwork across all occupations when he stated:

> Virtually every person on this planet either is or should be involved in team building, because we were designed to function in connected, interdependent relationships with other people. We were made to be team players. A family is a team. A ball club is a team. A business is a team. A church is a team. A hospital staff is a team. Even a military unit is a team. [8, p. 3]

LESSONS FROM THE MILITARY

Strategies for life success have been applied from well known military philosophies and practices to be used for success in business and in life. For example, there are books that apply Sun Tzu's *The Art of War* teaching and principles to improve marketing [12], managing [13], and business [14]. Sun-Tzu was a fifth-century BC military general for King Ho Lu's army, whose "incisive blueprint for battlefield strategy is as relevant to today's combatant's in business, politics, and everyday life as it once was to the warlords of ancient China" [15].

Other resources long quoted and cited from military leaders turned authors include General Norman Schwarzkopf's autobiography, *It Doesn't Take a Hero* [16], and General George S. Patton's *War As I Knew It* [17]. And let us not forget the literary contributions from four global leaders from the world of business; namely, Bill Gates (see *The Road Ahead* and *Business at the Speed of Thought* [18, 19]), Donald Trump (see *The Art of the Deal*, or *Think Big and Kick Ass in Business and Life* [20, 21]), Warren Buffett (see *The Essays of Warren Buffett: Lessons for Corporate America* [22]), and Jack Welch (see *Winning* [23]).

STORY TELLING

I believe at the core of our motivation to read the discourse from the worlds of coaching, business, and the military contains the drive to learn from each other's experiences, expertise, and strategies for success. To greatly enhance the 'cross-over' popularity, the majority of the writers apply the content to the masses, including anecdotes and real-life experiences which cross all walks of life to better identify and clarify the main points and life strategies the author is attempting to convey. It is these stories that tend to stay with readers long after the book has been returned to the library or book shelves at home. Much has been written about the many benefits of educating people through the telling of stories and sharing of anecdotes [24, 25]. According to Pat Williams, who speaks extensively about team-building and leadership:

> ...stories are the best way to make your point forcefully and memorably. When people hear you tell a story, their imaginations are engaged, forming pictures in their minds, triggering emotions that cause your message to be imprinted on their minds. [8, p. 60]

Utilizing stories and poetic representations appears to be becoming more popular in physical activity programming and coach education workshops and seminars [26, 27]. Douglas and Carless [28] utilized stories to improve coaches' reflective skills and holistic coaching practices at their professional development seminars. For these coach education seminars, the stories that were shared comprised of performance (sport was the main theme), discovery (sport was additive to one's life), or relational (focused more on relationships in sport) narrative stories. Coaches in this study responded to these stories by either asking questions, providing a summary of the story, or by incorporating the story within their own experience. Subsequent analyses of the use of narratives in this fashion suggested that "stories can provide a catalyst for coaches to explore their own subjective, moral and ethical beliefs in a supportive environment which more closely aligns with the dynamic nature of their work" [28, p. 46].

A quotation by Ellis and Bochner [29] shared in the Douglas and Carless [28] article exemplifies the learning potential of stories, in that we allow ourselves to resonate with the story, reflect on it, become part of it" (p. 753). Douglas and Carless [28] also found that the stories had three interrelated qualities which were useful in stimulating reflection and learning in their coach education programming: openness (being open to new ideas and methods), replay (being able to still-frame the reflective thought to compare it with own experiences), and promoting an ethical standpoint (reflecting on our own moral compass).

EXPLORATORY STUDY

I conducted an informal, exploratory survey in an attempt to ascertain the motives that coaches and consultants have for seeking out and reading business and military books, articles, and other resources. I contacted fifteen of my friends and colleagues who are either coaches at some level (n = 12) or sport psychology consultants (n = 3) and asked them two questions: (1) Do you read or watch resources from business or military leaders? (2) How do you use material from these leaders in business or the military?

In simple descriptive terms, the majority of those surveyed have over the past year watched an interview or read articles/books from business leaders (12 out of 15) and the military (8 out of 15). The majority of the coaches did profess to watching or reading material or interviews from top coaches in their sport and in other sports in the past year (9 out of 12 from coaches in the same sport, and 8 out of 12 from coaches in a different sport(s)).

These coaches and sport psychology consultants listed how they used the material from interviews and readings from leaders in business and the military. The numbers in parentheses represent the number of coaches who cited it: interesting reads (14); motivational ideas and strategies (13); managing of people, including staff (12); leadership advice-experiences (12); humorous stories (11); inspirational stories (10); communication strategies (10); quotations (9); problem solving-conflict management (7); coping with adversity (6); 'coaching' strategies – adjustments (6); philosophy (5); and establishing vision for teams (2).

MOTIVATIONAL QUOTATIONS

A question that could be asked is, 'How do you use motivating quotations from business and military leaders?' Whenever I travel, I read the "Successories - The source for employee motivation and recognition" advertisement in *Skymall* magazine, which matches breathtaking scenery with motivating and inspiring quotations. There is one featuring a bald eagle soaring with a snow-capped mountain in the background. Underneath the "Dare to Soar" title is the quotation: "Your attitude, almost always determines your altitude in life."

Anson Dorrance, the highly successful women's soccer coach referred to earlier, shared in his book [10] how he used a quotation from George Bernard Shaw, the noted Irish playwright who authored more than sixty plays. Coach Dorrance would have players who he felt were not giving their maximal effort recite this quotation to the entire team: "Be a force of fortune instead of a feverish, selfish little clod of ailments and grievances complaining that the world will not devote itself to making you happy."(p. 54) Although he wrote that in some cases this exercise did not have the desired effect, it exemplifies the use of quotations on the practice field and not simply reading them in a book or leaving them on a wall somewhere.

Pat Williams [8] shared a passage that Phil Jackson, the winningest NBA coach for the Chicago Bulls and the LA Lakers, would use with the Bulls prior to their annual playoff run which stressed the importance of relying on each member of the team. This passage was from Rudyard Kipling's *Second Jungle Book*:

> "Now this is the Law of the Jungle - as old and as true as the sky; And the wolf that shall keep it may prosper, but the Wolf that shall break it must die. As the creeper that girdles the tree trunk, the Law runneth forward and back. For the strength of the Pack is the Wolf, and the strength of the Wolf is the Pack."

In another example involving Phil Jackson, he mentioned in one of his books how he not only uses certain quotations to drive his teams and hands out particular books with messages for certain players, but also how he carefully chooses video clips to splice into the team's film sessions to invoke particular messages:

> For years I've spliced in clips from films or television shows to break up the monotony. Players would lose focus watching themselves race up and down the court for ten straight minutes. I often resort to comedies … Of course I'm not just trying to lighten the mood. Each clip comes with a message that registers, I hope. [30, p. 191]

Coach Pat Riley, who won NBA championships with the LA Lakers and the Miami Heat has also used quotations to inspire his team. He informed his team before a key Lakers-Celtics game the last words that his father told him before he passed away, which unfortunately was at Coach Riley's wedding: "Just remember what I taught you. There will come a time. And when that time comes, you go out there and kick somebody's ass. This is that time, Pat" [7, p. 133]. In the off-season, one of the star players, Michael Cooper, told Coach that the pre-game message "had gone so deep for him that the score was already five to nothing before the game started" (p. 134).

Let us not forget the historical pre-game ritual of the Notre Dame football players who touch the sign on their way to Notre Dame Stadium which says: "Play like a Champion Today." In similar fashion, in the basement of Heritage Hall on the campus of the University of Southern California, which houses the seven Heisman Trophies won by USC gridiron greats, there is a quotation painted on a wall leading to the exit (towards the practice field) which states: "129 All-Americans - whose next?"

With my team consulting at the University of Southern California and the University of Texas, the coaching staffs, captains, and I have used special quotations for many reasons, which include establishing a team vision, standards of execution, attitudes-in-action (similar to Lombardi's "character-in-action"), and daily reminders about what our ultimate goals are. In this vein, we use quotations that best represent the team's vision and standards and place them on the back of the practice shirts, so in times of adversity, fatigue, or frustration, they are to look to their teammates (and the quotation) for that needed inspiration and support. We also have players construct their own personal 'squares' (small posters) that are placed in their lockers or on the walls of the practice gym, or both; consisting of quotations and inspirational images special to them which are used to help inspire them prior to practice sessions.

There are so many sources of inspirational and motivating quotations from sport, business, and military leaders. There are many websites and books full of quotations from all different sources. [e.g. 31-30]

CONCLUSION

As a sports coach, if you are not in the habit of reaching for books or articles from a business or military leader, I hope this article has shown you the upside of going outside of the world of sport for some additional learning opportunities. I began an 'inspirational quotations file' when I first began coaching almost two decades ago and it has now morphed into a family of file folders housed in one of several file cabinets in my basement!

REFERENCES

1. Tzu, S., *The Art of War*, Oxford University Press, Oxford, 1971.

2. Krames, J., *The Jack Welch Lexicon of Leadership: Over 250 Terms, Concepts, and Strategies-Initiatives of the Legendary Leader*, McGraw Hill, New York, NY, 2001.

3. Slater, R., *Jack Welch and the G.E. Way: Insights and Leadership Secrets of the Legendary CEO*, McGraw Hill, New York, NY, 1998.

4. Henne, D. and Locke, E.A., Job Dissatisfaction: What are the Consequences? *International Journal of Psychology,* 1985, 20, 221-240.

5. Lawler, E., *Motivation in Work Organizations*, Jossey-Bass Inc., San Francisco, CA, 1994.

6. Locke, E.A. and Latham, G.P., Work Motivation: The High Performance Cycle, in: Kleinbeck, V., Quast, H., Thierry, H. and Hacker, H., eds., *Work Motivation,* Lawrence Erlbaum Associates, NJ, 1990,

7. Riley, P., *The Winner Within*, G.P. Putnam's Sons, New York, NY, 1993.

8. Williams, P., *The Magic of Teamwork,* Thomas Nelson, Inc., Nashville, TN, 1997.

9. Williams, P., *How to Be Like Mike: Lessons Learned About Basketball's Best,* HCI, New York, NY, 2001.

10. Dorrance, A., *Training Soccer Champions*, JTC Sports, Inc., Raleigh, NC, 1996.

11. Holtz, L. and Heisler, J., *A Championship Season at Notre Dame: The Fighting Spirit,* Pocket Books, New York, NY, 1989.

12. Michaelson, G. and Michaelson, S., *Strategies for Marketing*, McGraw-Hill, New York, NY, 2003.

13. Tzu, S. and Michaelson, G., *Sun Tzu: The Art of War for Managers - 50 Strategic Rules*, Oxford University Press, Oxford, 2001.

14. McNeilly, M., *Sun Tzu and the Art of Business*, Oxford University Press, Oxford, 1996.

15. Galvin, D., Synopsis, The Art of War (Barnes and Noble Classics Series), http://search.barnesandnoble.com/Art-of-War/Sunzi/e/9781593081720

16. Schwarzkopf, N., *It Doesn't Take a Hero: The Autobiography of General H. Normal Schwarzkopf*, Bantam Publishing, New York, NY, 1993.

17. Patton, G.S., *War as I Knew it*, Mariner Books, New York, NY, 1995.

18. Gates, B., *The Road Ahead*, Penguin, New York, NY, 1999.

19. Gates, B., *Business at the Speed of Thought: Succeeding in the Digital Economy*, Warner Business Books, New York, NY, 2000.

20. Trump, D.J., *The Art of the Deal*, Random House, New York, NY, 1987.

21. Trump, D.J. and Zanker, B., *Think Big and Kick Ass in Business and Life*, Collins, New York, NY, 2007.

22. Buffett, W. and Cunningham, L.A., *The Essays of Warren Buffett: Lessons for Corporate America*, 2nd edn., Cunningham Group, New York, NY, 2008.

23. Welch, J. and Welch, S., *Winning*, HarperCollins, New York, NY, 2005.

24. Cahnmann, M., The Craft, Practice, and Possibility of Poetry in Educational Research, *Educational Researcher,* 2002, 32, 29-36.

25. Richardson, L., Writing: A Method of Inquiry, in: Denzin, N. and Lincoln, Y., eds., *The Handbook of Qualitative Research*, 2nd edn., Sage, Thousand Oaks, CA, 2000,

26. Frank, A.W., Standpoint of Storyteller*, Qualitative Inquiry,* 2000, 10(3), 354-365.

27. Sparkes, A.C., *Telling Tales in Sport and Physical Activity*, Champaign, IL, 2002.

28. Douglas, K. and Carless, D., Using Stories in Coach Education, *International Journal of Sports Science and Coaching,* 2008, 3(1), 33-49.

29.   Ellis, C. and Bochner, A., Autoethnography, Personal Narrative and Reflexivity, in: Denzin, N. and Lincoln, Y., eds., *The Handbook of Qualitative Research*, 2nd edn., Sage, Thousand Oaks, CA,

30.   Jackson, P., *The Last Season: A Team in Search of its Soul*, Penguin Press, New York, NY, 2004.

31.   Ferguson, H.E., *The Edge*, Howard Ferguson, New York, NY, 1990.

32.   Brown, B., *1001 Motivational Messages and Quotations for Athletes and Coaches: Teaching Character Through Sport*, Coaches Choice, Monterey, CA, 1990.

33.   Wooden, J.R. and Jamison, S., *My Personal Best: Life Lessons from an All-American Journey*, McGraw-Hill, New York, NY, 2004.

Sports Coaches' Informal Learning from Business & Military Discourse:

A Commentary

David Whitaker
Performance Consultants
No. 1 Poultry, London, EC2R 8JR, UK
E-mail: David.W@performanceconsultants.co.uk

INTRODUCTION

There is no doubting Mike Voight's interest and passion in tapping into the experiences and wisdom of successful leaders to enhance the success of his personal interactions with his own performers. His openness to learning pervades his article and this in itself is an enticement to anyone who reads this to delve further and with greater energy into the literature. And what a wealth of literature it is; spanning time from the 5th century BC to the present day and encompassing business, military and sport.

Wisely, in his quest to enable coaches, teachers and consultants to explore and apply the wealth of potential learning in this sphere, Mike narrows his focus to a number of questions including:

- What intrigues us about these stories, quotations, interviews and videos?
- What do we derive from them?
- How do we use them in our work?
- Do we learn more about them as people or more about their practices, or both?
- Are these lessons inspiring enough to change us, our behaviours or our practices?
- Why do we love to recite, memorize and use quotes from business and military leaders?

THE POWER OF STORIES AND QUOTATIONS

The most powerful parts of the article for me are the insights that relate to the importance of stories and quotations (the best of which almost encapsulate a story) to people in the arena of maximising performance. Stories have been central to human societies as powerful methods of transferring knowledge, wisdom and culture from generation to generation and it is natural that they should also have an important part to play in generating and sustaining high performance in sport. Mike's research offers coaches insights into the reasons they are so valuable and how coaches have used them. His personal applications are also very valuable as practical examples of the areas in which stories and quotations can be used with performers.

Such is the potential power of these stories for both individual and team performance that I was left wanting answers to questions such as:

- What are the key principles to help coaches use this powerful process most effectively?
- If the personalisation of stories is important so that people are inspired, then what are the methods of helping performers personalise and apply the learning/messages?

PERSONAL USE OF STORIES AND QUOTATIONS

My own experience in Olympic sport and business has led me to use stories and quotations to challenge myself to understand more fully the learning processes that people need to experience in their search for sustained high performance. They also provided great challenges to my own perceptions and preferences that, when explored, invariably provided me with insights that enhanced my coaching and leadership. In my interactions with international team athletes, I found the use of quotations at the team level very powerful for emphasising the culture we set out to create; and with individuals or small groups to focus attention on specific ways of performing. Finally, in team preparation for international matches, I found the concept of 'stories' a powerful process as it puts the players and the team at the centre, as the subjects of the story. Involving the players in telling the story of the match coming up does not guarantee success, but it is truly engaging and has the power to achieve the appropriate emotional focus and balance that promotes high performance.

In business, stories and quotations can be very powerful vehicles for people to explore their own leadership and coaching principles and behaviours. Within this work, I find it important to enable the participants to personalise the insights they gain from their exploration of the story or quotation. With athletes, this transfer is more often done in the physical environment whereas in the business world this requires more focussed reflection and dialogue. The impact is the same, enhanced behaviours in the area of 'performance', but the processes are slightly different. Here are four quotations that have influenced me and my work:

- *'In matters of style, swim with the current; in matters of principle stand like a rock'* (Thomas Jefferson)

This has served me well in that it forced me to identify the principles upon which my work and my leadership were based. It is a continual 'touchstone' for me to establish whether a key issue is a matter of 'style' or 'principle'.

- *'Excellence is not an accomplishment. It is a spirit, a never-ending process'* (Lawrence M Miller)

This is perhaps the most important thing to remember as a coach to elite performers. It was the key factor that lay behind our progress from bronze medal to gold medal in the Olympics.

- *'All serious daring starts from within.'*
(Eudora Welty)
This is a constant reminder for me that I have to be continually working on the 'inner performance' in both myself and others if we are to achieve.

- *'Not everything that is faced can be changed. But nothing can be changed until it is faced'*
(James Baldwin)
High performance cannot be achieved without facing into a plethora of issues. Some are very pleasant to face and others are very painful, but face them we must!

CONCLUSION

I would not necessarily use these quotations with the people I am coaching, but they would underpin my interactions.

In my use of this informal learning, Mike left me with a few major questions for myself:

- What if my 'favourites' are merely my personal bias and do not resonate with the people with whom I am working?
- How do I enable people to 'personalise' the story or the message?
- How do I use 'my favourites' to help people identify the interpretation that works for them?

229

Sport Coaches' Informal Learning from Business and Military Discourse:

A Commentary

David Carless
Carnegie Research Institute
Leeds Metropolitan University
Headingley Campus
Leeds, LS6 3QS, UK
E-mail: d.carless@leedsmet.ac.uk

INTRODUCTION

Mike Voight has provided us with an interesting insight into the ways in which stories – in the broadest sense of the word – are drawn upon and used by sport coaches and psychologists in their day-to-day practice. Mike shares personal reflections on his own sport psychology consulting practice and provides exploratory data on the reasons that fifteen coaches and sport psychologists gave for turning to the stories, quotations, and anecdotes of business and military personnel. The combination of Mike's reflections and the participants' responses show, amongst other things, team building, motivational strategies, people management, leadership and inspiration as areas in which ideas from business and military discourse are perceived to be relevant and helpful. I do not wish to quibble with the points that Mike has raised; indeed I would agree with him that the kinds of examples he provides can be (and probably are) important features of many coaches' and sport psychologists' work. However, I would like to broaden the debate by asking whether the examples Mike provides are exclusively and necessarily a 'good thing' when translated into sport contexts.

CELEBRATION VERSUS CRITICAL ENGAGEMENT

I recently attended a keynote presentation by the sports historian Andre Odendaal from the University of the Western Cape, South Africa. With simultaneous reference to contemporary academic and socio-political contexts, Andre cautioned of the dangers of engaging in excessive *celebration* at the expense of *critical engagement*. His remarks have had a powerful effect on me and caused me to reconsider the extent to which contemporary culture – both within and outside academia – can tend to 'jump on the bandwagon' by wholeheartedly celebrating particular practices as 'a good thing' without seriously considering the problems that may arise as a direct or indirect result of these practices.

Relating this general point to the specific context of Mike's article, caution is in order because the beneficial use of stories (or quotations, anecdotes etc.) depends upon careful consideration of the *kinds* of stories that are offered. A relevant question then becomes what might be the limits or problems of business and military discourse when translated to the sporting lives of adults and young people? It is important, I think, to note that stories (and the effects of those stories) are not inherently *good*. Instead, as narrative research has shown in recent years [e.g., 1, 2], stories can bring positive or negative consequences depending on an interaction between the *kind* of story that is offered (for example, its plot or narrative type), the social context in which it is offered, and the particular life experiences of each individual hearing the story. Put another way, a particular story may have one effect on a one individual, but a very different effect on someone else. Thus, I suggest that the consequences of recounting business or military stories to different people in sport *will not* necessarily be positive and may lead to problems which we, as reflective professionals, would do well to consider.

To give this point a more specific meaning, I will relate it to the narrative research Kitrina Douglas and I have conducted in sport contexts. We have identified a dominant narrative (or discourse) in elite sport which we describe as a *performance narrative* [2]. In a performance story, talk of performance outcomes, winning, total commitment, and an overriding focus on sport are defining characteristics and war metaphors are frequently used [2, 3]. We have suggested that within contemporary sport culture, this story comes dangerously close to being the *only* story which is heard and voiced – at the expense of alternative stories. As a result, those people whose lives and experiences do not conform to the plot of the performance narrative risk becoming invisible as their alternative stories are silenced or dismissed as impossible.

For me, the primary job of stories is to provide a platform for *alternative* experiences and ways of living to be recounted and heard. Contemporary sport culture already tells and retells performance stories as if this plot is the *only* way to be an elite sportsperson. Within the current socio-cultural environment of sport, it makes little sense to further publicise performance stories – the 'story market' (so to speak) is already saturated with performance stories. More pressing, I believe, is the need to tell and share alternative stories: namely stories which challenge, transgress, question or subvert the dominant (performance) discourse. These alternative stories offer the potential to educate individuals in sport through showing other ways of living as and being an elite sportsperson [4].

I am wary of some of the quotations, anecdotes and stories that Mike provides which, while being interesting, seem to me to tend towards a singular view of life which is very much in line with the dominant performance narrative. To my ear, these stories *conform* to what we hear again and again in the sport media and in sports clubs and training facilities. Through being told and retold, these stories risk re-inscribing a singular way of being which, recent research suggests [e.g., 4, 5], can bring with it some worrying and dangerous consequences.

CONCLUSION

As reflective professionals, I think two tasks are required of us in our ongoing work. First, we need to consider and reflect upon the kinds of adverse consequences which can arise from emphasizing and privileging performance-oriented stories, whether they are drawn from sport, business or military contexts. Several publications have begun to explore these consequences [see 2-5]. Second, we need to find ways to broaden the stock of story types which are made available to sportspeople through finding ways of telling *different* kinds of stories – such as discovery and relational stories [2] – which challenge the dominance of performance stories. Simply making alternative stories – based on the lived experiences of others – available within sport environments is the first step in this process. Our research, alongside the tenets of narrative theory, has taught me that it is through sharing the kinds of stories which allow room for diversity and difference – as opposed to promoting a singular orientation or perspective – that the success, well-being and personal development of sportspeople is most likely to be supported and nurtured.

REFERENCES

1. Frank, A. W., *The Wounded Storyteller,* University of Chicago Press, Chicago, 1995.

2. Douglas, K. and Carless, D., Performance, Discovery, and Relational Narratives Among Women Professional Tournament Golfers, *Women in Sport and Physical Activity Journal,* 2006, 15(2), 14-27.

3. Douglas, K. and Carless, D., Training or Education? Negotiating a Fuzzy Line Between What "We" Want and "They" Might Need, *Annual Review of Golf Coaching 2008,* 1-13.

4. Douglas, K. and Carless, D., Using Stories in Coach Education, *International Journal of Sports Science and Coaching,* 2008, 3(1), 33-49.

5. Carless, D. and Douglas, K., "We Haven't Got a Seat on the Bus for You" or "All the Seats are Mine": Narratives and Career Transition in Professional Golf, *Qualitative Research in Sport and Exercise, 2009,* 1(1), 51-66.